Liberating
Shakespeare

SHAKESPEARE AND ADAPTATION

Shakespeare and Adaptation provides in-depth discussions of a dynamic field and showcases the ways in which, with each act of adaptation, a new Shakespeare is generated. The series addresses the phenomenon of Shakespeare and adaptation in all its guises and explores how Shakespeare continues as a reference-point in a generically diverse body of representations and forms, including fiction, film, drama, theatre, performance and mass media. Including sole authored books as well as edited collections, the series embraces a mix of methodologies and espouses a global perspective that brings into conversation adaptations from different nations, languages and cultures.

Series Editor:
Mark Thornton Burnett (Queen's University Belfast, UK)

Advisory Board:
Professor Ariane M. Balizet (Texas Christian University, USA)
Professor Sarah Hatchuel (Université Paul-Valéry Montpellier, 3, France)
Dr Peter Kirwan (Mary Baldwin University, USA)
Professor Douglas Lanier (University of New Hampshire, USA)
Professor Adele Lee (Emerson College, USA)
Dr Stephen O'Neill (Maynooth University, Ireland)
Professor Shormishtha Panja (University of Delhi, India)
Professor Lisa Starks (University of South Florida)
Professor Nathalie Vienne-Guerrin (Université Paul-Valéry Montpellier 3, France)
Professor Sandra Young (University of Cape Town, South Africa)

Published Titles:

Lockdown Shakespeare
Edited by Gemma Allred, Benjamin Broadribb and Erin Sullivan
Women and Indian Shakespeares
Edited by Thea Buckley, Mark Thornton Burnett, Sangeeta Datta and
Rosa García-Periago
Adapting Macbeth
William C. Carroll
Romeo and Juliet, *Adaptation and the Arts*
Edited by Julia Reinhard Lupton and Ariane Helou

Forthcoming Titles:

Shakespeare, Ecology and Adaptation: A Practical Guide
Alys Daroy and Paul Prescott
Shakespeare and Ballet
David Fuller
Shakespearean Biofiction on the Contemporary Stage and Screen
Edited by Ronan Hatfull and Edel Semple
Shakespeare's Histories on Screen: Adaptation, Race and Intersectionality
Jennie M. Votava

Liberating Shakespeare

Adaptation and Empowerment for Young Adult Audiences

Edited by
Jennifer Flaherty and
Deborah Uman

THE ARDEN SHAKESPEARE
LONDON • NEW YORK • OXFORD • NEW DELHI • SYDNEY

THE ARDEN SHAKESPEARE
Bloomsbury Publishing Plc
50 Bedford Square, London, WC1B 3DP, UK
1385 Broadway, New York, NY 10018, USA
29 Earlsfort Terrace, Dublin 2, Ireland

BLOOMSBURY, THE ARDEN SHAKESPEARE and the Arden Shakespeare logo
are trademarks of Bloomsbury Publishing Plc

First published in Great Britain 2023

Series design by Ben Anslow and Tjaša Krivec.
Cover image: AND JULIET by Max Martin © Johan Persson /ArenaPAL

A catalogue record for this book is available from the British Library.

A catalog record for this book is available from the Library of Congress.

ISBN: HB: 978-1-3503-2026-0
PB: 978-1-3503-2025-3
ePDF: 978-1-3503-2028-4
eBook: 978-1-3503-2027-7

Series: Shakespeare and Adaptation

Typeset by Deanta Global Publishing Services, Chennai, India
Printed and bound in Great Britain

To find out more about our authors and books visit www.bloomsbury.com and
sign up for our newsletters.

To our teachers and our students

CONTENTS

FIGURES

CONTRIBUTORS

Ariane Balizet is Professor of English and Associate Dean for Faculty and DEI in the AddRan School of Liberal Arts at TCU in Fort Worth, Texas. Her teaching and research interests include games and colonial competition in the early modern literary Caribbean, Shakespeare in adaptation, and intersectional approaches to teaching Shakespeare. She is the author of two monographs – *Shakespeare and Girls' Studies* (2019) and *Blood and Home in Early Modern Drama: Domestic Identity on the Renaissance Stage* (2014) – and many articles on blood, embodiment, and identities in the literature of the English Renaissance and its afterlives.

Jennifer Flaherty is Professor of English at Georgia College. She co-edited Arden's *The Taming of the Shrew: The State of Play* (2021) with Heather C. Easterling. Her research emphasizes adaptation, global Shakespeare, and girlhood, and her publications include chapters in the volumes *Shakespeare and Millennial Fiction* (2017), *Shakespeare and Global Appropriation* (2019), and *Shakespeare and Geek Culture* (2020). She has also published in journals such as *Borrowers and Lenders*, *Interdisciplinary Literary Studies*, *Comparative Drama*, and *Shakespeare Bulletin*.

Melissa Johnson is Visiting Lecturer in English at Texas Christian University. Her research centres on identity politics and diverse representation in young adult and pop-culture adaptations of Shakespeare. She has also appeared onstage in numerous productions of Shakespeare's plays.

Alexa Alice Joubin is Professor of English, Women's, Gender and Sexuality Studies, Theatre, International Affairs, and East Asian Languages and Literatures at George Washington University in Washington, DC, where she serves as founding co-director of the

Digital Humanities Institute. Her recent books include *Shakespeare and East Asia* (2021), *Race* (2018), *Onscreen Allusions to Shakespeare* (co-edited, 2022), *Local and Global Myths in Shakespearean Performance* (co-edited, 2018) and *Shakespeare and the Ethics of Appropriation* (co-edited, 2014).

Natalie Loper is Senior Instructor and Associate Director of First-Year Writing at the University of Alabama, where she mentors new teachers and teaches first-year writing, British literature, and Shakespeare. She co-edited *Shakespeare/Not Shakespeare* (2016) with Christy Desmet and Jim Casey. Her essays on adaptation, Shakespearean teen films, Baz Luhrmann, #metoo, the academic job market, and pedagogy have appeared in *Upstart Crow*, *The Pedagogy of Adaptation* (2010), and in forthcoming volumes on gendered violence and Shakespeare pedagogy.

Lawrence Manley is William R. Kenan, Jr Professor of English Emeritus at Yale University. He is the author of *Literature and Culture in Early Modern London* (1995) and co-author, with Sally-Beth MacLean, of *Lord Strange's Men and Their Plays* (2013).

Jesus Montaño is Associate Professor of English at Hope College, a liberal arts college in Holland, Michigan. His primary teaching and research interests include Latinx young adult literature and Latinx/Latin American literary confluences. His recently published book *Tactics of Hope in Latinx Children's and Young Adult Literature* (with Regan Postma-Montaño, 2022) highlights the reparative power of books and the transformational possibilities of reading for young readers to survive and thrive in the challenging spaces of our Americas. His current project, *Young Latinx Shakespeares: Race, Justice, and Literary Appropriation* (forthcoming), examines how contemporary Latinx young adult novels utilize Shakespeare as a locus for cultural and literary production while simultaneously signalling, in their divergence from the informing texts, the intention to wilfully open and create new terrains.

Sara Morrison is Professor of English and Associate Dean of the Core Curriculum at William Jewell College. Her teaching and research interests include intersectional methodologies for teaching early modern literature, adaptations of Shakespeare across various genres, and film studies. She co-edited *Staging the Blazon in Early Modern English Theater* (2013) with Deborah Uman and has published essays on blazons and gender in early modern drama and poetry.

Laurie E. Osborne is the Zacamy Professor of English at Colby College. Her research has ranged from nineteenth-century performance editions to Shakespeare on film, on television, and in contemporary popular culture. Her recent publications include 'The Paranormal Bard: Shakespeare Is/As Undead' in *Shakespeare and Millennial Fiction* (2017), 'Teaching Global Shakespeare: Visual Culture Projects in Action' in *Global Shakespeares* (2019), and 'Canon Fodder and Conscripted Genres: The Hogarth Project and the Modern Shakespeare Novel' (*Critical Survey*, 2021). She is also co-editor of and contributor to *Shakespeare and the 'Live' Theatre Broadcast Experience* (2018).

Jules Pigott is a screenwriter and director currently located in New York City. She graduated from Smith College in 2021 with a degree in Film and Media Studies, and she has produced multiple literature-based web series since the age of fifteen, including the Shakespeare adaptations *Like, As It Is* and *Twelfth Grade (or Whatever)*.

M. Tyler Sasser is Assistant Professor of Honors at the University of Alabama, where he teaches and researches Shakespeare, Renaissance literature, childhood studies, children's literature, and film. His research appears in *Medieval and Renaissance Drama in England, Shakespeare Bulletin, Shakespeare Newsletter, The Tennessee Williams Annual Review, Children's Literature Association Quarterly, Children's Literature in Education,* and *Children's Literature.* He has contributed essays to *Shakespeare and Geek Culture* (2020), *Queering Childhood in Early Modern English Drama and Culture* (2018), and *Shakespeare and Millennial Fiction* (2017).

Charlotte Speilman is a classroom teacher who specializes in English literature and politics. She teaches young adults at the middle school, high school and university levels. She is also a PhD candidate in the Department of English at York University, where her areas of research focus include the interplay of youth empowerment and Young Adult Shakespeare.

Laura Turchi is a teacher educator specializing in English language arts. She co-authored *Teaching Shakespeare with Purpose: A Student-Centered Approach* (2016) with Ayanna Thompson and recently completed *Teaching Shakespeare with Interactive Editions* (forthcoming). She is the curriculum director for 'RaceB4Race: Sustaining, Building, Innovating' at the Arizona Center for Medieval and Renaissance Studies. Dr Turchi is also co-directing the DOE-funded *Shakespeare and Social Justice Project* at the Shakespeare Center of Los Angeles.

Deborah Uman is Professor of English and Dean of the Lindquist College of Arts & Humanities at Weber State University. In addition to her monograph, *Women Translators in Early Modern England* (2011), she co-edited *Staging the Blazon in Early Modern English Theater* (2013) with Sara Morrison, served as the founding co-editor of *Seneca Falls Dialogues Journal*, and has published numerous essays on translation, adaptation, and gender in early modern literature.

Jane Wanninger is Assistant Professor of Literature at Bard College at Simon's Rock. Her research focuses on performance, embodiment, gender, and agency in early modern drama. Recent publications have explored ambiguous and unresolved representations of pregnancy in medieval and early modern literature (chapter in *Gendered Temporalities in the Early Modern World*, co-authored with Bethany Packard and Holly Barbaccia) and the staging of confession in *Romeo and Juliet* and *'Tis Pity She's a Whore* (article in *Early Theatre* 25.2) As a Fellow of the Bard Institute for Writing and Thinking Center for the Study of Liberal Arts Pedagogy (CLASP), she also researches and writes about writing-based pedagogy and assessment in secondary and post-secondary academic settings.

ACKNOWLEDGEMENTS

This collection had many beginnings, including a Facebook inquiry, several grant proposals, and a seminar on Young Adult Shakespeare at the 2020 meeting of the Shakespeare Association of America. That meeting was scheduled to take place in Colorado but, like so many things, was disrupted by the Covid-19 pandemic. Our participants made the jump to Zoom with us, and we enjoyed lively and thoughtful conversations in a virtual setting. We are grateful to all of our participants, whose ideas and questions confirmed our interest in pursuing the topic of adaptations of Shakespeare. Many of our seminar participants have contributed chapters to this volume, and we are especially appreciative of their intellectual acuity and tenacity, which has led to chapters that are both timely and necessary.

In the middle of editing this collection, we received news that a companion proposal to host an NEH Institute on a similar topic would be funded for the summer of 2022. This institute, Transforming Shakespeare's Tragedies: Adaptation, Education, and Diversity, brought twenty-four high school and middle school ELA and theatre teachers to Weber State University to study adaptations of *Hamlet* and *Othello* and explore ways to enliven their classrooms with a variety of materials and strategies. We are grateful to the National Endowment for the Humanities for their support and would like to offer our thanks to our visiting faculty, including Ariane Balizet, Vanessa Corredera, Alexa Joubin, Douglas Lanier, Mark Miazga, and Jesus Montaño, who generously shared their expertise as scholars and teachers with us. We especially thank our colleague, Scott O'Neil, whose title of Technology Expert inadequately describes the centrality of his many contributions to the project.

Most of all, we extend our gratitude to teachers, those who joined us for the institute and those who show up every day to share their passion, wisdom, and support to our students. Teaching has always been a difficult and underappreciated profession, but the last few years have drastically increased the challenges faced by classroom frontline workers who are doing all that they can to support students through health and mental health crises while being dragged into political battles not of their own making. When saying goodbyes at the institute, our participants spoke of the renewed sense of hope that the experience provided. In turn, we thank them for reminding us of the vital role that education, particularly in the humanities, plays during even the most difficult times.

Introduction

Taking Young Adult Shakespeare seriously

Jennifer Flaherty and Deborah Uman

When we first began to advertise our seminar on 'Young Adult Shakespeare' for the 2020 meeting of the Shakespeare Association of America (SAA), the reaction that we got most often from colleagues was 'What a fun topic!' It was a valid response – YA Shakespeare is an engaging subject for scholars and young audiences. Students in our Shakespeare classes often express surprise and delight that they 'get' to write papers about *10 Things I Hate about You* (1999), *Gnomeo & Juliet* (2011), *The Fault in Our Stars* (2012), or Taylor Swift's 'Love Story' (2008). In the *Shakespeare and the Teenage Girl* course at Georgia College, the assigned coursework includes reading YA novels such as Cat Winters's *The Steep and Thorny Way* (2016) and watching YouTube series that reimagine Shakespeare's plays as first-person video diaries narrated by the young characters themselves. Students enjoy Shakespeare-inspired video games, including *Elsinore* (2018), which features Ophelia as the playable main character who seeks to rewrite the tragedy of *Hamlet*. Even students who initially see Shakespeare's plays as boring or difficult often find his work more appealing after they experience YA adaptations of the texts (Figure I.1).

FIGURE I.1 *Cover art for* Elsinore. Elsinore, *produced by Golden Glitch (2018).*

The widespread appropriation of Shakespeare's plots, characters, and language into YA media is not an indictment of Shakespeare as inaccessible. It is an illustration of how adaptable and accessible his plays are for contemporary youth audiences. In the past thirty years, the number of screen Shakespeare adaptations targeting adolescent audiences has grown significantly, branching out from the teen films of the 1990s and early 2000s that Richard Burt identified as teen 'Shakesploitation'[1] and Robert L. York dubbed 'Teen Shakespirit'[2] to include video games, music videos, vlogs, fan fiction, and other new media. In the same time frame, YA authors have published more than two hundred YA novels based on Shakespeare's plays,[3] matching the pace of the expanding market for teen fiction, which 'has exploded into a global economic powerhouse as young adult texts continue to grow in sales'.[4] Shakespeare has also been used to speak to young people on stage, starting with plays such as *Shakespeare's R&J* (1999), by Joe Calarco, and continuing today with the current Broadway and West End productions of *& Juliet* (2019). As a sequel/revision of *Romeo and Juliet*, the jukebox musical features a diverse cast of young people singing pop anthems made famous by stars such as Britney Spears and Katy Perry. Content creators – who range from large-scale studios and bestselling authors to start-up production companies and emerging writers – connect Shakespeare with contemporary experiences, using humour and accessibility to appeal to the young target audience. The enthusiasm generated by YA Shakespeare can be an inspiring motivator in high school and college classrooms, particularly in a time when student and teacher morale is low. That is the power of a fun topic.

We would argue, however, that fun is not synonymous with inconsequential or frivolous. Contemporary adaptations of Shakespeare for young people address the darker and more uncomfortable aspects of adolescence, drawing on a practice dating back to the nineteenth century, when Mary Cowden Clarke published *The Girlhood of Shakespeare's Heroines* (1854). Cowden Clarke's novellas incorporated serious topics, such as sexual assault, suicide, poverty, and injustice, into stories of Shakespeare's female characters during their imagined childhoods. As Laurie Osborne notes, Clarke's text 'offered Victorian girls a cautionary education about masculine sexual predation', while also enacting a 'subversive pre-feminist exploration of female autonomy'.[5] The 1994 publication of Mary Pipher's *Reviving Ophelia* established the practice of using Shakespeare's characters as blueprints for examining and contextualizing the challenges faced by contemporary youth, particularly young women, when Pipher compared her young female patients who were suffering from depression and anxiety to Ophelia.[6] Fictional adaptations of Shakespeare aimed at young people echoed this process, connecting the experiences of Shakespeare's characters with the challenges and exhilarations of the contemporary teenage experience.[7] Like today's young people, characters in YA Shakespeare adaptations face oppression and trauma, and some of them manage to defy cultural limitations in ways that Shakespeare's characters could not. Some of these reworkings use the creative dissonance of adaptation to reference gaps or silences in their Shakespearean sources, giving new voices to marginalized characters. Others place recognizable Shakespearean plotlines, characters, or quotations within new contexts, weaving their perceived cultural authority into the diverse stories of young people, past and present. These works use Shakespeare to address some of the most pressing questions in contemporary culture, exploring themes of violence, media, race relations, gender dynamics, and intersectionality.

Because our seminar for the SAA was scheduled for April 2020, our conversation about addressing contemporary issues through

YA Shakespeare was held virtually due to the cancellation of the in-person SAA conference. Since then, the world has experienced challenges we could not have imagined when we began this project. Under the restrictions and uncertainties caused by the Covid-19 pandemic, students and teachers are struggling. After months, even years, of learning in isolation and interacting under the threat of contagion, young people are experiencing anxiety and depression in record numbers. Returning to in-person education has also renewed the threat of violence in our schools; the week before we submitted our final draft of this volume, a shooter killed nineteen children and two teachers in an elementary school in Uvalde, Texas. The growing social unrest and political polarization in the United States has also led to legal disputes over the inclusion of books dealing with race and sexual orientation and identity in libraries, classrooms, and curricula. When Black Lives Matter and #MeToo movements amplified serious conversations about racism and misogyny, parental groups and state governments countered with censorship of lesson plans that might make (some) students feel uncomfortable. Among the heated debate about secondary school texts and curricula, we do not currently hear calls to eliminate Shakespeare. Our seminar conversation about how Shakespeare can be used to address trauma for young adult audiences takes on new significance in this changing social climate. While we started out with the goal of sharing ideas to make Shakespeare more engaging to young people, we are now additionally motivated by the urgent need from teachers to develop tools to discuss our histories and realities with their students in ways that are attentive to students' and teachers' precarious positions.

In the summer of 2022, we led an institute entitled 'Transforming Shakespeare's Tragedies: Adaptation, Education, and Diversity' for the National Endowment for the Humanities. Twenty-four high school and middle school English language arts (ELA) and theatre teachers came to Utah to study adaptations of *Hamlet* and *Othello* and to explore ways to enliven their classrooms with a variety of contemporary materials and comparative strategies. After more than two years of teaching through Covid-19, our participants were understandably exhausted. They were apprehensive about the growing challenges to teacher autonomy. Yet each one of these teachers embraced the study of Shakespeare and adaptation with renewed energy, curiosity, and compassion. They were generous in sharing their own expertise and experiences with us and with each other. For nearly three weeks, they kept to a rigorous schedule of classes with us and our visiting faculty (many of whom were also contributors in this volume), as well as workshops and performances at the Utah Shakespeare Festival, and they met every challenge with enthusiasm. Their excitement about introducing these adaptations to their students confirms our belief that Shakespeare can make a compelling contribution to high school and middle school curricula, particularly in connection with adaptation. Our institute, like this volume, explores how Shakespeare's plays can be transformed to address contemporary topics that matter to teachers and young people living through this challenging cultural moment.

By imbuing contemporary topics with the canonical authority of Shakespeare, YA Shakespeare adaptations are uniquely positioned to strike a balance between demands for innovation and tradition in high school curricula. In *Teaching Shakespeare with a Purpose*, Ayanna Thompson and Laura Turchi make a case for teachers to 'recognize the value in continuing to explore and challenge the relevance of Shakespeare's works' by arguing that 'without a twenty-first-century approach, Shakespeare in schools really will cease to matter – it will be a dead subject like Latin – and will be replaced by texts that are "relevant" and easily accessible, like *The Hunger Games*'.[8] Victor Malo-Juvera, Paula Greathouse, and Brooke Eisenbach acknowledge the currency of YA literature, but note that even 'some educators feel that young adult literature is inferior in quality when compared to canonical texts', despite the fact that the standards of preparation for two major accreditation agencies 'require that teacher candidates be knowledgeable with young adult literature'.[9] This collection grew out of our desire to promote engaging ways to teach Shakespeare in high school, ways that spark students' imaginations and speak to their lived experiences. YA Shakespeare can tackle challenging issues for audiences of young people, using the canonical power and 'the comfortable distance of the Shakespearean source text . . . to address contemporary social concerns'.[10] At a time when banned book lists are growing in size and number, young adult adaptations of Shakespeare can be a way to teach close reading and comparison with a source (common objectives and requirements in secondary and higher education) while also engaging students in challenging conversations that encourage critical thinking.

In the context of this project, it matters a great deal to understand the relationship of the adapted work to the original because of the cultural imperative to teach Shakespeare throughout the educational landscape. Before publishing her oft-cited *A Theory of Adaptation*, Linda Hutcheon points out that 'when we adapt, we create using all the tools that creators have always used', and she challenges the 'postromantic valuing of the originary' by asking whether or not it matters whether a piece of art is new or adapted.[11] Douglas Lanier expands on Hutcheon's point, challenging the emphasis on the relationship of adaptation to original and offering the botanic metaphor of the rhizome as a theoretical model that facilitates the 'study of the vast web of adaptations, allusion and (re)productions that comprises the ever-changing cultural phenomenon we call "Shakespeare"' and situates authority 'not in the Shakespearean text at all, but in the accrued power of Shakespearean adaptation'.[12] Lanier's rhizomatic model provides ways for teachers, scholars, and students to reconsider notions of authority and ownership.

The wide range of adaptations addressed in this volume use Shakespeare's plays as a jumping-off point by including familiar plots, frequent allusions, or even direct quotations. These texts are not 'faithful' retellings of Shakespeare; as Douglas Lanier notes in *The Arden Research Handbook of Shakespeare and Adaptation*, 'strictly speaking, there is no such thing as a faithful adaptation. . . . To be faithful to some element of the original is not to duplicate it in its entirety, but rather to strike a relation of similarity to some quality of the source that the adaptation identifies as essentially or distinctively Shakespearean'.[13] In their efforts to understand the relationship between adaptation and appropriation, Christy Desmet and Sujata Iyengar note that both practices can be viewed both as forms of theft and acts of self-assertion. Without arguing for adherence to one term or another, Desmet and Iyengar suggest exploring 'the oscillation between these concepts as attitudes toward artistic production, consumption, and social regulation'.[14] Desmet has pointed to the 'personal urgency' that drives creators of Shakespearean adaptations and appropriations for whom such work can be seen as 'acts of survival'.[15] While Desmet and Iyenger focus on the creative acts of adaptation and appropriation, the interest of this collection is primarily on the impact for the readers and audiences of adaptive content. Instead of thinking about adaptation as theft, we argue that placing the works of Shakespeare in contemporary and diverse settings makes clear that some version of Shakespeare already belongs to everyone.

Liberating Shakespeare demonstrates the value of adapting Shakespeare for young adults, focusing on adaptations that seek to engage young audiences by depicting examples of oppression, trauma, and resistance. By examining adaptations that deal with urgently relevant issues for young people who are struggling today, we assert that Young Adult Shakespeare can create crucial connections. Chapters in this collection consider whether such representations empower young adult audiences and how these works can be used as companion texts within educational settings. As the authors of *Shakespeare and Young Adult Literature* note, Shakespeare can achieve a symbiotic relationship with YA media and culture, 'allowing teachers to combine some of the best the Bard has to offer while at the same time increasing the relevance and engagement for their teen readers, and in many cases, for themselves'.[16] We argue that YA Shakespeare should be taken seriously as art that speaks to the complexities of a broken world, offering glimmers of hope for an uncertain future.

The chapters in the collection are arranged in two sections. The first focuses on trauma as represented in Shakespeare's plays, various adaptations, and students' lives. While many of Shakespeare's plays revel in tragedy, the chapters in this section turn towards themes of survival, often emphasized in modern adaptations. Speaking directly to our unprecedented moment, Ariane Balizet's chapter examines the challenges and opportunities of teaching *Romeo and Juliet*, a play that takes place during a plague, during the Covid-19 pandemic. With great sensitivity to the trauma faced by her students in their educational and personal lives and with attentiveness to the unexpected benefits of virtual and online instruction, Balizet considers the important role that trauma-informed pedagogy can play in acknowledging students' experiences and empowering students to engage with literature in meaningful ways.[17]

The next two chapters, by Laurie Osborne and Sara Morrison, direct our attention to the gender-based violence of Shakespeare's *Much Ado about Nothing* and *The Winter's Tale*, examining how much has changed and how much remains the same across centuries, genres, and modalities. Osborne explores the plethora of adaptations of *Much Ado* in YA fiction – at least fourteen versions since 2006 – and remarks on the damaging power of digital forms of surveillance and misinformation detailed in these novels. After considering how Shakespeare himself adapted Robert Greene's *Pandosto* (1588), Morrison centres on E. K. Johnston's *Exit, Pursued by a Bear* (2016) and its hopeful view of the support women can receive in the face of unspeakable violence.

Turning to concerns of race and national identity, Charlotte Speilman and Jesus Montaño focus on adaptations of Shakespeare's most-taught tragedies, including *Hamlet*, *Othello*, and *Romeo and Juliet*. Speilman compares YA novelizations of each of those plays, addressing the use of racialized language and the ways in which each text can be traumatic for young readers of colour, even if the adaptations are designed to reveal and condemn racist behaviours and policies. Montaño reads Guadalupe García McCall's reimagining of *Romeo and Juliet*, set in Texas during the Mexican Revolution, as a 'counter-story' that challenges white supremacist notions of history and offers a rare platform for young Latinx readers to see themselves and their histories reflected.

Completing Section I, M. Tyler Sasser offers a wide-ranging discussion of numerous adaptations of a variety of plays, identifying a pattern in which a young protagonist experiences a traumatic event and, through engagement with Shakespeare, overcomes that trauma to achieve a happy, comedic ending. Sasser's analysis is cautionary, and he warns that such bardolatry can be harmful to young readers who seek solace in Shakespeare rather than in the hands of mental health professionals. With this advice in mind, we centre the second section on the ways that YA Shakespeare adaptations can empower young people as consumers, creators, scholars, and teachers.

Natalie Loper, Melissa Johnson, and Lawrence Manley return to questions of gender, now focusing on the potential for female empowerment and agency in adaptations. Comparing Lisa Klein's novel *Ophelia* (2006) to Claire McCarthy's film adaptation (2018), Loper sees the first as offering models for women who help each other overcome trauma and the latter as missing an opportunity and preventing its female characters from forging alliances and collectively challenging their limitations. Johnson concentrates on the representation of witches in novelizations of *Macbeth* and argues that these works participate in a feminist reclamation of witches that can, in turn, offer a message of empowerment for young women. In his analysis of Aoibheann Sweeney's *Among Other Things, I've Taken Up Smoking* (2017), a loose adaptation of *The Tempest*,

Lawrence Manley attends to the novel's interest in questions of gender, sexuality, and race as central to its treatment of identity formation among young people. Manley links this intersectional approach to a model of 'queer pedagogy' that can help young adult readers rethink their ideas of normalcy and understand identity as dynamic and relational.

The affordances provided by the internet and social media, particularly web series and vlogs, are examined in chapters by Jane Wanninger and web series creator Jules Pigott. In discussing the 2014 YouTube series, *Nothing Much to Do*, created by a group of four young women calling themselves The Candle Wasters, Wanninger learns from her students and from The Candle Wasters themselves; she argues that this multi-modal and interactive model not only provides new opportunities to engage with traditional texts but also helps decentre traditional notions of understanding and literary interpretation. Inspired by the work of other young adult content creators, including The Candle Wasters, film and media student Pigott began developing web series adaptations of Shakespeare when she was still in high school with the creation of *Like, as It Is* and then *Twelfth Grade (or Whatever)* (2016). In her chapter, Pigott looks back on the ways her series used Shakespeare's comedies to reflect the emotional roller coasters of adolescence and explore contemporary questions of gender identity, anxiety, and societal pressure that young people face in their daily lives.

As a professor who regularly interacts with pre-service ELA teachers, Laura Turchi also engages directly with the young people for whom YA adaptations are designed. In her chapter, Turchi details her experience with an assignment for education students requiring them to create a 'book talk' on a YA novel that could serve as a companion text when teaching *Romeo and Juliet* and could connect to the potential high school students' lives. While acknowledging some of the challenges and shortcomings in her students' work, Turchi is optimistic that these future teachers want to be a force for good in their future students' lives and that there is room for the works of Shakespeare in their endeavours.

We conclude the collection with an afterword that comes full circle to where the book begins, focusing on pedagogies that are responsive to the traumas of our current moment and work towards social justice by promoting mutual understanding. In this concluding chapter, Alexa Alice Joubin details a variety of what she calls interactive pedagogies, such as radical listening and communal writings assignments, offering specific examples of activities and demonstrating how Shakespeare and adaptations provide 'fertile ground for training students to listen intently and compassionately' and for us all to contribute to a model of reparative education. Joubin's emphasis on listening to the experiences and perspectives of others highlights an important tension that runs throughout this collection. Many of the chapters point to the value of YA adaptations because students can relate to the characters and their experiences.

Like relevance, relatability can be an uncomfortable measure for Shakespeare's plays. In her 2014 *New Yorker* article on 'The Scourge of Relatability',[18] Rebecca Mead argues that 'the notion of relatability implies that the work in question serves like a selfie: a flattering confirmation of an individual's solipsism. To appreciate "King Lear" – or even "The Catcher in the Rye" or "The Fault in Our Stars" – only to the extent that the work functions as one's mirror would make for a hopelessly reductive experience'.[19] In her plenary address for the 2018 Shakespeare Association of America, Marjorie Garber quotes Mead's article, challenging the general trend to 'sex [Shakespeare] up and dumb it down' and calling the practice 'the deplorable relatable'.[20] Garber uses several examples relating to YA Shakespeare while speaking more broadly about producing, teaching, adapting, or reading Shakespeare today, and her words are reminiscent of other arguments against adaptations made for young audiences.[21] Gregory M. Colòn Semenza examines the assumptions behind this criticism of teen Shakespeare films in his analysis of animated Shakespeare:

> A common argument in the subfield of Shakespeare film scholarship is that so-called 'teenpics' exploit the shallow sensibility and economic viability of their primary audience through a process of 'dumbing down' Shakespearean playtexts . . . the assumption seems to be that because the films inevitably subtract words/action present in the plays, they also remove much of the complexity that more words and action are intuited to represent.[22]

Similar arguments about quality persist about any medium or genre where young people are the target audience, and we are far from the first to challenge such criticism and say that YA Shakespeare is worthy of study.[23] We would add to this conversation that the very things that make YA Shakespeare compelling in the classroom can also lead to adaptations being dismissed as oversimplified Shakespeare or disparaged as pandering to self-centred audiences who only want to see themselves reflected back at them.

In the publication based on her plenary, Garber argues that Shakespeare's 'plays are full of diverse characters, each with his or her own language and style. It's not even all about Hamlet, much less all about you'.[24] As a solution, she suggests the Brechtian concept of alienation, with its emphasis on 'defamiliarization or estrangement' as a way for teachers and readers to reclaim and relish the 'unfamiliar' in Shakespeare.[25] Garber's emphasis on the importance of reading Shakespeare with a sense of the strange and unusual is valuable. While we can hope that the argument that adapting Shakespeare for young audiences equates to 'dumbing him down' has lost its dismissive potency, the point about the need to read for a range of voices and experiences is well taken, particularly in the current polarized political climate. Efforts to include diverse voices in our classrooms are based on the belief in the inherent value of learning about cultures and experiences that reflect our own *and* those that are significantly different. Teaching Shakespeare's plays alongside adaptations allows us to offer both approaches to our students simultaneously. As the chapters in this collection show, situating the work of Shakespeare with and against the responses of other creators and of our students provides us with powerful tools to explore the foreign and strange and to understand the immediate and familiar. In this way we hope to liberate Shakespeare from centuries of bardolatrous expectations and show that his works belong to all of us.

Notes

1 Richard Burt, 'Afterword: Te(e)n Things I Hate about Girlene Shakesploitation Flicks in the Late 1990s, or Not-So-Fast Times at Shakespeare High', in *Spectacular Shakespeare: Critical Theory and Popular Culture*, ed. Courtney Lehmann and Lisa S. Starks (Teaneck: Fairleigh Dickinson University Press, 2002), 205.

2 Robert L. York, '"Smells Like Teen Shakespirit" Or, the Shakespearean Films of Julia Stiles', in *Shakespeare and Youth Culture*, ed. Jennifer

Hulbert, Kevin J. Wetmore Jr., and Robert L. York (New York: Palgrave Macmillan, 2006).

3 Laurie Osborne, 'Reviving Cowden Clarke: Rewriting Shakespeare's Heroines in Young Adult Fiction', in *Shakespearean Echoes*, ed. Adam Hansen and Kevin J. Wetmore (New York: Palgrave Macmillan, 2015), 21.

4 Victor Malo-Juvera, Paula Greathouse, and Brooke Eisenbach, *Shakespeare and Young Adult Literature* (London: Rowman & Littlefield, 2021), vii.

5 Osborne, 'Reviving Cowden Clarke', 22.

6 For the updated edition, see Mary Pipher and Sara Pipher Gilliam, *Reviving Ophelia: Saving the Selves of Adolescent Girls* (New York: Riverhead Books, 2019).

7 See Ariane M. Balizet, *Shakespeare and Girls' Studies* (New York: New York University Press, 2014); Jennifer Hulbert, Kevin J. Wetmore Jr., and Robert L. York, *Shakespeare and Youth Culture* (New York: Palgrave Macmillan, 2006); and Sarah Projansky, *Spectacular Girls: Media Fascination and Celebrity Culture* (New York: Routledge, 2020), among others.

8 Ayanna Thompson and Laura Turchi, *Teaching Shakespeare with Purpose: A Student-Centred Approach* (London: Bloomsbury Arden Shakespeare, 2016), 7.

9 Malo-Juvera, Greathouse, and Eisenbach, *Shakespeare and Young Adult Literature*, viii.

10 Jennifer Flaherty, 'Reviving Ophelia: Reaching Adolescent Girls through Shakespeare's Doomed Heroine', *Borrowers and Lenders: A Journal of Shakespeare and Appropriation* 9, no. 1 (1 May 2014): n.p.

11 Linda Hutcheon, 'On the Art of Adaptation', *Daedalus* 133, iss. 2 (Spring 2003): 108–111.

12 Douglas Lanier, 'Shakespearean Rhizomatics: Adaptation, Ethics, Value', in *Shakespeare and the Ethics of Appropriation*, ed. Alexa Huang and Elizabeth Rivlin (New York: Palgrave Macmillan, 2014), 29. *The Arden Research Handbook of Shakespeare and Adaptation*.

13 Douglas Lanier, 'Shakespeare and Adaptation Theory: Unfinished Business', in *The Arden Research Handbook of Shakespeare and Adaptation*, ed. Diana E. Henderson and Stephen O'Neill (London: Bloomsbury Arden Shakespeare, 2022), 50.

14 Christy Desmet and Sujata Iyengar, 'Adaptation, Appropriation, or What you Will', *Shakespeare* 11, no. 1 (2015): 19.

15 Christy Desmet, 'Introduction', *Shakespeare and Appropriation*, ed. Christy Desmet and Robert Sawyer (London: Routledge, 1999), 15.

16 Malo-Juvera, Greathouse and Eisenbach, *Shakespeare and Young Adult Literature*, ix.

17 For another take on the impact of the Covid-19 pandemic on Shakespeare studies, see the volume *Lockdown Shakespeare*, in this series.

18 The year 2014 was also the publication year of Deanne Williams's special issue on 'Girls and Girlhood in Adaptations of Shakespeare' for *Borrowers and Lenders*. When Jennifer Flaherty received the final edit suggestions on her essay 'Reviving Ophelia', one reviewer suggested that she remove the word 'relatable' as a descriptor for the heroines in the YA Shakespeare novels because of Mead's article denouncing relatability.

19 Rebecca Mead, 'The Scourge of "Relatability"', *The New Yorker*, 1 August 2014.

20 We were both in attendance at Garber's talk, and we are grateful to Gregory Watkins for the quotations, which are taken from specific references to her speech in his 2022 workshop reflection. Gregory Watkins, 'Speaking the Speech: Cultivating a Space Somewhere Between Literature and Performance in the General Education Classroom', *Shakespeare and General Education Workshop, Annual Meeting of the Shakespeare Association of American* (2022): 3.

21 See Burt, 'Afterword' and York, '"Smells Like Teen Shakespirit"', among others.

22 Gregory M. Colòn Semenza, 'Teens, Shakespeare, and the Dumbing Down Cliché: The Case of "The Animated Tales"', *Shakespeare Bulletin* 26, no. 2 (Summer 2008): 37–68.

23 See Balizet, *Shakespeare and Girls' Studies* and Erica Hateley, *Shakespeare in Children's Literature: Gender and Cultural Capital* (New York and London: Routledge, 2009), among others.

24 Marjorie Garber, 'Relatable', *Raritan* 38, no. 4 (Spring 2019): 125.

25 Ibid., 126.

SECTION I

Trauma and survival

1

Teaching *Romeo and Juliet* in plague time

A trauma-informed approach

Ariane Balizet

This chapter addresses the study of Shakespeare's *Romeo and Juliet* in the years 2020–22, during the global pandemic of Covid-19. In what follows, I acknowledge and consider various forms of trauma, including widespread community trauma like the overwhelming threat of illness and death, grief and loss of loved ones, the abuse and murder of Black and Brown people at the hands of police and white supremacists, economic instability, unemployment, and decreased access to social services including basic medical care. Within this context my subject is Shakespeare's *Romeo and Juliet*, a play that includes descriptions of sexual assault, sexist and racist language, and depictions of suicide, grief, bloody violence, and child loss.

My intent in describing the contents of this chapter is not to avoid these issues but rather to address them directly as forms of trauma and support increased access to trauma-informed pedagogical approaches to Shakespeare's plays for readers whose engagement with this subject may be informed by individual, collective, or intergenerational histories of trauma. As Alison Kafer has proposed,

> [P]erhaps part of our task in thinking pedagogically about trigger warnings and trauma, disability and disclosure, is to think about the work of such warnings. What exactly might they make room for or allow? What work can they do?[1]

In part, content warnings can enrich and expand our pedagogy when employed as dynamic operations of accessibility. For students with intrusive thoughts of self-harm, for example, a syllabus statement alerting readers to the presence of suicide in *Romeo and Juliet* may not prevent a panic attack if the professor shows a film version of the final scenes in class or when a peer casually weighs the relative pain thresholds of the two protagonists in discussion. In addition to static warnings, our pedagogy could work towards a shared understanding that some content holds the potential to generate pain, panic, anxiety, and suffering in students. To accomplish this, we must acknowledge that Romeo and Juliet's suicides are both *traumatic* and *traumatizing* events and direct our pedagogy towards empowering all students to develop meaningful ways of accessing and engaging with the tragedy. Teaching *Romeo and Juliet* during plague time has revealed to me the urgency of developing a pedagogical approach that acknowledges the broad impact of trauma on the Shakespeare classroom – especially as the ubiquitous rhetoric of plague, contagion, and pestilence in Renaissance literature draws students' attention to historical experiences of suffering and disease.

In this chapter, I argue that recognizing the force of trauma in students' lives and in *Romeo and Juliet* can make the Shakespeare classroom more accessible and support a more meaningful engagement with early modern affect. I focus on teaching *Romeo and Juliet* between 2020 and 2022 as a critical frame; this period of plague time has revealed how trauma transforms students' experiences in the literature classroom and demanded that instructors rethink accessibility in all aspects of their teaching. In characterizing recent history and an ongoing pandemic as plague time, I mean to acknowledge the language of plague in early modern drama as an expression of trauma and register its salience to the teaching of *Romeo and Juliet* during the pandemic (ongoing at the time of this writing). This is certainly not to suggest that the nature and effects of Covid-19 and the bubonic plague are the same but rather that we can make meaningful connections between our students' experiences of a global pandemic and the cycles of plague that shaped attitudes towards illness and loss in Shakespeare's plays.

Trauma and triggers in plague time

The widespread but heterogenous effects of the Covid-19 pandemic demand a reckoning with how trauma shapes our students' experiences in the classroom. In the midst of designing virtual courses or managing socially distanced classrooms, educators were made increasingly aware of how students' emotional and physical well-being affected their access to and success in the classroom. When nearly all university classes went virtual, many students' lack of access to a personal computer, private study space, and a reliable internet connection made it impossible to successfully complete their studies. As colleges and universities went back to in-person instruction, students returned with new experiences of illness and loss of friends, family members, and loved ones. Knowing that many of our students are suffering financially, emotionally, mentally, and/or physically as a result of the pandemic must prompt us to consider how we expect all students to engage with depictions of trauma or potentially traumatizing material.

Trauma-informed pedagogy increases access to educational spaces that would otherwise exclude or harm students with trauma histories. At the same time, a trauma-informed pedagogy accepts that not all students will experience trauma in similar ways, recognize shared events *as* trauma, or fully understand their own attitudes towards trauma. In other words, a trauma-informed approach to teaching *Romeo and Juliet* in plague time does not assume that all students experience traumatic effects as a result of the pandemic or that the study of literature in the context of sixteenth- and seventeenth-century cycles of plague will trigger uniform responses in the classroom. Scholars of trauma and pedagogy in the social sciences have noted that teaching about trauma as an aesthetic category can, in some cases, ignore or even promote traumatic effects. A trauma-informed pedagogy addresses *trauma* in content and students' lives from the position that *traumatization* should be consciously and deliberately avoided. For Janice Carello and Lisa Butler,

> To be *trauma-informed*, in any context, is to understand how violence, victimization, and other traumatic experiences may have figured in the lives of the individuals involved and to apply that understanding to the provision of services and the design of systems so that they accommodate the needs and vulnerabilities of trauma survivors. . . . A central tenet of this view is that individual safety must be ensured through efforts to minimize the possibilities for inadvertent retraumatization, secondary traumatization, or wholly new traumatizations in the delivery of services.[2]

Carello and Butler take particular issue with pedagogical approaches to trauma in non-clinical disciplines that exalt or exploit traumatic effects as learning 'breakthroughs'. A trauma-informed approach to teaching *Romeo and Juliet* in plague time should thus recognize the potential for students to make meaningful connections between life during sixteenth- and twenty-first-century pandemics but should not take for granted uniformity among students in their own experiences of Covid-19, nor expect personal disclosures of trauma as necessary for success in the class.

The 'first, do no harm' pedagogical approach advocated by Carello and Butler reflects early models of trauma-informed systems in healthcare and legal institutions. The US Substance Abuse and Mental Health Services Administration (SAMHSA) has developed a model for trauma-informed care that

> *realizes* the widespread impact of trauma and understands potential paths for recovery; *recognizes* the signs and symptoms of trauma . . . and *responds* by fully integrating knowledge about trauma into policies, procedures, and practices, and seeks to actively *resist re-traumatization*.[3]

Although students may not be prepared to disclose their personal trauma histories in the first weeks of a class on early British literature, the SAMHSA model does prompt educators to consider how pedagogical policies, procedures, and practices engage with or ignore the effects of trauma. Students who experience (or anticipate) re-traumatization in the classroom are not only denied access to learning but may be acutely harmed by the experience. In an essay on 'Weepy Rhetoric' with Neil Simpkins, Sarah Orem describes a harrowing panic attack triggered by a fellow student's presentation on 'the rhetoric of the suicide letter' in the work of David Foster Wallace. Orem writes, 'I spent the class, mentally, somewhere else, struggling to hold on against an onslaught of electrifying fears.'[4] I will return to Orem and Simpkins's notion of 'weepy rhetoric' later in this chapter, but here I want to stress how the effects of re-traumatization can utterly deprive a student of meaningful access to the classroom in a manner that may be invisible to their peers and professor. A trauma-informed pedagogy would encourage collaboration with students on strategies for dealing with the threat of re-traumatization (including, but not limited to, allowing students to define the terms of their engagement with potentially traumatizing texts).

Teaching *Romeo and Juliet* in plague time demands that we not only consider the forms of trauma students may bring to the classroom but also recognize their counterparts in Renaissance drama *as trauma*. To illustrate, I want to turn briefly to a description of rape in *Romeo and Juliet*. Given the high incidence of sexual assault on college campuses,[5] a trauma-informed approach to teaching *Romeo and Juliet* should consider how we draw attention *to* or *from* the traumatic effects of sexual violence in sixteenth-century drama. As I have argued elsewhere, attending to intersections of gender, age, race, and class in *Romeo and Juliet* reveals students' beliefs that 'everyone got married earlier in those days' and that girls and women had no expectation of bodily autonomy in the Renaissance.[6] In discussions of gender and violence, students at all levels often begin from the assumption that sexual violence was not experienced as trauma in Shakespeare's time. Alerting students to the fact that the play includes descriptions of sexual assault through a written content note will not sufficiently counter these assumptions, and students may overlook or, crucially, internalize the promise of assault in this exchange between two Capulet men in the opening scene of the play:

> SAMSON [W]omen, being the weaker vessels, are ever thrust
>   to the wall; therefore I will push Montague's men from the
>   wall, and thrust his maids to the wall.
> GREGORY The quarrel is between our masters and us their men.

SAMSON 'Tis all one. I will show myself a tyrant: when I have fought with the men, I will be civil with the maids, I will cut off their heads.
GREGORY The heads of the maids?
SAMSON Ay, the heads of the maids, or their maidenheads, take it in what sense thou wilt. (1.1.15–26)[7]

Samson's boast describes his aggression towards the Montague patriarch as a form of gendered violence: 'women, being the weaker vessels, are ever thrust to the wall; therefore I will . . . thrust [Montague's] maids to the wall.' His pun on 'heads of the maids/ maidenheads' pairs a fantasy of sexual assault with that of murder. A trauma-informed pedagogy acknowledges that this passage not only depicts a traumatizing act in the past but also has the potential to activate a trauma response in a present-day survivor. In her essay 'Sexual Violence, Trigger Warnings, and the Early Modern Classroom', Kristen Mendoza explains how educators often deliberately avoid addressing the violence in Shakespeare's works *as traumatic*, which can alienate and isolate sexual assault survivors in the classroom:

> When instructors underscore the ubiquity of violence in early modern works without voicing and responding to its continued pervasiveness in our contemporary moment, these silences and inaction neglect those in the classroom who are working through the aftermath of trauma, and suggest that the issues raised in analyses of early modern literature are ultimately limited to Shakespeare's time.[8]

Instructors can bring a trauma-informed approach to *Romeo and Juliet* by addressing the exchange between Samson and Gregory initially through asynchronous learning opportunities – such as a paper handout, online content, or brief recorded lecture – that students can engage with on their own terms in preparation for a scheduled class discussion. The development of asynchronous lessons has become familiar to most educators two years into a pandemic, and the introduction of asynchronous learning specifically when dealing with traumatizing content builds trust between the instructor and students that they will not be surprised by potentially triggering content in the classroom. This approach conveys to all students that they should discuss such content with care and concern for their peers.

By offering multiple modalities (and temporalities) for engaging with potentially traumatic material, instructors can use trigger warnings to 'enable student autonomy by giving students the time and space to discover what they are capable of doing and when they require assistance'.[9] Disability Studies scholars have further theorized trigger warning as a rhetorical form that registers trauma and resists ableist assumptions about who belongs in the classroom. Orem and Simpkins describe the trigger warning as 'weepy rhetoric . . . a method of calling attention to pain through language':

> Reclaiming pathologizing notions about the over-sensitivity of the mentally ill, a trigger warning is a form of reverse discourse – a political strategy whereby a marginalized group speaks back to power in the same terms that have historically been used to oppress them.[10]

Adopting a trauma-informed pedagogy establishes pathways for students with varied experiences of trauma to engage with historical accounts of emotion or violence without ignoring or dismissing their own pain.

Plague and points of entry

Teaching *Romeo and Juliet* in plague time means noticing – perhaps more poignantly than ever before – that although the language of plague and pestilence was ubiquitous, Renaissance dramatists rarely depicted the suffering of plague victims. *Romeo and Juliet* was likely first performed around 1594, not long after the theatres reopened after the 1592–3 outbreak of plague had passed. Early audiences would have included mothers and fathers grieving the loss of their children, and those fortunate enough to have survived an infection may have carried visible marks and scars from carbuncles, necrosis, and, of course, the painful, swollen, discoloured lymph nodes or *buboes* that give the plague its name.

Mercutio's dying words – 'A plague a' both your houses!' (3.1.108) – seem freshly cruel in the context of a post-pandemic theatrical audience, but even in the accidental quarantine of Friar

John at the end of the play, Shakespeare resists confirming a single case of plague in Verona. Friar John explains his inability to deliver the letter in a narrative that briefly raises the spectre of contagion:

> Going to find a barefoot brother out,
> One of our order, to associate me,
> Here in this city visiting the sick,
> And finding him, the searchers of the town,
> Suspecting that we both were in a house
> Where the infectious pestilence did reign,
> Sealed up the doors and would not let us forth,
> So that my speed to Mantua there was stayed. (5.2.5–12)

Believing Friar John and his colleague to be coming from a house struck by plague, the 'searchers of the town' force them to remain inside. Friar John claims he was unable to get a messenger to deliver the letter, 'so fearful were they of infection' (5.2.16). Despite this, however, Friar John emerges the following day, implying that 'the infectious pestilence' did *not*, in fact, 'reign' in the house he was visiting. As Barbara Traister observes, '[i]n these scattered references to plague there is no recorded concern for those who may be (but in fact never are) suffering and dying. Rather the concern is for preventative measures to protect those not infected'.[11] Mercutio's invocation of 'A plague a' both your houses!' is decidedly *not* a statement of concern or a warning. But Traister's characterization of *Romeo and Juliet*'s plague references as 'preventative measures' given the absence of plague victims on the early modern stage suggests that dramatists drew a bright line between engaging with the traumatic communal effects of plague and staging the infected body.

This brings me once again to the questions about trigger warnings posed by Kafer at the beginning of this chapter: 'What exactly might they make room for or allow? What work can they do?' Reading Mercutio's line through the lens of traumatization 'makes room' for audience members who seek to recuperate a sense of control – through effective quarantine practices, perhaps – over their houses. This reading builds upon Mendoza's model of trigger warnings as pedagogical tools that can 'frame classroom conversations, provide points of entry for discussion of early modern works, and optimize access, learning, equity, and respect in the classroom'.[12] As Mendoza observes, a single 'catch-all' statement does not meaningfully increase access to a pedagogical experience for students with a mental illness or trauma history that might be triggered by specific topics. Rather, she argues:

> Teachers can increase accessibility for students and heighten their intellectual engagement by using trigger warnings as introductions, framing the session's lesson plan, and giving students multiple strategies for beginning analysis and entering conversations.[13]

Although both Kafer and Mendoza advocate for dynamic and critical practices of content framing, their work also acknowledges a surprising array of voices and positions in the debate over trigger warnings in academic spaces. Some believe the practice of identifying and alerting students to potentially distressing content promotes and rewards 'weakness'; some fear that such warnings will allow students and educators to ignore challenging material; and some express concern that the policing of distressing content, especially at the institutional level, will inevitably silence already-marginalized educators who teach about racial injustice, sexual violence, or other histories of oppression and will ultimately prioritize the comfort of the most privileged students and faculty.[14] Indeed, because the first summer of the Covid-19 pandemic coincided with the rise of Black Lives Matter as one of the most prominent social justice movements in US history, educators who teach about racism, intersectionality, or white supremacy in plague time are already subject to overt attempts to ban texts that challenge white comfort. While trauma-informed pedagogy can help us 'explain the difference between pedagogically productive discomfort and trigger-induced re-traumatization',[15] instructors who use a trauma-informed pedagogy to promote accessibility remain vulnerable to condemnation (and worse) by educational and political administrations.

Teaching *Romeo and Juliet* in plague time

In the last section of this chapter, I offer an example of a trauma-informed lesson on *Romeo and Juliet*. This example reflects an evolving approach to teaching *Romeo and Juliet* in two upper-division courses on the Plague Years and Plague in the Humanities (spring 2021, synchronously online) and a lower-division *Introduction to Shakespeare* class during the summer of 2020 (asynchronously), winter 2020 (synchronously online), and fall 2021 (in-person). I begin with some practical advice on developing trauma-informed frameworks for teaching early modern drama in plague time. I then sketch out a single day's lesson that invites students to consider the prologue to *Romeo and Juliet* as a dramatic trigger warning, alerting a post-pandemic audience to the content and nature of the play, and framing the tragedy as meaningful because the star-crossed lovers' death buries the feud. I pair passages from Shakespeare's play with Arthur Brooke's 1562 verse translation of Bandello, *The tragicall historye of Romeus and Iuliet*, and follow each passage with a set of critical questions that emerged in my own experience teaching the play during 2020 and 2021. This lesson attends to three overlapping pedagogical priorities: reading the language of plague as an expression of trauma, acknowledging the salience of this interpretation to the study of the play during the Covid-19 pandemic, and actively resisting re-traumatization of students in my classroom.

A trauma-informed approach to *Romeo and Juliet* comprises a range of opportunities to reflect on and accommodate the effects of trauma, including written and verbal content notes (updated as needed), open and ongoing communication about potential triggers, and an invitation to bring objects or gadgets that provide sensory comfort to class. Crucially, these reflections are not limited to students who come to the course prepared to disclose a disability and/or trauma history; all students should be invited to reflect on the impacts of trauma on the classroom.

Developing a trauma-informed perspective might begin with keeping an archive of content warnings for assigned texts and taking the time to reflect on and update these warnings as the semester goes on. Similarly, I include a statement (excerpted here) on how the class will approach potentially traumatic content on the syllabus and online course presence:

> It is my aim to provide a safe and supportive learning environment for all students. As a teacher-scholar of colour, I am keenly aware that the hierarchies of racial, gender, and class oppression celebrated in Renaissance literature will be troubling

for many students. It is my belief that *naming* and *understanding* these hierarchies is a more liberating educational practice than dismissing them with 'things were different back then.' As a professor with over two decades of teaching experience, I am also sensitive to the fact that certain ideas, images, concepts, and acts (especially those having to do with violence or suffering) can trigger a trauma response in some students that makes it difficult – if not impossible – to learn. I hope that you will use content notes as an opportunity to communicate with me about how I can best support your learning.

In our study of each play, we will be learning about plague in the Renaissance, including descriptions of symptoms, mortality rates, and cultural responses. Notes on potentially traumatizing content appear [online]. I will usually signal content with depictions of or references to racism, sexual assault, gendered violence, homophobia, suicide, physical violence, and pregnancy/ infant loss. Please let me know if it would be helpful for your learning to signal other forms of content.

As I noted earlier on the exchange between Samson and Gregory, creating handouts, short videos, or online modules that directly address traumatic content gives students freedom to access important material at a time and place that supports their learning. Explaining why these materials are available and trusting students to engage with them in healthy ways builds trust between students and the instructor; similarly, inviting students to reflect periodically on their verbal contributions to class from a trauma-informed perspective demonstrates the value placed on communal support and collaboration.

In all of the courses I listed earlier, *Romeo and Juliet* was the first play on the syllabus, and the aim of this lesson is to begin developing students' ability to recognize trauma in Shakespeare's plays and its potential impact on the classroom relatively early in the semester. I typically devote at least half an hour on the first day of class to invite students to close read the prologue and note what we learn about the play's plot, setting, and language from its first fourteen lines. Inevitably, students wonder why Shakespeare 'spoils' the ending before the play has begun. The lesson I propose begins after we have completed the play, about a week into the semester. I invite students to return to the question of why the prologue not only sets the scene (as in *Troilus and Cressida*, the only other tragedy that opens with an omniscient chorus) but also gives away the play's ending. In class, students examine two passages from Brooke's poem and two similar passages from Shakespeare's play (typically, we read all four passages as a large group, but depending on class size and time available, this exercise could also be done through small groups). I have arranged them in the following in what might be called chronological order (Brooke's 1562 'Argument' and then a passage from much later in his poem, followed by the prologue to *Romeo and Juliet* and the 'infectious pestilence' passage from Act 5), but in practice I prefer to conclude the discussion with Shakespeare's prologue to explore questions of how that text *specifically* manages the emotional weight of the audience's grief in a post-pandemic theatrical experience.

Passage 1

The Argument

Love hath inflamed twain by sudden sight.
And both do grant the thing that both desire.
They wed in shrift by counsel of a frier.
Yong Romeus climes fayre Juliet's bower by night.
Three months he doth enjoy his chief delight.
By Tybalt's rage, provoked unto ire,
He payeth death to Tybalt for his hire.
A banished man he scapes by secret flight.
New marriage is offered to his wife.
She drinks a drink that seems to [stop] her breath.
They bury her, that sleeping yet hath life.
Her husband hearte the tidings of her death.
He drinks his bane. And she with Romeus knife,
When she awakes, her self (alas) she slayeth.[16]

Critical Questions: How does Brooke's Argument introduce the protagonists? How does their story resemble Shakespeare's tragic pair, and how is it different? Although the characters come from feuding households, Brooke does not mention this in the Argument. What aspects of the story are essential to this passage? What does this passage prepare us to focus on as we read Brooke's poem?

Passage 2

For that a brother of the house,
a day before or twain.
Dyed of the plague (a sickness which
they greatly fear and hate)
So were the brethren charged to keep
within their convent gate,
Bard of their fellowship,
that in the town do wonne,
The town folk eke commanded are,
the fryers house to shun:
Till they that had the care of health,
their freedom should renew,
Whereof, as you shall shortly hear,
a mischief great there grew.
The fryer by this restraint,
beset with dread and sorrow,
Not knowing what the letters held,
deferred until the morrow.[17]

Critical Questions: Unlike Shakespeare's *Romeo and Juliet*, Brooke notes that one of the holy brothers did, in fact, die of plague during the course of the action. Does this brief mention of a plague victim in Brooke's poem change our sense of the narrative? Why might a playwright retain this scene's function in the plot but leave out the actual victim? Why does drama approach descriptions of plague differently than verse?

Passage 3

Two households, both alike in dignity,
In fair Verona, where we lay our scene,
From ancient grudge break to new mutiny,
Where civil blood makes civil hands unclean.
From forth the fatal loins of these two foes
A pair of star-crossed lovers take their life,
Whose misadventured piteous overthrows
Doth with their death bury their parents' strife.

The fearful passage of their death-marked love,
And the continuance of their parents' rage,
Which but their children's end naught could remove,
Is now the two hours' traffic of our stage;
The which, if you with patient ears attend,
What here shall miss, our toil shall strive to mend. (1.0.1–14)

Critical Questions: How does the prologue depict the plot of *Romeo and Juliet*? Having finished the play, are there aspects of the prologue that you now find misleading? Were both houses depicted 'alike in dignity?' How effective is the play at showing that the deaths of Romeo and Juliet have 'bur[ied] their parents' strife?' What does this passage prepare us to focus on as we watch the play?

Passage 4

the searchers of the town,
Suspecting that we both were in a house
Where the infectious pestilence did reign,
Sealed up the doors and would not let us forth
So that my speed to Mantua there was stayed. (5.2.8–12)

Critical Questions: How does thinking about *Romeo and Juliet* as taking place during a pandemic shape our understanding of the play? The protagonists meet at an 'old accustomed feast' (1.2.19) at the Capulet house. Do the Capulets (and gate-crashing Montagues) not realize that there is plague in Verona? Do party-goers assume they will not be affected by plague, or do they willingly accept this risk? Even though Mercutio famously curses both houses with 'a plague', this passage spoken by Friar John is the first we have heard about an 'infectious pestilence' in Verona. Why does this occur so late in the play?

To conclude, I ask students to consider the prologue of *Romeo and Juliet* as a dramatic trigger warning. Students' responses to this possibility have been remarkable: they note, for example, how the prologue twice asserts that the deaths of Romeo and Juliet will end the feud and 'heal' Verona, preparing audience members from the first lines to find meaning in the tragic loss of two children. The prologue, in fact, invites us to grieve for Romeo and Juliet on behalf of their parents, placing the audience in a position of compassion as we witness multiple scenes of violence and trauma. These passages also show students, however, that Shakespeare treats the threat of plague with ambivalence: contagion lurks in Verona, but we are only aware of the plague once the lovers have been separated and Romeo has been tragically misled by news of Juliet's death.

Not all of my students are convinced that Romeo and Juliet's deaths will end the feud and heal the 'ancient grudge' in Verona; indeed, some note that the dialogue between Montague and Capulet patriarchs in the final scene indicates a festering resentment. I am reminded of Orem and Simpkins's conclusion that the weepy rhetoric of trigger warnings can generate healing that is not altogether neat or clean:

> Wounds weep when they heal. Just like a mending sore leaks pus and fluid, a trigger warning brings into the world (via text) the nasty, painful histories that someone who might use a trigger warning has lived through while allowing mentally ill students to find a way to navigate the world around them. Trigger warnings ask us to consider how reading and writing make the body and mind vulnerable together.[18]

Shakespeare's *Romeo and Juliet* habitually employs weepy rhetoric, insisting on the interrelation between the emotional pain of grief and the physical peril of contagion, or the acute fear of sexual assault as retribution for the chronic violence between two foes. Reading the first fourteen lines of the play as a dramatic trigger warning helps students recognize and empathize with trauma in the distant past and the current moment.

Teaching *Romeo and Juliet* in plague time has made clear to me that trauma-informed pedagogy can radically transform students' engagement with Shakespeare and support a more meaningful sense of community in the literature classroom. To be sure, students attending class via Zoom after being exposed to Covid-19 identify with Shakespeare's depiction of Friar John 'sealed up' in a house to prevent infection in a way that very few could have in 2019. Yet the spread of bubonic plague in early modern England usually tapered off significantly in the winter, and some periods of plague (like that which preceded the first performances of *Romeo and Juliet*) could be measured in months, not years. The relentless waves of Covid-19 mutations will likely shape our students' college experience from beginning to end. Teaching in plague time demands pedagogies that cultivate empathy, make room for vulnerability, and actively build trust between educators and learners. This is how our classrooms may, in time, support our collective healing.

Notes

1 Alison Kafer, 'Un/Safe Disclosures: Scenes of Disability and Trauma', *Journal of Literary & Cultural Disability Studies* 10, no. 1 (2016): 16.

2 Janice Carello and Lisa D. Butler, 'Potentially Perilous Pedagogies: Teaching Trauma Is Not the Same as Trauma-Informed Teaching', *Journal of Trauma & Dissociation* 15 (2014): 156.

3 Substance Abuse and Mental Health Services Administration (SAMHSA). *SAMHSA's Concept of Trauma and Guidance for a Trauma-Informed Approach.* HHS Publication No. (SMA) 14-4884 (Rockville, MD: Substance Abuse and Mental Health Services Administration, 2014), 9 (emphasis in original).

4 Sarah Orem and Neil Simpkins, 'Weepy Rhetoric, Trigger Warnings, and the Work of Making Mental Illness Visible in the Writing Classroom', *Enculturation: A Journal of Rhetoric, Writing, and Culture*, 16 December (2015): n.p. http://enculturation.net/weepy-rhetoric.

5 According to the Association of American Universities, over 20 per cent of all fourth-year undergraduates have experienced sexual assault while in college. D. Cantor, et al., *Report on the AAU Climate Survey on Sexual Assault and Sexual Misconduct.* Association of American Universities (2019): 41.

6 See Ariane Balizet, 'An Intersectional Approach to Girls and Girlhoods in Shakespeare's Verona', in *MLA Approaches to Teaching Romeo and Juliet*, ed. Joseph Ortiz (forthcoming).

7 William Shakespeare, *Romeo and Juliet*, ed. René Weis, in *The Arden Shakespeare, Third Series, Complete Works* (London, New York, Oxford, New Delhi, and Sydney: Bloomsbury, 2020). All references to the play are to this edition.

8 Kristen N. Mendoza, 'Sexual Violence, Trigger Warnings, and the Early Modern Classroom', in *Teaching Social Justice Through Shakespeare: Why Renaissance Literature Matters Now*, ed. Hillary

Eklund and Wendy Beth Hyman (Edinburgh: Edinburgh University Press, 2019), 100.

9 Ibid., 99.

10 Orem and Simpkins, 'Weepy Rhetoric', n.p.

11 Barbara H. Traister, '"A Plague on Both Your Houses": Sites of Comfort and Terror in Early Modern Drama', in *Representing the Plague in Early Modern England*, ed. Rebecca Totaro and Ernest B. Gilman (Oxford and New York: Routledge, 2010), 178.

12 Mendoza, 'Sexual Violence', 98.

13 Ibid., 100–1.

14 Mendoza outlines the debate on trigger warnings in the classroom in 'Sexual Violence', 97–9. See also Angela M. Carter, 'Teaching with Trauma: Trigger Warnings, Feminism, and Disability Pedagogy', *Disability Studies Quarterly* 35, no. 2 (2015): n.p. https://doi-org.ezproxy.tcu.edu/10.18061/dsq.v35i2.4652 and Kafer, 'Un/Safe Disclosures', 1–2.

15 Carter, 'Teaching with Trauma', n.p.

16 Arthur Brooke, *The tragicall historye of Romeus and Iuliet written first in Italian by Bandell[o], and nowe in Englishe by Ar. Br* (London, 1562): unnumbered page.

17 Brooke, *The tragicall historye of Romeus and Iuliet*, fo. 70ʳ.

18 Orem and Simpkins, 'Weepy Rhetoric', n.p.

2

Nothing/Something

YA *Much Ado* novels in the world of digital shaming and virtual outcasts

Laurie E. Osborne

Something or nothing? Noting or oblivious? Interest or disdain? The questions at the core of Shakespeare's *Much Ado about Nothing* align serendipitously with issues that inspire YA novelists to adapt the comedy's characters and multiple slander narratives. The recent proliferation of *Much Ado* novels suggests that Shakespeare's comedy offers YA novelists a near irresistible blend of romantic manipulation, sexual shaming, bullying, and outsider status. Even though Hero's disgrace has much more extreme social consequences than reputations created (and destroyed) in current Western social media, the widespread access to personal information through internet circulation enables new explorations of how false report and image manipulation influence public identities, particularly among adolescents. Ultimately, eavesdropping, false reports, and staged representations of betrayal *and* attraction in Shakespeare's *Much Ado about Nothing* prove both invaluable for adaptation and usefully varied in detail. Consequently, the comedy has become an important site for working through current reputation building and surveillance.

The technologies of sexual shaming and false report surface in YA *Much Ado* novels as early as 2006. Since then Shakespeare's comedy has been adapted into fiction at least fourteen times: J. C. Burke's *Faking Sweet* (2006), Jenny Oldfield's *Much Ado about Nothing* (2008), Jody Gehrman's *Triple Shot Betty* (2008), Kjersten Beck's *Much Ado about Magic* (2012)*, Michelle Mankin's *Love Revolution* (2012)*, Alison May's *Much Ado about Sweet Something* (2013), C. E. Wilson's *Much Ado about Nothing: Shakespeare for Everyone Else* (2013)*, Tara Eglington's *How to Keep a Boy from Kissing You* (2013), Marion Cheatham's *Ruined* (2014)*, Marina Fiorata's *Beatrice and Benedick* (2014), Michelle Ray's *Much Ado about Something* (2016)*, Lily Anderson's *The Only Thing Worse Than Me Is You* (2016), McKelle George's *Speak Easy, Speak Love* (2017), and Molly Booth's *Nothing Happened* (2018).[1] Two are historical novels that target both YA and adult audiences (*Beatrice and Benedick* and *Speak Easy, Speak Love*), but most are Young Adult or New Adult novels.[2] These writers pick up on the potential links between this comedy and social media so vividly realized in the YouTube vlog production *Nothing Much to Do* (2014).[3]

The specific deployment changes, but digital slander has deleterious effects that are, surprisingly, as consistent across platforms as across time: posting doctored pictures on MySpace in Gehrman's 2008 *Triple Shot Betty* still resonates with current practices even without the up-to-date technological allusions in Lily Anderson's 2016 *The Only Thing Worse Than You Is Me*. Even so, evolving digital manipulations of reputation/identity enable increasingly complex depictions of how social media and instant communications both harm and benefit adolescents.

While the semi-amorous hostilities of Beatrice and Benedick typically remain intact and central to these narratives and other characters, like Don John, are reworked in telling ways, Hero, Shakespeare's virtuous but largely passive heroine, has provoked the most wide-ranging adaptation and elaboration. Hero – aka Henrietta, Hope, Heaven, Bonni (to Beatrice's Blythe), Sarah, Samantha, Harper, and Hana – undergoes almost as much character revision as her name does. These fictional reworkings of Hero and her experience of slander emerge concurrently with developments in psychological and behavioural studies that are now reaching the popular press. In August 2019 Mary Pipher and Sarah Pipher Gilliam ascribed 'The Lonely Burden of Today's Teenage Girls' to 'today's huge unplanned experiment with social media'.[4] Already well known in Shakespearean feminist and girl studies for her work in *Reviving Ophelia: Saving the Selves of Adolescent Girls*, Pipher directs her attention to the dangerous effects of social media on girls' sense of personal identity and self-sufficiency. Their article draws on a relatively small, largely Midwestern sample of one hundred interviews but parallels many recent social science studies of online adolescent dating. Though often seeming to plumb the depths of the obvious, this work ranges from hypotheses about the technological potential for slander and increased anxiety that young couples can experience in their first romantic explorations to the possible linkage of 'technology-assisted adolescent dating violence and abuse (TAADVA)' with more general abusive adolescent relationships.[5] Adopting the less clunky phrasing of digital dating abuse (DDA), Lauren Reed and her fellow researchers bring gender differences into their analysis and in the process discern significant gender alignments in different online actions.[6] The most widely visible abuse – circulating or creating reputation-damaging online material – replays in virtual form the slander of Hero in Shakespeare's *Much Ado*. In current online dating, as in the play, such behaviour originates more often in young men and does more psychological damage to young women. Reed's findings provide a useful context for the online slanders and visual misrepresentations that appear in many YA *Much Ado* adaptations.[7]

The subtleties of this research have even broader implications. For example, beyond examining the sexting abuses often ascribed to young men and most luridly familiar in the press, Reed and her co-authors also research excessive surveillance as well as gendered emotional responses to both digitally invasive behaviours.[8] The gender disparities in both the abuse and the reactions to it suggest that young women may suffer more anxieties about online treatment but, at the same time, they are more likely to engage in versions of online stalking, including tracking their partners with cell phones and haunting their social media.[9] Young women's apparently larger stake in online surveillance aligns surprisingly well with treatment of Beatrice in the play. While the trick on her succeeds as quickly as the one on Benedick, it is substantially shorter and grounded as much in commentary on her shrewish nature as on Benedick's ostensible love for her. Benedick, in contrast, seems to require highly visual descriptions of Beatrice's emotional state, the early modern counterpart to the current circulation of provocative images. The first three of these *Much Ado* novels identify technology and internet communication as the new arenas for eavesdropping and sexual shaming across different national audiences. Published in Australia, J. C. Burke's *Faking Sweet* is both earliest and most explicit in reimagining adolescent reputation building and destruction within technological contexts. *Faking Sweet* deploys email, texting, and an electronic diary to engage with the play. These materials present conflicting narratives that demand the readers' attention to alternative versions of the possibly 'evil' characters, Jess or Calypso. Admittedly, the naiveté of the central protagonist, Holly, almost immediately provokes readers to doubt her supposed friend, Calypso, who wants revenge on Jess for everything from stealing her boyfriend to shoplifting with her and abandoning her. The novel locates the establishment of rumour and reputation in social media interactions: miles away in Melbourne, Calypso uses texts, email, and phone calls to destroy Jess's reputation as thoroughly as she can. Holly spends as much time worrying over and interpreting these communications as the novel spends offering them. All this interpretation occurs in the context of Mrs Gideon's classes on *Much Ado*, as the play ultimately leads Holly to understand her role as a Borachio in Calypso's revenge plan.

Just as important, the novel puts its readers into a state of uncertainty, embroiling them in misjudging Jess. Though Calypso is obviously tricking Holly, texts and digital materials nonetheless obscure both Jess's reputation and her relationship with Scott. Calypso's story portrays Scott and her as a couple until 'One Saturday afternoon when Calypso was meant to meet Scott at his place, she walked in to find Scott and Jess together. There was her boyfriend with her best friend rolling around on the floor of his parents' bedroom'.[10] Burke includes Jess's diary entries that seem to support this account. Not until the end of the novel do Holly and the reader discover that Scott is Jess's cousin, stalked by Calypso. Burke ensures that her readers are as misled by the digital exchanges as Holly herself is and as implicated in the effects of technological reputation creation/destruction.

Two years later, in a British YA *Much Ado* adaptation, Jenny
Oldfield foregrounds the visual dimension of publicity culture
through her somewhat unusual narrator, a tabloid-style reporter
for *Lite Entertainment*. Claudia Ricci observes and reports the
action with her paparazzi cameraman. Their presence implies
ongoing technological reproduction of all the misunderstandings
and tricks. For example, in Act 3 she describes 'picking up the
next scrap of scandal when we come across Pedro chatting with
Benedick, Claudio and Leonardo in the hot tub' and overhearing
Claudio's promise to 'shame [Hero] in front of everyone in the
church'.[11] However, although Ricci freely criticizes Claudio's hot-
headedness and John's villainy and even asks 'when is it ever Pedro's
and Claudio's fault? Answer: Never',[12] she herself never intervenes
to defend Hero. Oldfield's novel uses the surveillance implicit in
current celebrity culture to emphasize the ways in which her
readers/audience members, like Burke's readers, are continuously
implicated in the surreptitious surveillance, resulting assumptions,
and crucial inactions within Shakespeare's play. Similar publicity-
based reputation destruction surfaces in Michelle Mankin's New
Adult novel, *Love Revolution* (2013), which puts the comedy's
characters in a rock-and-roll world: JR's (Claudio's) shaming of
innocent intern Sarah (Hero) takes place in the public space of
a televised interview. Unlike Mankin's single publicity moment,
Oldfield's ubiquitous video journalist *and* painstaking adherence to
Much Ado place the comedy solidly within current reproducible
television and social media.

In Jody Gehrman's 2008 *Triple Shot Betty*, published in
the United States, the shaming and its resolution demonstrate
how visual technologies can both create and dispel destructive
characterizations. After being rejected by the naïve Hero, who
prefers Claudio, a charming Italian vintner intern, John circulates a
photoshopped image of Amber (Margaret) in Hero's boots to ruin
Hero's reputation and relationship. Unlike the relative privacy of
the overheard phone conversations that encourage Geena (Beatrice)
and Ben (Benedick) to recognize their interest in each other, John's
visual misrepresentation circulates widely. It also leads the three
baristas to realize that several other young women widely 'known'
as sexually promiscuous in their social circle have suffered from
comparable slander at John's hands after rejecting him. The young
women exploit and expand John's strategy of using video evidence.

With the help of his latest young target, the Betties Against Men (BAMs) and their allies lure John into the forest, tie him to a tree, and coerce him into confessing his crimes as each victim recounts what he did to ruin her reputation. By filming the entire episode and publicly screening John's humiliation, they turn the technology that he has used against Hero into the mechanism for exposing his callous serial slanders. Long before the #MeToo Movement, Gehrman's novel both identifies the mistreatment of female reputations as a reiterative strategy of masculine control and posits collective public testimony as the most powerful response.

Released early in the history of digitized adolescence, these novels anticipate the more complex explorations that later *Much Ado* novels offer. The six adaptations published in 2012–13 by Beck, Mankin, May, Eglington, Wilson, and Cheatham consistently explore the implications of digital (mis)representation and slut-shaming, though the last two novels offer more limited versions and Eglington invokes Facebook misrepresentation of Aurora (Beatrice) by her mother rather than social media generally. Beck's and May's novels offer the most intriguing permutations on the sexual shaming, reputation surveillance, and status contests that give Shakespeare's comedy its ongoing adaptive currency.

Kjersten Beck's YA *Much Ado about Magic* translates the comedy's status issues into teenage magical conflicts between clans controlling different spells. Pedro Aragon's money making/ stealing spell ensures his superior status, and Claudio Florentine's strength spell helps the soccer team, while Bee (Beatrice) resists using the Hero clan's beauty/image alteration spell as Sarah (Hero) and Leonata (Leonato and Borachio) do. Ben Paduan's truth spell causes the rift between Bee and him when he enspells her to tell Pedro about her crush on him. Since these spells represent the clans' claims to power and superiority over the 'normals', leaking them is cause for extreme punishment. In fact, Sarah's supposed theft of the money spell is her 'betrayal' and leads to her public shaming. Despite its magical focus, this novel's conflict nonetheless centres around videotaped evidence of Sarah's theft, thus indirectly underscoring the self-photoshopping inherent in the Hero clan's magic. Their image manipulation not only enables Leonata to adopt Sarah's appearance to frame her as a spell-stealer but also helps Sarah and Bee 'disappear' by removing their beauty spells to become invisible as 'normal' kids in their school. While the slander in this novel has shifted away from sexual transgression, a move that some later novels also adopt, Bee's resistance to beautifying herself as a Hero clan member and the increasing focus on body image align this novel in subtle ways with the mechanism of digital shaming.

In *Much Ado about Sweet Nothing*, Alison May elaborates on *Much Ado*'s characters by positing digital relationships and by foregrounding the importance of 'nothing' in ways that resonate with digitalization – Ben, a mathematician, has just published a book about zero and the importance of nothing, which Trixie (Beatrice) reluctantly promotes at the library where both she and Henrietta (Hero) work. Of the adaptations up till 2013, May's novel takes up most fully the biggest challenge that this play poses for current readers: Hero's submissive nature. While the fierce independence of Benedick and Beatrice translates well into contemporary relationships, the high social value and vulnerability of Hero's chastity and, more disturbing, her willingness to marry Claudio despite humiliating public shaming utterly contravene current mores.

Perhaps as a result, Henrietta's (Hero's) passivity receives much fuller treatment than it does in the play. Scarred by the death of her mother and consequently committed to perfection as a defence mechanism against abandonment, Henrietta first engages Claudio's interest before he goes abroad; their relationship flourishes in their texting while he is away. When he almost immediately proposes after they reunite, she devotes herself to creating the perfect wedding, which he then ruins by publicly rejecting her at the altar, based on the slenderest evidence presented in any of these novels. Once the error is resolved and Claudio barrels ahead with renewed wedding plans, May's Henrietta seems poised to exemplify the original Hero's easy acceptance of her marriage to the man who shamed her. Initially, she even more vigorously tries to achieve perfect fiancée/wife status by agreeing to marry in Italy and move away from her family, job, and friends to follow his job offer. This characterization of Hero resonates with Pipher's diagnosis of social media's effects on young women: excessive anxieties, impaired self-sufficiency, and a weakened sense of self.

May also reimagines *both* Claudio and Hero. Her Claudio notices that Henrietta always agrees with his plans and asks her to choose. Faced with the decision of getting on the plane with him or not, Henrietta realizes that both options are *Claudio's* alternatives, without any real attention to what she might want. However, her decision to stay rather than go with Claudio is not the most interesting revision that May offers. When Claudio emails Henrietta three months later to ask for a new start, the novel closes with her receipt of his message and a truly open choice:

> From: Claudio Messina
> Subject: Sorry. New start?
> And those two little buttons. Open and delete.
> Open or delete?[13]

Because May leaves Henrietta's decision undetermined, her novel simultaneously focuses on the difficult question of Hero's easy re-acceptance of Claudio in the play and leaves her agency open to interpretation. The novel's pervasive use of virtual communication, May's fully realized Hero-protagonist, and the final unanswered binary virtual choice all challenge any easy assessment of Henrietta (Hero). The ending even raises the question of whether this last option merely entraps Henrietta again in Claudio's alternatives.

Despite the relatively limited digital interactions in May's novel, Henrietta's experience fits with the DDA examined by Lauren Reed and her co-authors. Beyond their predictable assertions that 'digital media use in adolescence is frequent, varied, and integrated into daily life and relationships', Reed tracks gender differences in digital dating and points out that sexual images and 'intrusive digital dating behaviours' trouble young women more than young men.[14] Their study neatly dovetails with Henrietta's experiences, especially during the courtship and its aftermath.

The two novels published in 2016, Michelle Ray's *Much Ado about Something* and Lily Anderson's *The Only Thing Worse Than Me Is You*, deepen and re-envision both the possibilities of digital slander and potential variations of plot and character. Consequently, both expand social media contexts while addressing issues created by recent possibilities in digital manipulations and permanence. These shifts underscore the flexibility of the comedy as an adaptive source, not only as a site for negotiating with the patriarchal stereotyping in digital interactions that researchers like Reed have identified but also as a source for exploring the varied influence and duration of digital representations.

Michelle Ray followed her well-received *Falling for Hamlet* by self-publishing *Much Ado* in *Much Ado about Something*. In addition to diverging from all other YA adaptations in a key aspect of the plot – her Hero actually does die, albeit accidentally by rushing into traffic after an argument with her irate father – Ray's novel represents a pinnacle in technological slut-shaming for these novels. Following up on the clever use of media in *Falling for Hamlet*, Ray deploys social media and texting extensively in *Much Ado about Something*. In fact, she emphasizes technology as the dominant mechanism for *both* social interaction and deception. Each chapter opens with a text exchange, much of the rumour circulation occurs via texting, and Beatrix even 'overhears' a butt-dialled conversation.

Most significant, Hope's (Hero's) shaming at the dance involves the video that implies her promiscuity by splicing her image with Maggie *in flagrante*, the public circulation of that video at the dance, and Clay's (Claudio's) public rejection of her. The compression of all the trick's elements – presentation of visual proof, circulation of rumour throughout Hero's social circle, and publicly humiliating rejection – foregrounds technology's role. Ray goes further and incorporates the ways that public policing has entered the social media picture. Though all the boys are in trouble for their public treatment of the video, Clay faces criminal child pornography charges for supposedly circulating it until another piece of video evidence proves that John actually stole Clay's phone and used it for the public distribution. Ben, too, runs into difficulties, both with Hope's parents who demand that the school ruin his college chances and with Beatriz who has realized that he knew about the video before Clay received it. The real-world consequences of the video shaming thus threaten the futures of Clay, Ben, and Beatriz, not just Hope.

Ray's updating of *Much Ado* also insists on the unintended, extended, and tragic consequences of specifically *digital* shaming in Hope's death. Beyond that shocking resolution – which realizes in full the deadly effects of Hero's humiliation that Shakespeare's comedy merely pretends – Ray's novel posits text, email, images, *and* video as the pervasive social world which these characters inhabit. Even stepping back from that virtual engagement has destructive consequences. When Beatriz refuses to call or text her parents while she and Ben drive back to Los Angeles from Hope's funeral, her parents send the police to arrest Ben for kidnapping, even though Beatriz is of age. At the same time, video technology advances their relationship: the resolution involves a video of Beatriz's confessing she has only broken up with Ben to save him from being suspended at her uncle's behest and Pedro's film of Ben, still in love with Beatriz, demanding that Pedro NOT ask her to the dance. Even the final scene is represented as video: Beatriz and Ben on film for the digital yearbook. All in all, Ray depicts a world both aligned with *Much Ado*'s culture of surveillance, interpretation, and social consequences and expressive of even more pervasive, destructive effects for such social interactions in virtual communities.

Lily Anderson's *The Only Thing Worse Than Me Is You* sustains Ray's view of a pervasive and influential virtual world but reimagines its consequences. Anderson recasts the ruin and the rescue of Harper's (Hero's) reputation wholly within technological contexts: the 'cheating' here is changing grades on the school computer server in order to frame some students for plagiarism and reshape the relentlessly reported class rankings of the top five students. As it turns out, the only intentional slanders in this novel are academic; their purpose is to punish bullies and to dethrone inconveniently top-ranked students by getting them suspended for plagiarism and lowering their class ranking. In fact, Harper is only accidentally identified as the school's computer hacker because her IP address is used. Replacing sexual slander with a hacking scandal designed to manipulate class rank relocates social ruin in the loss of both status and access to top-tier colleges for students at the Messina School for the Highly Gifted.

Not only does this strategy exploit the most intense current adolescent anxieties – fears about getting into college – but also Anderson identifies technology itself as governing the various slanders. Falsifying internet information to manipulate relationships lies at the core of this novel. Moreover, virtual interactions have intended and unintended consequences, benefiting some relationships and characters while harming others. John is initially accused of plagiarism himself, but he researches the hacking and identifies Harper as the source of the destructive technological misbehaviour. At first this move seems like a clever double fake for a character who has the reputation as 'the evil twin'. However, John is *not* slandering Harper, and his own bad reputation arises from a psychology project in which he has been experimenting with rumour. Instead, Michael, an ex-friend of Ben's not based on any character in the source narrative, has been trying to regain Ben's friendship by 'helping' him become valedictorian. As a result, this novel consistently demonstrates that even well-intended technological approaches to relationships can be destructive – Michael's inadvertent digital slander of Harper does as much harm to her relationship with Cornell (Claudio) as Don John's manipulations in Shakespeare's play, albeit not in the realm of sexual shaming.

More important, when Harper blames the hyper-competitiveness at the school for what has happened, she identifies the larger social world, with its enforced grade hierarchies and resulting pressures, as the real source of the scandal. Her point is persuasive – the duels at Messina involve sharing the forbidden knowledge of student IQs (Trixie's and Ben's are identical!).[15] Harper even takes Cornell's reaction to her apparent hacking to mean that he cares more for his class rank than for her. In turn he seeks to refute that view by sabotaging his own top ranking through complex manipulations of the points he stands to gain – or lose – from club membership. The considerable disorder generated by the hacking scandal, particularly in terms of rank/status and male friendships, extends well beyond Harper's humiliation and suspension. As a consequence, the novel reframes the situations in Shakespeare's comedy outside the arena of sexuality and romance yet still solidly anchored within manipulable digital reputation.

At the same time, *The Only Thing Worse Than Me Is You* adapts the mixed consequences of rumour and slander in Shakespeare's *Much Ado about Nothing* to explore the many facets of adolescent cyber relationships. Marissa Mosley and Morgan Lancaster have recently observed that 'Technology use in adolescent relationships is more complex than most research may suggest; it is neither all good nor all bad, but both positives and negatives can be experienced concurrently throughout this important developmental stage'.[16] Just as telling, they note that '[b]y encouraging an "either-or" stance on the benefits *or* adverse impacts of technology, the researchers have noticed that couples begin to feel as if we do not quite understand their lived experience'.[17] Supported with a large data set (though predominantly white and heterosexual) that includes 5,647 seventh through twelfth graders with 84 per cent response rate,[18] their study is particularly pertinent to YA *Much Ado* novels because of its balanced examination of the benefits *and* dangers of technologically assisted relationships. What these novels explore is the complexities of young adult 'lived experience'. Both their plots and their characters work through which kinds of social surveillance and (mis)representations enable and which ones destroy relationships and individuals.

For example, in Anderson's novel Trixie articulates her changing perceptions of Ben's physique and character in computer metaphors – 'I could not stop myself from cataloguing all of it, overriding the existing Ben West folder in my head'.[19] Moreover, texting very quickly becomes the grounds for their relationship. In an orgy of nerd-bonding, Trixie and Ben text back and forth for several pages about their mutual interest in comic books. As Trixie herself notes, unlike the normal school email communications, 'texting felt personal, unregulated'.[20] In fact, a few chapters later they are texting each other *while together*. Even the revelation that they have been tricked into liking each other resolves after he sends her a text message asking her to sit with him. These virtual interactions adapt both the imagined letter writing that incites their love and the sonnets that prove it in Shakespeare's comedy. These novels re-contextualize Benedick's comment, 'A miracle! Here's our own hands against our hearts'.[21] Essentially, concrete records in Shakespeare's comedy resonate in digital records that also potentially persist and influence identities and relationships.

The most recent *Much Ado* novel, Molly Booth's *Nothing Happened*, starts out eschewing the trend of aligning the comedy with current internet dating behaviours. The Maine summer camp where this novel takes place combines a ban on technology with camp, a conventional hotbed of teenage romance away from home. Initially, Booth seems more concerned with diversifying *Much Ado*'s characters than with the play's potential resonance with social media: Beatrice is an Ethiopian adoptee who grapples with a largely white culture in Maine, Donald and his illegitimate brother John are both mixed race, and Beatrice's bisexual sister Hana (Hero) is falling in love with Claudia, who has herself grappled with homophobic prejudice in her high school. However, Hana's relationship with Claudia, like Henrietta's with Claudio in (*Much Ado about*) *Sweet Nothing*, develops in texts and email while they are apart during the school year. More important,

John engineers Hana's supposed cheating initially by exploiting the ways her texts to her ex-boyfriend imply their continued intimacy. *Nothing Happened* also invokes texting, which is so destructive for Hana and Claudia, as the crucial resolution for Bee and Ben after their friends reveal their trickery. Ben pulls out their phones where they have texted each other their feelings 'in writing, remember?'[22] These intrusions of technology demonstrate the potential to enable as well as destroy intimate relationships, with both possibilities most strongly influencing the female characters.

Ben's comment reinforces the effects implied in Anderson's adaptation: putting feelings 'in writing' virtually is just as determinative now as in *Much Ado*, even though these records are currently digital. The problem – or opportunity – created by the permanent record appears most strikingly in Shakespeare's comedy when Beatrice and Benedick's private sonnets, once exposed, overrule their public declarations of disinterest. Though none of these novels notes it explicitly, these adapters are beginning to grapple with how the new photographic or video or IP evidence that ruins the reputations of the several Hero-figures also possesses a problematic semi-permanent digital footprint.

As YA *Much Ado* novels demonstrate, social practices in Shakespeare's comedy that may seem dated actually prove both persistent and currently coercive. These novelists adopt different approaches to digital manipulations of reputation, status, and identity to engage the evolving virtual social lives of adolescents. Their fictions stage increasingly nuanced explorations of how social media and instant communications benefit *and* endanger adolescent relationships and identities. Just as significant, these interactions, like those in Shakespeare's play, have both transient and potentially permanent effects. Even as adapters move beyond the obvious social media relevance of eavesdropping, false reports, and staged representations of betrayal *and* attraction in the comedy, Shakespeare's *Much Ado about Nothing* continues to offer YA adapters provocative and cautionary material, particularly for young women. After all, Benedick follows his observation that his and Beatrice's private written words overrule their public disdain by silencing Beatrice: 'Peace, I will stop your mouth' (5.4.96). We should be grateful that YA novelists who engage this comedy so frequently show no sign of stopping.

Notes

1 J. C. Burke's *Faking Sweet* (Sydney: Random House Australia, 2006), Jenny Oldfield's *Much Ado About Nothing* (London: A&C Black, 2008), Jody Gehrman's *Triple Shot Betty* (New York: Dial Books for Young Readers, 2008), Kjersten Beck's *Much Ado about Magic* (Amazon Digital Services, 2012)*, Michelle Mankin's *Love Revolution* (Amazon Digital Services, 2012)*, Alison May's *Much Ado about Sweet Something* (UK: ChocLit, 2013, reissued in 2021)*, C. E. Wilson's *Much Ado about Nothing: Shakespeare for Everyone Else* (Amazon Digital Services, 2013)*, Tara Eglington's *How to Keep a Boy from Kissing You* (Sydney: St. Martin's, 2013), Marion Cheatham's *Ruined* (Amazon Digital Services, 2014)*, Marina Fiorata's *Beatrice and Benedick* (London: Hodder & Stoughton, 2014), Michelle Ray's *Much Ado about Something* (Amazon Digital Services, 2016)*, Lily Anderson's *The Only Thing Worse Than Me Is You* (New York: St. Martin's Griffin, 2016), McKelle George's *Speak Easy, Speak Love* (New York: HarperCollins: Greenwillow Books, 2017), and Molly Booth's *Nothing Happened* (New York: Hyperion Books, 2018). Self-published novels have asterisks.

2 Booksellers identify 'New Adult novels' as those geared for YA readers who have aged beyond novels addressed and populated by teens.

3 See Jane Wanninger '"Hello, people of the Internet!": *Nothing Much to Do* and the Young Adult Creators and Communities of Vlog-Shakespeare' in this volume and Douglas M. Lanier, 'Text, Performance, Screen: Shakespeare and Critical Media Literacy', *Cahiers Élisabéthains* 105, no. 1 (2021): 124.

4 Mary Pipher and Sara Pipher Gilliam. 'The Lonely Burden of Today's Teenage Girls', *Wall Street Journal* (17 August 2019): C3.

5 Karlie E. Stonard, et al. '"They'll Always Find a Way to Get to You": Technology Use in Adolescent Romantic Relationships and Its Role in Dating Violence and Abuse', *Journal of Interpersonal Violence* 32 (2017): 2083.

6 These research papers typically cite *all* the previous work in the field, so I am limiting my review here to a few key articles.

7 Lauren A. Reed, 'Gender Matters: Experiences and Consequences of Digital Dating Abuse Victimization in Adolescent Dating Relationships', *Journal of Adolescence* 59, no. 1 (August 2017): 79–89.

8 Ibid.

9 The 2021 Facebook scandal underscores these effects on young women.

10 Burke, *Faking*, 30.

11 Oldfield, *Much Ado,* 54.

12 Ibid., 83.

13 May, *Much Ado about Sweet Nothing*, 307.

14 Reed, 'Gender Matters', 79, 80.

15 Anderson, *The Only Thing*, 53.

16 Marissa A. Mosley and Morgan Lancaster, 'Affection and Abuse: Technology Use in Adolescent Romantic Relationships', *American Journal of Family Therapy* 47, no. 1 (2019): 62.

17 Ibid., 55–6.

18 Ibid., 56.

19 Anderson, *The Only Thing*, 153.

20 Ibid., 165.

21 William Shakespeare, *Much Ado about Nothing*, ed. Claire McEachern, in *The Arden Shakespeare, Third Series, Complete Works* (London, New York, Oxford, New Delhi, and Sydney: Bloomsbury, 2020). All references to the play are to this edition (5.4.91).

22 Booth, *Nothing*, 319.

3

'I will not be a frozen example, a statued monument'

Self-actualization after trauma in *Pandosto*, *The Winter's Tale*, and *Exit, Pursued by a Bear*

Sara Morrison

Central to Robert Greene's *Pandosto*, William Shakespeare's *The Winter's Tale*, and E. K. Johnston's *Exit, Pursued by a Bear* is gendered violence, in each case involving a male victimizer and a female victim or survivor. These three texts form a genealogy of adaptations that reveal the consequences of women's isolation when confronted with violence and subsequent trauma, clarifying the significance of supportive intersectional networks to post-traumatic healing and actualization. Considered chronologically, these texts reflect historically situated ideologies of gender, charting forward progress towards female self-actualization, the process of emergent recreation of one's particular autonomy, even as the characters reckon with trauma and its consequences. Greene's *Pandosto* (1588) offers the least glimmer of hope, as Bellaria does not survive the eponymous character's unrestrained jealousy. Shakespeare's *Winter's Tale* (1610) adapts Greene's plot, providing inroads for hope, optimism, and healing. Hermione survives, owing to Paulina's wise counsel and advocacy; in this case, she has an ally whose own autonomy facilitates Hermione's restoration of self. In Johnston's novel (2016), the most hopeful of the three texts, Hermione Winters mobilizes her trauma to restore her strength and recreate herself, self-actualizing in cooperation with a supportive coalition of friends, family, law enforcement, and the medical community. In Shakespeare's play and Johnston's novel, intersectional alliances facilitate women's and girls' healing and renewed, emergent self-discovery. The gap over the distance between victim and survivor is filled for Hermione and her namesake in *Exit* by allies and advocates who provide counsel, safety, and support, facilitating post-traumatic healing that contends with the physical remnants and emotional consequences of violent trauma. Johnston's novel offers the clearest expression of hope, as Hermione Winters is a co-creator of her autonomous self, engaging with empathetic allies and skilled advocates and healers, whose trust and strength facilitate her therapeutic movement back to self-confident autonomy. The novel's optimism is particularly important for young readers, who themselves may be navigating through post-traumatic healing or serving as an ally in a supportive network.

In her discussion of Shakespeare's *Othello* and Jordan Peele's *Get Out*, Vanessa Corredera productively suggests that 'placing [them] in conversation with each other, or at least having the racial dynamics of the latter inform one's reading of the former invite "cross-historical" tracing that might foster reflection upon what strategies for Othering may have been successful in the early modern period . . . even if there was not a precise vocabulary to define them'.[1] The same model may be overlaid onto reading backward from *Exit* to *The Winter's Tale* to *Pandosto*; Johnston has access to a vocabulary that is responsive to twenty-first-century social dynamics, critical theory, legal arguments and decisions, and medical responses to trauma, among others, that can be brought to bear on Shakespeare's and Greene's texts. Such interpretive strategies do not foreclose differences in historical context, nor do they expect early modern writers and texts to think, act like, and reflect twenty-first-century ideologies. Yet, they do 'invite "cross-historical" tracing' to revisit pan-historical consequences of power differences and, in the case of these three texts, post-traumatic traces of gendered and sexual violence.

'My power is such as I may compel by force': The foreclosure of female recovery after trauma in *Pandosto*

In *Pandosto*, the language of masculine love and desire is equivalent to the language of violence and control.[2] Moreover, gendered violence is generational. Pandosto violently threatens his wife, Bellaria, when he feels betrayed or rejected or, perhaps even more disturbingly, as an overture to love. Dorastus, Egistus's son, treats Fawnia, Pandosto's daughter, in the same way. Both mother and daughter are subjected to gendered violence, which results, ultimately, in Bellaria's death and Fawnia's inexplicable absence from the text's ending. Compellingly, the queen and her daughter, a girl of sixteen, actively resist both Pandosto's false accusations and unwanted advances and Dorastus's misguided and violent love language, yet both women's lives end tragically. Although mother and daughter are self-aware and strong, both resisting all unwelcome sexual advances and violent death threats, there is no possibility of post-traumatic self-actualization. Neither woman has an ally or advocate to support her, including each other, as they are separated in Fawnia's infancy, during which time Bellaria dies. In large part, both women are isolated.

Pandosto's violent actions arise from jealousy and licentiousness, traumatizing both his wife and his daughter. After accusing Bellaria of infidelity with his friend Egistus, Pandosto imprisons her and puts her on trial. While imprisoned, Bellaria gives birth to a baby girl, whom Pandosto rejects and sends into exile on a boat. Although Bellaria insists on her innocence, she dies immediately upon learning of her son, Garinter's, untimely death, another casualty of Pandosto's rage. After Pandosto buries his wife and son together, the narrative turns to Fawnia and Dorastus, Egistus's son. Fawnia's relationships with both Dorastus and Pandosto disturbingly repeat patterns of male violence as endemic to rituals of courtship. Upon first seeing Fawnia, Dorastus is seduced by her beauty, which surprises him, exposing his biases rooted in social class, given that she is the daughter of a shepherd and he a prince. He expresses his desire for her by thinking about her in degrading ways, calling her a 'country slut', and suggesting that she cannot reject him: 'Why Fawnia, perhaps I love thee, and then thou must needs yield, for thou knowest I can command and constrain.'[3] Fawnia sees this for what it is – threats of rape masquerading as love behind justifications of class privilege – replying, 'I had rather die than be a concubine, even to a king'.[4] That Fawnia eventually marries Dorastus can help us to understand the reasons that she similarly does not condemn Pandosto. Moreover, her internalization of these various aggressions brings into focus the consequences of women's isolation and forced silence in response to masculine violence.

Fawnia encounters violent overtures to sexual assault again, this time instigated by her father. Upon Fawnia's return to Bohemia sixteen years later, Pandosto attempts to coerce her into a sexual liaison before he is aware of her identity; he is therefore guilty of sexual misconduct even as he is unwittingly soliciting incest. Pandosto repeats Dorastus's strategies, attempting to coerce her into a sexual encounter, warning her, 'My power is such as I may compel by force'.[5] Like her mother, Fawnia resists gendered violence by relying on herself – her personal ethics and individual strength. And like her mother, Fawnia is the singular woman in her own story. After Fawnia successfully rebuffs her father's advances, Pandosto vows to execute her, unknowingly revisiting his threats against her when she was an infant sixteen years earlier. Yet upon learning the truth of Fawnia's identity, Pandosto recants, and the narrative turns to reconciliation – though troubled – as Fawnia and Dorastus marry.

It would seem, then, that Fawnia moves beyond trauma towards self-actualization. Yet, the ending of Greene's romance is ambiguous. The narrative concludes with Dorastus alone: 'Dorastus . . . went with his wife and the dead corpse into Bohemia where, after *they* were sumptuously entombed, Dorastus ended his days in contented quiet'[6] (italics mine). Katharine Wilson considers the violent parallels between Dorastus and Pandosto:

> Dorastus achieves 'contented quiet', but only apparently after 'they' (logically his wife and father-in-law) are safely below

ground. . . . the joint burial is eerily reminiscent of Pandosto's dispatch of Bellaria and Garinter at the end of the first half of the narrative. . . . Dorastus somehow rids himself of women and lives in solitary bliss. Fawnia – who never comments on her father's actions – is thus as effectively silenced as her mother before her.[7]

Like her mother, Fawnia dies in isolation from other women, and as Wilson persuasively suggests, perhaps at Dorastus's hand or will. Given *Pandosto*'s pervasive culture of gendered violence, Dorastus's permanent silencing of his wife is consistent with the text's patterns of marital dynamics. Given these patterns, readers can map Pandosto's violent 'courtship' of Fawnia backward onto his early relationship with Bellaria, suggesting that Bellaria may likely be a long-term survivor of gendered trauma rooted in sexual coercion. This may help us rethink and reframe her interactions with Egistus. Although both women exert their powerful voices and wills against their perpetrators, in their isolation they are forced into silence to endure their trauma alone.

'Be stone no more; approach': Women's alliances as facilitators of post-traumatic actualization in *The Winter's Tale*

Shakespeare's dramatic romance, *The Winter's Tale*, is patterned closely after Greene's *Pandosto*, with notable differences when it comes to women's responses to gendered trauma. As in Greene's play, the gendered violence in *The Winter's Tale* is generational. Leontes abuses his wife and daughter, and having survived exile in Bohemia, Perdita is also threatened with bodily harm by Polixenes. Both kings respond with violence when they feel a loss of control. Like Pandosto, Leontes initiates his wife's trauma by triangulating their marriage. At his request, Hermione bids Polixenes to delay his departure from Sicilia, successfully achieving what her husband could not, thereby convincing Leontes that his wife and friend have betrayed him. Leontes imprisons Hermione, his wrath focused on questions of fidelity and paternity, which catalyses the generational effects of gendered violence – their son, Mamillius, dies and Leontes banishes their daughter, Perdita. Sixteen years later, in Bohemia,

Polixenes exercises similar cycles of paternal and royal violence, threatening to disinherit his son Florizel and disfigure Perdita, warning, 'I'll have thy beauty scratched with briars',[8] should they marry without his permission. Polixenes's violent threats directed at both Perdita and Florizel align him with Leontes's capacity for violence carried out on a woman's, and his son's, bodies. Although both Hermione and Perdita suffer violence and ongoing trauma at the hands of men who should instead champion them, their stories end differently than do Bellaria's and Fawnia's, as both have allies and advocates. Most significantly, having witnessed the violent injustice of Leontes's actions and its consequences, in Act 2, Paulina steps into the role of actionist.[9]

Considering Paulina's interventions into Leontes's actions and Hermione's ultimate 'rebirth' in this way shifts the focus of the play onto Paulina herself. In allying herself with Hermione, speaking truth to Leontes's power, arranging Hermione's sixteen-year safe house, and directing her ultimate reconciliation with Perdita, Paulina's actionism facilitates her own self-actualization. Paulina is a skilful counsellor; her powerful, persuasive language drives Leontes's penance and Hermione's return to the social world. Insofar as she protects Hermione, assisting her through her trauma, Paulina is both healer and counsellor. Ian Sabroe and Phil Withington consider the significance of counsel to early modern and modern medical practice, addressing the centrality of the dialogic doctor/patient relationship in both eras. Grounding their analysis of early modern medicine in Thomas Elyot's *The Castle of Health* (1539) – 'the foundational text of the vernacular medical humanism' – they argue that 'Elyot was giving his readers a voice – one that allowed them to become patients who counselled *with* rather than simply took counsel *from* physicians'.[10] Although Paulina is neither physician nor patient, her counsel instructs and, though perhaps not entirely satisfyingly, heals. Included in Sabroe and Withington's taxonomy of early modern medical practitioners are 'healers', including 'wise-women', who can be understood as 'peripherals, amateurs and unlicensed marginal healers'.[11] They argue that, in the sixteenth century, counsel 'meant to make for more equal and dialogic consultations between patients and doctors'.[12] The word 'counsel' means authoritatively beyond medical discourse, of course, including 'a single person with whom one consults or advises', 'advocate'.[13] Considering together these contexts for understanding

Paulina's powerful counsel – she advises Leontes, advocates for Hermione, and directs the performative healing at the play's end – can be instructive for understanding the ways in which Hermione's trauma activates Paulina's actionism and expressions of autonomy and also for looking ahead to the networks of healers, allies, and advocates who facilitate Hermione Winters's post-traumatic healing in *Exit, Pursued by a Bear*.

Leontes's imprisonment of Hermione activates Paulina's role as counsellor, advocate, and healer. Upon learning of the king's unjust treatment of his wife, Paulina resolves to advise him of the truth, using the baby Perdita as proof of Hermione's fidelity. She insists that counsel 'becomes a woman best', promising that if Hermione trusts her with Perdita, she will 'be / Her advocate to th'loudest' (2.2.31, 37–8). Paulina's plan initially backfires, though; upon presenting Perdita to Leontes, he recoils from the baby, calling Paulina 'a mankind witch! . . . A most intelligencing bawd!' (2.3.66, 67) and ordering Antigonus to convey Perdita into exile. Should Antigonus refuse, Leontes will kill Perdita himself: 'The bastard brains with these my proper hands / Shall I dash out' (2.3.138–9). Like Bellaria, Hermione insists on her innocence, acting with Polixenes only as Leontes had instructed her. Yet, he is not moved. Leontes's abuse of Hermione catalyses Mamillius's death, which in turn causes Hermione to faint. Leontes, ironically, characterizes Paulina as Hermione's physician, insisting, 'Her heart is but o'ercharged. She will recover. /. . ./ Beseech you, tenderly apply to her / Some remedies for life' (3.2.147, 149–50). Paulina exits with Hermione, only to return to chastise Leontes, insisting that the queen is dead at his hand. Yet, unbeknownst to all, including first-time readers and playgoers, Paulina will serve as Hermione's healer, providing 'remedies for life', though not those that are possible in Leontes's imagination.

Instantiated as Hermione's healer, Paulina hides her for sixteen years, protecting her from her abusive husband, until, at the play's end, she reveals and vivifies Hermione's 'statue' (5.3.10). Before Paulina draws the curtain, she unsettles Leontes's epistemological position, warning Leontes that he may not be able to understand what he sees.[14] And this is bourne out by his silence upon seeing Hermione for the first time. Paulina shakes him from his 'wonder', instructing him to speak (5.3.22). Leontes and Polixenes, who has also returned to Sicilia, describe her using standard blazonic tropes and Petrarchan conventions, though their use of such language cannot activate her. Instead, Paulina, as Hermione's co-creator, successfully coaxes her back to animation, saying, 'be stone no more; approach' (5.3.99). Through counsel, advocacy, and creative healing, Paulina assists Hermione's re-actualization. Although Hermione defended herself against Leontes's false accusations, she could not save herself without a fiercely devoted ally; and it is in this powerful role that Paulina herself actualizes, as she creates space for her own and Hermione's female subjectivity in a world that otherwise would seek to silence and marginalize them throughout and in the aftermath of traumatic violence.

Intersectional alliances as facilitators of post-traumatic self-actualization in *Exit, Pursued by a Bear*

E. K. Johnston's YA novel, *Exit, Pursued by a Bear*, chronicles adolescent sexual assault and its consequences. In the novel, high school senior Hermione Winters is drugged and raped while she is away at cheerleading camp; the assault results in pregnancy, and Hermione resolutely chooses to have an abortion. The novel does not minimize the traumatic consequences of sexual assault, but it is optimistic in its modelling of personal, systemic, and institutional support that can be important for young readers. Hermione's ability to process violent sexual trauma is bolstered by an extensive support network, all actionists who refuse to stand by, including her best friend, Polly Olivier, her parents, her cheer coach, Coach Caledon, Officer Caroline Plummer, and Dr Malcolm Hutt, a psychiatrist, whose dialogic healing encourages her to return to herself, a self who grows more resilient having experienced and survived traumatic sexual assault and its aftermath. Hermione Winters's alliance network crosses age and gender lines as well as ideologies and practices of law enforcement and medicine. With the support of her extended coalition of advocates, Hermione can self-actualize after trauma, regaining her confident sense of self even when confronted with people like Leo, her boyfriend, who seek to victim-blame her.

Hermione's trajectory through trauma is facilitated by a matrix of allies, including legal and medical professionals. It is significant that Hermione's support network extends beyond friends and family to include the institutional support of officers of the law, nurses, and doctors. Johnston's novel characterizes the structures of policing not as idealistic but as trustworthy and tenacious when faced with gross injustices and violations of the law. The novel similarly depicts the medical professionals with whom Hermione interacts. Officer Caroline Plummer makes clear to Hermione from the outset that she will be her champion, providing sound counsel that will help Hermione think objectively about the consequences of her trauma. She tells Hermione that even though the lake has eroded genetic evidence of the assault, should the rape have resulted in pregnancy, DNA samples could be taken from the foetus. Officer Plummer gives Hermione confidence that it may be possible to identify her attacker, which gives her a framework for thinking about her trauma and preparing for the pregnancy test. She recalls Officer Plummer's counsel, thinking, 'I can think of it as being legal, not personal, and that helps me cope'.[15] Armed with strategic coping mechanisms, Hermione makes good choices that productively advance her case. She selects the medical clinic for the abortion that is closest to the DNA testing lab, for example, to preserve the sample. Hermione's decisions are underpinned by her confidence in Officer Plummer, who likewise treats Hermione with dignity and respect. Johnston's characterization of a supportive legal system is mirrored in the novel's medical practitioners and institutions. The medical clinic in fact functions intersectionally, serving both medical and legal purposes. Just before her abortion, the doctor, a woman, enters the room carrying a 'special collection bag . . . [with] the OPP seal on it'. Hermione thinks, 'My fetus might not get to be a full person, but it's sure as hell going to be official.'[16] Hermione considers contrasting ideas of personhood, considering the ways in which the abortion will determine the foetus' future potentialities. The foetus will not grow into an autonomous person, yet Hermione will ensure that its existence will be logged into official records, playing a significant role in identifying her attacker and achieving justice. In a novel that is invested in young women's post-traumatic healing strategies, Hermione's choice preserves the intrinsic value of the foetus' identity, made possible by consistent systemic support systems.

Following the abortion, Hermione receives care from Dr Malcolm Hutt, a psychiatrist, who therefore specializes in counsel, in dialogic healing. Dr Hutt's healing process aligns with 'a strengths perspective' in working with survivors of sexual assault.[17] Carol McCarthy and Joycee Kennedy cite Bell (2003), who 'identifie[s] three assumptions of such a perspective: clients have inherent strengths individually and within their communities, and they are more likely to act on these strengths when they are fully supported and affirmed; clients are experts of their own experiences; and the therapist is a collaborator in partnership with the client'.[18] This perspective on counsel is markedly different from Paulina's methods in Shakespeare's play. *The Winter's Tale*'s particular characterization of counsel is largely unidirectional, as healing involves advocacy and instruction. Sabroe and Withington argue that dialogic healing bridges early modern and modern ideologies of good counsel, observing that 'early modern and postmodern conceptions of counsel both suggest genuine communication between patient and doctor [is] engendered through conversation'.[19] In Shakespeare's play, that dialogic counselling is hidden from the audience's view. In hiding Hermione for sixteen years, the play does not perform the mechanisms of effective counsel. Modelling this process for young readers is integral to Johnston's novel; she makes the collaborative process visible, centralizing Hermione in her own recovery, as Dr Hutt, her psychiatrist, empowers her from a 'strengths perspective'. When they first meet, he recognizes that her memory is vague, fuzzy from being drugged, but also perhaps to protect her from traumatic pain. He tells her early in their provider–patient relationship, 'At some point, if your memories resurface, you'll break. That doesn't make you weak. That's just how it goes. And when it happens, I will already know who you are and how you think, and therefore be in a position to help you heal.'[20] Central to his philosophy is assisted healing through interpersonal dialogue. This is particularly significant as the patient has doubts or experiences post-traumatic fear. Hermione's recovery is not linear, yet she knows that she has a network of support on whom she can rely as the legal case lags and she re-experiences trauma. Like Officer Plummer, Dr Hutt is trustworthy and safe, facilitating Hermione's post-traumatic healing through active counsel that respects her personhood and life experiences.

Although Hermione's post-traumatic healing process facilitated throughout by supportive networks is *Exit*'s central focus, she is not the novel's only adolescent girl invested in self-actualized authenticity. Like Shakespeare's Paulina, Polly, too, is significantly more than just a support for her best friend. Following Officer Plummer's news that the investigation has hit a roadblock, Polly counsels Hermione, the conversation leading to Polly's confiding in her best friend that she is lesbian. This trusted sharing of intimate knowledge forges greater connection between the two friends, as Polly shares her authentic self with Hermione, and this news causes Hermione to step outside of her own circumstances to genuinely see her friend. Her first thought upon hearing this news is, 'my best friend is a lesbian and I [have been] too self-involved to notice', later apologizing to Polly, saying, 'I've been a pretty lousy friend lately, in terms of reciprocation'.[21] This moment is significant to the novel's characterization of healing in that it focuses on the importance of giving back to one's allies as well as receiving support from them. Stepping outside of the self to recognize someone else's needs can also be central to growth and healing. In *Precarious Life*, Judith Butler writes, 'Loss and vulnerability seem to follow from our being socially constituted bodies, attached to others, at risk of losing those attachments, exposed to others, at risk of violence by virtue of that exposure'.[22] Butler is concerned with the ways in which loss, vulnerability, and desire shape human interaction. As 'socially constituted bodies', humans at once are embedded in social networks and vulnerable to them. Hermione's vulnerability to her attacker is located in the context of people, place, and shared sport. At Camp Manitouwabing, a place she loves, she is competing with her trusted cheer teammates, yet she is also physically vulnerable to the violence of a stranger. Yet, in *Exit*, the relationships in Hermione's support networks deepen as a result of vulnerability conjoined with trust, authenticity, and counsel. Hermione experiences the value of empathetic communication from both patient and provider position, recognizing that genuine, good counsel (involving both talking and listening) forges strong, intimate connections and facilitates authentic expressions of self.

Exit opens with a preface that introduces Hermione as a runner. She is a body in motion from the outset, mapping Palermo and its surroundings with her footsteps and actively resisting becoming 'a frozen example, a statued monument': 'I run up and down the streets of Palermo . . . trying to hold on to the feeling that my body is my own and limitless.'[23] Although running can be a team sport, for Hermione it is a solo activity. As an athlete, she understands that physical progress takes hard work and consistent perseverance; she also knows that athletic progress isn't always linear. As a flyer on her cheer squad, Hermione takes risks, relying on her teammates to catch her as she falls. And, without doubt, practice and growth involve grit and failure, achievements made over time. In 'Whose Body Is It, Anyway?' Pamela R. Fletcher, an athlete herself, argues that taking back the body through physical activity, a reconnecting, a reclaiming, of the female body, is a strong driver of resisting ideologies of rape culture.[24] She also argues that this isn't enough, encouraging girls and women to knit together the body and the soul in resistance strategies. She writes, 'When our souls are connected to our bodies, we do not allow our bodies to be taken for granted or to be taken away from us – at least not without a struggle.'[25] Hermione's various healing strategies, including solo activities and working collaboratively with her support networks, chart a path towards renewed self-integration, body and soul, of a girl who insists on reclaiming herself. Amber Moore considers Johnston's novel's title: 'As [Wendy] Philips highlights, the story is aptly named because: "The novel's title, from a stage direction in Shakespeare's *A Winter's Tale* [sic], suggests the dangers young adults face in the real world" . . . in this case, the prevalence of sexual violence.'[26] While it's certainly true that in Shakespeare's play, the stage direction foretells Antigonus's brutal death, I read Johnston's title differently. Hermione is the bear, the Fighting Golden Bear, who pursues the truth and reclaims herself, self-actualizing with the help of an intersectional coalition of people, including her teammates whose loyalty and support, grounded in being part of a team that relies on trust, bolster her through her trauma. Near the novel's end, Hermione acknowledges the importance of their support, telling them before they leave for nationals held at Camp Manitouwabing, the site of her rape, 'you believed in me, when I didn't believe in myself. And now I believe in you. I believe in us'.[27] At the novel's end, at a serendipitous moment of recognition, Officer Plummer's procedural objectivity, Dr Hutt's convictions, Hermione's friends' and family's support, and Hermione's own self-confidence converge to enact justice. As the Fighting Golden Bears walk by the North York team, Hermione 'lock[s] eyes with one of the boys', recognizing him.[28] She sees him throw a water bottle into a trash can, certain that the DNA on the bottle will match the foetal sample. Hermione gives the bottle to Officer Plummer, who promises to run the tests immediately and move forward to an arrest.

This cluster of texts could be productively recruited as teaching tools for young audiences. Including *Exit* in a unit on *The Winter's Tale*, that also may include *Pandosto*, can substantively address the current lives of students who are facing trauma. While *Exit*'s optimistic characterization of Hermione's post-traumatic recovery is rosy and therefore somewhat challenging, perhaps that's what we should be striving for to reach students and communities. *Exit* offers hope, acknowledging that people experience trauma, but also that it's possible to come out the other side, to exit, bolstered by supportive communities. Johnston's novel suggests that we're now closer in the twenty-first century than in the early modern period. Greene's text characterizes Bellaria and Fawnia's trauma as fatal, foreclosing the possibility that women could respond productively to trauma and its consequences. And, absent the linguistic or ideological scaffolding to underpin conceptions of full post-traumatic recovery, Shakespeare may not really have been able to imagine a holistic recovery for Hermione or Perdita, one in which they are actively engaged, visible to their abusers and peers. Emilie Buchwald's essay, 'Raising Girls for the 21st Century', opens with an epigram from Freud, who writes to Marie Bonaparte *c.* 1935, 'The great question that has never been answered and which I have not yet been able to answer, despite my thirty years of research into the feminine soul, is *What does a woman want?*'[29] Buchwald's answer reveals Freud's blindness to gender equality, 'What a girl wants, what a woman wants, is what Freud knew is held precious by every man: self-determination, autonomy within reason, life without undue fear, liberty without causing harm to others, and the ability to pursue one's happiness'.[30] Yet these freedoms are severely limited in a culture whose political institutions and cultural ideologies actively constrain women's and girls' paths to self-actualization. *Exit*'s optimism, its expression of hope and survivalist ideology, opens doors for conversations about women's and girls' post-traumatic healing that is facilitated by supportive communities and intersectional alliances.

Notes

1 Vanessa Corredera, '*Get Out* and the Remediation of Othello's Sunken Place: Beholding White Supremacy's Coagula', *Borrowers and Lenders* 13, no. 1 (2020): 6.

2 Robert Greene, 'Pandosto', *An Anthology of Elizabethan Prose Fiction*, ed. Paul Salzman (Oxford: Oxford University Press, 1987).

3 Ibid., 185.

4 Ibid.

5 Ibid., 200.

6 Ibid., 204.

7 Katharine Wilson, 'Revenge and Romance: George Pettie's *Palace of Pleasure* and Robert Greene's *Pandosto*', in *The Oxford Handbook of Tudor Literature, 1485-1603*, ed. Mike Pincombe and Cathy Shrank (Oxford: Oxford University Press, 2009), 702.

8 William Shakespeare, *The Winter's Tale*, ed. John Pitcher, in *The Arden Shakespeare, Third Series, Complete Works* (London, New York, Oxford, New Delhi, and Sydney: Bloomsbury, 2020). All references to the play are to this edition (4.4.429).

9 Victoria L. Banyard, Andrew J. Rizzo, and Katie M. Edwards define 'actionists' as 'a term used to specify third parties who help as opposed to those who stand by', thereby distinguishing actionists from bystanders in their article, 'Community Actionists: Understanding Adult Bystanders to Sexual and Domestic Violence Prevention in Communities', *Psychology of Violence* 10, no. 5 (2020): 531.

10 Ian Sabroe and Phil Withington, 'Language Matters: "Counsel" in Early Modern and Modern Medicine', in *The Edinburgh Companion to the Critical Medical Humanities*, ed. Anne Whitehead and Angela Woods (Edinburgh: Edinburgh University Press, 2016), 512, 517.

11 Ibid., 511.

12 Ibid., 523.

13 *Oxford English Dictionary*, online edition. II.7.b; II.8.b.

14 For a discussion of the relationship between speech and truth, see Lynn Enterline, *The Rhetoric of the Body from Ovid to Shakespeare* (Cambridge: Cambridge University Press, 2000), esp. 206, 210–26.

15 E. K. Johnston, *Exit, Pursued by a Bear* (New York: Penguin, 2016), 66.

16 Ibid., 136.

17 Carol J. McCarthy and Joycee Kennedy, 'Transforming Trauma Responses to Sexual Abuse in Adolescents', in *Trauma Transformed: An Empowerment Response*, ed. Marian Bussey and Judith Bula Wise (New York: Columbia University Press, 2007), 41.

18 Ibid.

19 Sabroe and Withington, 'Language Matters', 523.

20 Johnston, *Exit, Pursued by a Bear*, 146.

21 Ibid., 155, 158.

22 Judith Butler, *Precarious Life: The Powers of Mourning and Violence* (London: Verso, 2004), 20.

23 E. K. Johnston, *Exit, Pursued by a Bear*, Preface, unpaginated.

24 Pamela R. Fletcher, 'Whose Body Is It, Anyway?' in *Transforming A Rape Culture*, ed. Emilie Buchwald, Pamela R. Fletcher, and Martha Roth (Minneapolis: Milkweed Editions, 1993), 439.

25 Ibid.

26 Amber Moore, '"I Knew You Were Trouble": Considering Childism(s), Shame Resilience, and Adult Caretaker Characters Surrounding YA Rape Survivor Protagonists', *New Review of Children's Literature and Librarianship* 24, no. 2 (2018): 149.

27 Johnston, *Exit, Pursued by a Bear*, 201.

28 Ibid., 239.

29 Emilie Buchwald, 'Raising Girls for the 21st Century', in *Transforming A Rape Culture*, ed. Emilie Buchwald, Pamela R. Fletcher and Martha Roth (Minneapolis: Milkweed Editions, 1993), 181.

30 Ibid., 181.

4

Exposing hate

Violence of racialized slurs in Young Adult adaptations of Shakespeare

Charlotte Speilman

As Sephy, a main character in Malorie Blackman's *Noughts and Crosses*, tells us, 'Whoever came up with the saying that "sticks and stones may break my bones but words will never hurt me" was talking out of his or her armpit'.[1] Words have great power. They can heal, and they can hurt. Words have the power to justify action and perpetrate violence. Words, which may seem simple on their surface, can reinforce social norms and political structures. Names can tell people who they are and how they are connected to their community. Conversely, they can alienate people from the community and devalue their existence, which is especially true for racial slurs.

In February 2018, Princeton University cancelled the course 'Cultural Freedoms: Hate Speech, Blasphemy, and Pornography' after students protested the professor's use of 'the n-word'. He 'defended his use of the word as "necessary" and intended to "deliver a gut punch" but by lecture's end, several students had walked out in protest'.[2] It appears that he meant to use the word to shock his students. However, when his students voiced distress, he failed to stop or to listen. He may have wanted to be provocative but, in not hearing his students' concerns, he missed a learning opportunity about the painful reality of racial slurs. He knew the hurt his words could cause, but he did not understand that, as a white man teaching Black students, his words were a *real* threat.

It is easy to say that racial slurs have no place in the classroom and to leave it at that. Yet, if we want to start societal reconciliation in our classrooms, we need to be able to discuss issues of racial discrimination with students.[3] How do we do this without causing unnecessary trauma for our students? In this chapter, I will discuss three Young Adult (YA) novelizations of Shakespeare plays as spaces for the exploration of social trauma. The texts each use racial slurs and hate speech to provoke a sense of injustice from their audiences and teach empathy for those who have experienced these types of slurs. This chapter will also explore the authors' different approaches to racialized slurs. In analysing these three texts, I hope to provide an initial framework for teachers to use when selecting texts for their classrooms.

The Shakespearean Young Adult adaptations, *Exposure* (2009), *The Steep and Thorny Way* (2016), and *Noughts and Crosses* (2001), all explore anti-Black racial violence through the stories of, and allusions to, Shakespeare's *Othello*, *Hamlet*, and *Romeo and Juliet*. To do so, each author makes a different choice in addressing the use of hate language. Mal Peet's villains in *Exposure* reveal their hateful nature through their open use of racial slurs. Cat Winters uses the voice of her main character as narrator in *The Steep and Thorny Way* to edit the conversations which she hears around her, alluding to racial slurs without quoting them directly. Finally, Malorie Blackman exposes the power of hate speech in her dystopian world of *Noughts and Crosses* by creating a dialogue of racial slurs that is unique to the reimagined world.

Texts as spaces for discussing social trauma

Each of the YA adaptations discussed in this chapter places Shakespearian plots in cultural settings torn apart by racism and bigotry. The trauma happens both on the individual and societal levels. In these new settings, societies are dealing with the collective trauma of racial prejudice. As Jeffery Alexander explains in *Trauma: A Social Theory*, 'For traumas to emerge at the level of the collectivity, social crises must become cultural crises . . . Trauma is not the result of a group experiencing pain. It is the result of this acute discomfort entering into the core of the collectivity's sense of its own identity'.[4] In these YA texts, discriminating slurs are used to make the characters and readers aware of the 'acute discomfort' breaking the community's connectivity. The slurs are more than 'name-calling'. While both 'name-calling' and slurs are painful to the individual experiencing them, name-calling is meant to hurt that individual but does not necessarily connect to larger social discrimination. By contrast, a slur is meant to alienate and hurt a person by ostracizing them from a particular society. In this 'acute discomfort', the victim is both experiencing this hate as an individual and is part of a collective experience of discrimination.

These YA texts serve as trauma narratives, which Alexander defines as 'naturally occurring events that shatter an individual and collective actor's sense of well-being'.[5] First, each text describes different characters' individual traumas of being discriminated against in their fictional landscapes. In these texts, characters face discrimination based on skin colour, which shatters their sense of well-being. As we follow the characters, we witness examples of social trauma described in these fictional worlds. In addition, as these texts represent real-world racial, sexual, class, and religious prejudice, they are stories of collective trauma ensuring readers hear of these injustices and are made aware of the 'acute discomfort' that is (or should be) present in their own collective identities. Just as fictional characters are made to recognize the collective trauma of racial injustice in their societies, the reader bears witness to a collective trauma in one's own society.

Who is the baddie? Racial slurs as markers for 'evil'

Mal Peet, a white author, does not shy away from the use of racial slurs in *Exposure*, his YA retelling of *Othello*. Peet's novel is set in a fictionalized South American country divided by racial tensions between a Black northern population, which celebrates its African heritage, and a white southern population. Although one would think in an *Othello* retelling that 'Otello', the Black football star, would be the main character, *Exposure* is part of a series of books that follow the career of the white sports journalist character Paul Faustino. In the opening of Peet's story, Faustino introduces us to Otello by saying: 'Born in the North, and famously proud of his African heritage, Otello has done much to silence (in the stadium, at least) the racist jeers directed at black northerners'.[6] Otello is a proud northerner who has just been signed for millions of dollars with a southern football (or soccer) team. He soon falls in love and marries a white politician's pop-star daughter, Desmerelda. Here, the reader is not only directed to the racism that northern players face but also that (according to local news) this racism can only be silenced with exceptionality. It is clear that Otello's talent as a player has not stopped the racism that northerners face but has instead quieted such overt behaviour. We see a world willing to hide its racism if a player is winning.

Yet despite this introduction from Faustino, we soon see that Otello is operating in a world he does not understand. He has taken the praise received on the pitch to mean that his world is no longer racist. When another character explains that there will be bitterness for selling a white player (Luis) to pay for Otello's spot on the team, Otello is surprised. When Otello is asked what he thinks of this, he is 'too taken aback to say anything'.[7] Soon after this, Brabanta (a senator, team owner, and Otello's future father-in-law) describes racism in their society and in sport to Otello saying, 'On the field, these matters are of no consequence. Off the field. . . . well you know. But what I want you to understand is this: I believe absolutely that individual ability transcends race. You are a great player. Your colour is irrelevant'.[8] Brabanta uses the toxic 'colour-blind' approach to race issues in their country; in reaction Otello's 'thoughts are tumbling like leaves in the wind'.[9] Brabanta has reintroduced Otello to the racism that Otello thought the world had moved beyond. Because of the 'silencing' on the pitch, Otello thought that he was living in a world which was progressing beyond historic racial tensions and was accepting of him now as a Black man. Brabanta is quick to bring Otello and the reader into the reality of racism in this world, pointing out the way talent may silence racism in certain arenas but not eradicate it.

Brabanta represents the white society that publicly attempts to ignore or dismiss race, while privately believing and reinforcing racist ideas. Brabanta says to Otello: 'I have no time for racism. A primitive emotion. But as I said, you will experience some hostility.'[10] By using the term 'primitive' to describe 'racism' Peet signals that Brabanta is using the historic language of racism to pretend to discredit it. In other words, the reader and Otello are becoming quickly aware of a society that is 'saying' it is not racist, while at the same time practising ideas that form racist ideologies. Otello slowly becomes more aware that those around him view him as an 'investment',[11] and he wonders 'if there will be any other black guests. It bothers him that the question has even occurred to him, he's not used to thinking this way'.[12]

Where Otello is left to parse out racism from the coded 'colour-blind' messaging around him, the reader soon realizes the racist motivations of the book's villains (Brabanta and Diego). In Otello's absence, their language shifts from careful elevated speech into racial slurs. Diego calls Otello 'King Kong', one of several references to Otello that compares him and people of his heritage to animals.[13] Later, at the height of Brabanta's anger, he refers to Otello by the 'n' word.[14] In their private speech, Peet shows his villains acting not out of reason but deep-seated racial hatred. Peet's characters openly use racial slurs to indicate that Otello cannot be a successful part of their society and that they see him as a threat because of his race. As their plots to bring Otello down advance, Otello becomes more silenced, confused, and uncomfortable with the community in which he thought he belonged. Peet's unforgiving use of radicalized language is jarring, marking for readers the individual trauma that Otello is experiencing in a society based on racial oppression. Although *Exposure* is fictional, readers are faced with the real radicalized language that represents the collective trauma of many actual racially divided communities.

The deeply unsettling use of racial slurs and the resulting silence of Otello allow readers to reflect on their own communities' use of hate speech to silence and oppress. Otello's world is a racist community functioning under the ideology that racism is not an issue. Yet, Peet does not explore the subtle ways that systemic racism can affect characters' everyday lives. Instead, he focuses on the idea that overt racism is motivation for evil acts. Otello is a famous player and widely loved, but the world (or at least several characters) conspires against him. Peet explains the motivations of these characters through their hidden (private from Otello but obvious to the reader) conversations where they spew racist opinions and use racial slurs. In this way, Otello is exposed to the consequences of racially motivated discrimination (his world is destroyed; he loses everything, including his wife, and is traded to a team in the States). Desmerelda loves Otello, but she never openly discusses his race, other than a few paragraphs of internal dialogue fetishizing his skin. She is unable to see her own privilege as a wealthy white woman or understand (as the reader does) that racism is the cause of his struggles. Instead, when Otello's world starts to crumble and he needs her the most, she insists the situation 'is about *you*' (meaning Otello) and that she has 'done nothing'.[15] Otello may not be able to avoid his problems, but Desmerelda can, and she leaves him. Peet uses racial slurs to reveal the evil nature of the villains in the book and the way that 'colour blindness' can use 'bad luck' as a mask for racially motivated oppression. The reader, and not our main character, is left to deal with the pain this language causes. Peet's villains are evil for the sake of being evil and racist for the sake of being racist, but his 'good' white characters also choose to be oblivious to race and to abandon Otello. There is no emotional or social development for these characters. Thus, the audience is given no path forward away from the pain of these racial slurs.

Racial slurs and authorial editing in historical fiction

Cat Winters's novel *The Steep and Thorny Way* is a retelling of Shakespeare's *Hamlet* set in a small town in the State of Oregon in the 1920s. As Winters, a white resident of Oregon, explains in her author's note, she was inspired to write her novel after discovering the lesser-known history of racialized laws in Oregon and the 1920s KKK takeover of the state. In this prohibition-era town, the main characters of Hanalee and Joe face discrimination due to their race and sexual orientation. Hanalee (our Hamlet-esque main character) is the daughter of a white mother and an African American father living in a state that has outlawed such marriages. Joe has known from an early age that he was attracted to boys and yet also knows that he could be arrested for acting on his feelings. Both characters struggle with being simultaneously a part of society and ostracized by that society. As the local chapter of the KKK gains more power in their small town, Hanalee and Joe are targeted, not for anything they have done but for being who they are. Hanalee explains her own situation as the only person of mixed racial heritage in the area: 'we all know I can't marry anyone around here, unless a nonwhite young man actually moves into the region. I'm not sure anyone will hire me for work. . . . What on earth am I supposed to do for the rest of my life.'[16] Winters makes her characters aware of the social violence that eugenics is inflicting on society. And yet, her characters become more aware of the hate that fuels these social structures of discrimination when they are called slurs. When Joe tells Hanalee what his father called him when he discovered he was gay, 'his voice cracked' in revealing that his father 'called me an abomination'.[17] Hanalee herself had to 'swallow down an ugly taste'[18] when she recounts Joe's experience. Early on in her story, Winters shows how the use of slurs both dehumanizes and deeply hurts her characters. When Joe is called an 'abomination', his place in the social order is eliminated: he is no longer part of a loving family, and (as his father is also the local minister) he is no longer part of a religious community.

When using the term 'abomination', Winters introduces the pain of slurs without using a word that would offend most young readers. The use of this insult does not directly name his gay identity. The term is hurtful and meant to alienate, but it draws attention to the speaker of the term more than to the person at whom it is directed. Winters reveals the hurt caused by this word through Joe and Hanalee's discussion of the incident, but she does not censor the word. The word itself does not 'deliver a gut punch' for contemporary readers. It teaches readers about the pain felt from slurs, but it is unlikely to trigger a trauma response in a reader. In *The Steep and Thorny Way*, slurs are clear markers for hate and mark the moments that these characters are no longer safe. Winters's story, published in 2016, is fiction set in an historical backdrop meant to explore the racial laws of 1920s Oregon. According to Winters, her novel was developed after she 'unearthed the troubling exclusion laws and unofficial "sundown laws", the latter of which kept African Americans from passing through certain towns after dark'.[19] She goes on to say that she lived in Oregon as of 2006 and was shocked to learn of 'the Ku Klux Klan's takeover of the state in the 1920s'.[20]

When writing popular historical fiction, authors must find a balance between wanting to appeal to a current audience and creating a historical landscape. Although Winters refers to Black people in her author's note as African American, she uses the term 'Negro' without quotation marks as a description of (and a slight towards) Hanalee and her father. Where the term 'Negro' would have been the socially acceptable term in the 1920s, one cannot ignore that it is an offensive term to some today and has been used as a racialized slur. Winters uses the term throughout the book without contextualizing it. In her afterword, Winters says she wanted the language to 'reflect how people in that era would have described both Hanalee and Joe and to learn how the two of them would have identified themselves' but that 'there are some words, however, whose power to hurt and belittle goes beyond the need for historical accuracy'.[21] She goes on to add that 'no offense is intended by the inclusion of any derogatory and/or outdated words within this book'.[22] The use of the term could have a 'gut punch' effect on young people who do not understand this context before reading the book.

With some slurs, Winters chooses to silence the words on the page. When Hanalee asks her friend if she knows why people are threatening Joe, her friend says: 'They call him' – her ears turned pink, and she hunched over her shoulders – 'a word I'm not going to say, but I know what it implies'.[23] Later, when it is clear that the KKK was responsible for her father's death, and Hanalee is in the threatening clutches of the local Klan leader, he tells her that 'we hoisted him off the ground, that no part of that godforsaken Negro would linger in this state – that's for damn sure'. Hanalee's narration then adds: 'only he didn't say *Negro*'.[24] The reader is then made aware of the racial slur to which Hanalee is exposed though the word itself is not present.

Hanalee is given room to grow when she asks if people want Joe dead because he's 'not a real man?'.[25] Winters does not let her main character speak of this discrimination without pointing out that Hanalee 'felt the sudden urge to be cruel to him again' and that afterwards the words made her 'mouth taste rotten'.[26] By describing the emotional impact of these types of hate speech, Winters indicates that this language is inappropriate due to its derogatory nature. As such, a reader's emotional reaction to the language can be validated in the characters' equal discomfort. The only characters who use slurs against Hanalee and Joe in the book are KKK members indicating to the reader that these overt slurs are hate speech. These KKK members use slurs when threatening physical violence against the main characters. As such, these derogatory terms are actual threats of violence. It is also the victims of these terms, or their allies, who choose to silence or edit out these words for the reader. Yet, because Winters and her characters do not edit out the 'F' word in reference to Joe as a gay man, readers may be left feeling that this is an imbalance to these types of languages.[27] In noticing the silencing of racial slurs but not those used against gay men, the reader becomes acutely aware of a value system that Winters has put in place to protect some readers more than others. Still, hate speech in Winters's book both indicates social breaks and teaches about historical collective trauma. In her use of slurs, and then the silencing of slurs by her protagonists, Winters proposes a way forward: recognition of the hate that people can have for difference but also a choice that can be made to celebrate that difference and to heal with that difference.

Creating racial slurs to reduce trauma and build reader empathy

Unlike Winters, who edits and silences slurs, and Peet, who uses them to disturb the reader, Malorie Blackman creates an alternative language of racial slurs that allows for teaching the destructive power of such terms – without re-traumatizing readers who may have experienced such slurs. Blackman, a Black author, notes in her preface that she wrote *Noughts & Crosses* out of a 'desire to tackle racism head on'.[28] Set in a dystopian future London, Noughts are discriminated against and face racial prejudice because of their white skin colour. Noughts are denied higher-paying jobs, positions of power, and higher education. In contrast, Crosses run society and have complete control. They have access to education and privileges based on their black skin colour. Accomplishments by Noughts are erased from history as Crosses dictate a world that celebrates them and keeps safe their positions of power. In this loose reimagining of *Romeo and Juliet*, Sephy (a privileged Cross girl) and Callum (a

lower-class Nought boy) are best friends who fall in love in a world
that forbids their friendship, much less their romance.

Because this fictionalized world uses its own radicalized
language, readers are slowly introduced to the racial slurs of
the book's world. Callum's brother asks him if he was 'with his
dagger friend' to which Callum responds, 'Don't you call my best
friend that. . . . Say it again and I'll knock you flat'.[29] He goes on
to explain that his brother 'never called them Crosses. They were
always daggers'.[30] From this exchange, the reader learns that the
term 'dagger' is offensive. Readers also understand that Callum's
brother is likely deeply prejudiced because he only uses that term.
We realize that, for Callum's brother, Crosses are oppressors and
cannot be humanized. Later, Sephy hears her father use the racial
slur 'blanker' and she 'winced at the venom in Dad's voice' because
she had never heard him use the 'horrible word' before.[31] These
racial slurs are highlighted in the filtered commentary of our main
characters so that the readers recognize them as hate speech.

However, it is only later that Sephy is brought to fully realize
the power of slurs. She uses the word herself and Callum looks
at her with 'the strangest expression on his face' and tells her,
'Sephy, if you'd slapped me or punched me or even stabbed me,
sooner or later it would've stopped hurting. Sooner or later. But
I'll never forget what you called me, Sephy. Never'.[32] Sephy is left
with the realization that 'one word had caused all this trouble
between us'.[33] In this way, readers learn from the main characters
that racial slurs are painful, and they also experience the power
slurs have in their ability to divide friends and community. Racial
slurs in Noughts & Crosses act as the signifiers for the larger
communal discord. These words reinforce and create distances
that are almost impossible to mend. Additionally, by not using
the racial slurs of our current cultures, Blackman asks readers
to face their own relationships to these words. Readers can be
active, present learners in understanding the power of racial slurs
without being exposed to terms which may have already caused
traumatic experiences. Because both protagonist and antagonist
use these words, readers can empathize with the social struggles
characters are facing while viewing these characters as human.
Readers are taught to recognize 'acute discomfort' in a society
– a tool they can then use to recognize collective trauma in their
own communities. For Blackman, slurs are not markers of 'evil

people' but rather clear indicators of a broken society in need of reconciliation.

Implications of texts in the classroom: Moving towards empowerment and empathy

Many young people are exposed to violence. It would be a normal reaction to try to reduce the violence to which they are exposed in texts. Yet, it has been my experience that students have often connected with the violence of Shakespeare's texts – seeing their own lived experiences in the messy landscapes of Shakespeare's plays. YA Shakespearian adaptations that address racial violence allow students to process social trauma and connect their own lived experiences to a story that has been helping audiences confront social discord for centuries.[34] At the same time, we need to consider how we select texts that both empower students and reduce the harm of exposure to violence in texts. In using a trauma-informed teaching practice, we can also give students warning about triggering topics and safe spaces to opt out of difficult topics without penalty.[35] If we shift our focus away from the violence of the text, and instead look at how the trauma of that violence is discussed or experienced in a text and by the reader of that book, we can then consider if the text simply delivers a 'gut punch' or tries to move towards communal healing.

Mal Peet's *Exposure* thrusts the violence of racial slurs on its readers. In exposing readers to these slurs, even though they are only spoken by villains, the text raises awareness of large collective traumas, but it can re-traumatize readers who face these real-world words of violence daily. It is easy for some readers to dismiss these terms as those of 'racist' people, while more deeply reminding other readers of their own individual traumatic experiences with this language. As Otello falls more silent, we miss the moment of 'acute discomfort' where we become aware of the collective trauma of racism and instead dismiss his story as simply an individual tragedy of racism. Slurs are spoken by villains who are not meaningfully held accountable for their actions. As such, readers experience the 'gut punch' without any tools or means of moving forward.

Similarly, in Winters's *The Steep and Thorny Way* racial slurs are used only by members of the KKK (villains). Unlike in *Exposure*, Winters's characters describe and process the emotional pain that these words cause. In this way, the protagonists become aware of that 'acute discomfort' that is present in their culture. Readers can navigate through more of the emotional impact of these words. Careful consideration and warnings would need to be given to much of her text – as her selective editing only protects some and can deliver an unfortunate 'gut punch' to readers who realize some hate speech is allowed.

Finally, Malorie Blackman's *Noughts and Crosses*, written with an intention to educate, has both villains and protagonists using the racial slurs of their society. As each character explores the effects these words have on their relationships and explains these words to readers, readers can reflect on the collective trauma of the racism being described both in the fictionalized society and their own societies. As such, readers can recognize the 'acute discomfort' experienced by all characters in Blackman's books, opening an opportunity for readership to see the complex, nuanced, and systemic nature of the collective trauma culturally experienced by racism.

Teachers should use these texts with caution. In using a trauma-informed teaching practice teachers can decide if such material is appropriate for their class and the best means to introduce them. In selecting texts that use racial slurs (even reimagined ones), teachers should consider both the impact of the words on their students and how the word is treated in the text. Is space given to process the emotional impact of these words? Is there space to empower students to discuss these issues in a way that can work towards collective healing? Shakespeare does not have to be something that students 'survive'. Indeed, with adaptations that discuss contemporary issues of racial violence, Shakespeare can become a space of empowerment for students to discuss their own lived experiences.

Notes

1 Malorie Blackman, *Noughts and Crosses* (London: Penguin Books, 2001), 52.

2 Colin Dwyer, 'Professor Cancels Course on Hate Speech Amid Contention over His Use of Slur', *NPR*, 2 December 2018, https://www.npr.org/sections/thetwo-way/2018/02/13/585386694/professor-cancels-course-on-hate-speech-amid-contention-over-his-use-of-slur.

3 The term 'societal reconciliation' refers to the process that a society can use to heal historic wrongs. It recognizes that to reconcile, a society must be able to name past wrongs and move forward to change them. The classroom is one place where this process can take place using restorative justice practices. This idea draws on South Africa's and Canada's *Truth and Reconciliation Commissions*. See Linda Radzik and Colleen Murphy's entry on 'Reconciliation' in the *Stanford Encyclopedia of Philosophy*, ed. Edward N. Zalta (Fall 2021), https://plato.stanford.edu/archives/fall2021/entries/reconciliation/.

The Mosaic Institute also has resources on teaching restorative justice in the classroom.

4 Jeffery Alexander, *Trauma: A Social Theory* (Cambridge: Polity Press, 2012) https://ebookcentral.proquest.com/lib/york/reader.action?docID=1184137&ppg=6.

5 Ibid., 14.

6 Mal Peet, *Exposure* (Somerville: Candlewick Press, 2009), 8.

7 Ibid., 43.

8 Ibid., 44.

9 Ibid.

10 Ibid.

11 Ibid., 56.

12 Ibid., 58.

13 Ibid., 84.

14 Ibid., 247.

15 Ibid., 385.

16 Cat Winters, *The Steep and Thorny Way* (New York: Amulet Paperbacks, 2016), 53.

17 Ibid., 89.

18 Ibid.

19 Ibid., 328.

20 Ibid.

21 Ibid., 331.

22 Ibid.

23 Ibid., 103.

24 Ibid., 295.

25 Ibid., 72.

26 Ibid.

27 Ibid., 135.

28 Blackman, *Noughts and Crosses*.

29 Ibid., 26.

30 Ibid., 27.

31 Ibid., 36.

32 Ibid., 52.

33 Ibid., 53.

34 For lessons on how to introduce racial slurs in the classroom, see 'Addressing Racist and Dehumanizing Language', *Facing History and Ourselves*. https://www.facinghistory.org/resource-library/discussing -race-and-racism-classroom/addressing-racist-and-dehumanising -language (Accessed 6 March 2022).

35 There are many resources available to educators on trauma-informed or trauma-aware teaching strategies, which often focus on student choice, move away from zero-tolerance teaching practices, and support students when confronting triggering material. The Mosaic Institute (https://www.mosaicinstitute.ca/) and The Resilient Educator (https://resilienteducator.com/) have extensive resources.

5

When Romeo and Juliet fought the Texas Rangers

Race, justice, and appropriation in *Shame the Stars* by Guadalupe García McCall

Jesus Montaño

In *Medicine Stories: Essays for Radicals* Aurora Levins Morales states, 'the way we are taught our history is an endless repetition of the perpetrator's story, in which crusaders are shining knights, not massacring mercenaries, wars are glorious and heroic, not massive assaults on human beings and the natural world for the sake of domination'.[1] Resistance and recovery, in her view, require 'creating and telling another story about the experience of violence and the nature of the participants, a story powerful enough to restore a sense of our full humanity to the abused'.[2] From here, my chapter considers the young adult novel *Shame the Stars* (2016) by Guadalupe García McCall, a Latinx appropriation of

Shakespeare that reimagines *Romeo and Juliet* in Texas during the Mexican Revolution (1910–20) and tells the little-known history of murders and lynching of Mexicans and Mexican Americans by the Texas Rangers.[3] Though hundreds if not thousands of Mexicans and Mexican Americans were murdered by extra-legal and state-sanctioned means, little is remembered of these atrocities in the collective memory of the United States. Instead, the Texas Rangers have become 'shining knights'.[4] It thus is my argument that *Shame the Stars* enacts Levins Morales's directive to create and tell 'another story' with the understanding that justice takes place 'in the telling and the bearing witness, in the naming of trauma and in the grief and rage and defiance that follows'.[5]

The premise of my chapter is simple: Romeo and Juliet, via their literary appropriation in *Shame the Stars*, are deployed to fight against the brutality of the Texas Rangers, as well as the resultant injustices perpetrated by a national collective memory that embraces the myth of the Rangers for its state-building mechanisms. If white supremacy is the goal of statecrafting in the United States, appropriating Shakespeare becomes a vehicle to address injustices. In order for this counter-story to be successful, I argue, Shakespeare must be consumed, absorbed, and incorporated anew. What Oswald de Andrade aspired to in his 'Cannibalist Manifesto', as Anne Sophie Refskou and others in *Eating Shakespeare* note, is that the 'the absorbing, transforming, and incorporating of new elements – would foster a new order, allowing those traditions excluded and marginalized the opportunity to reclaim their agency'.[6] In such a cannibalistic feast, Shakespeare becomes the nutrient as *Romeo and Juliet* is transformed into a Critical Race Theory counter-story that engages issues of race and belonging, that challenges the whitewashing of historical memory, and that propels new culturally vibrant intertextual forms that function as platforms for social justice.

In this chapter I thus take a bold step in suggesting that we can wrestle with marginalization by addressing this cultural trauma through the lens of Shakespeare or rather the newly created Latinx Shakespeare that emerges at the cannibalized intermixing of Shakespeare and Latinx cultural production. This new co-created cultural product provides Latinx young readers with the courage to become agents as they engage with the text and, in this way, with a fractured social and national body. What is at stake, therefore, in this counter-story offered by *Shame the Stars* is righting the way Latinx young readers see themselves. In our grave contemporary situation where systemic racism on Brown and Black bodies is evidenced in official policies and practices including deportation, separation, incarceration, and death at the hands of law enforcement, this chapter shows how healing requires the medicinal powers of knowledge and artful narrative, as well as Shakespeare's role in such empowerment for young Latinx readers.[7]

An ancient grudge, or conflict at the intersection of race and ethnicity

Shame the Stars, written in novel form, echoes the original play in a few key ways. For instance, the novel begins with a cast of characters and a prologue. Also, akin to the ways in which the prologue of *Romeo and Juliet* is not merely about the setting, in *Shame the Stars* the Prologue depicts both the historical antagonisms at play in the novel and the current antagonisms that are the source of fighting between the families. Set two years before the action in the first chapter, the prologue begins with the head of the two families, Don Acevedo del Toro (Montague) and Don Rodrigo Villa (Capulet), drinking brandy and smoking cigars at an Easter Sunday celebration while discussing the impact of the Mexican Revolution on their *Tejano* town in the South Texas area known as the Rio Grande Valley. Del Toro, 'a giant of a man, light-haired and fair-skinned like an Anglo . . . [though] all *Mejicano-Tejano* to the core',[8] stands in contrast with Villa, 'small, dark, and so wiry you'd think he was a compressed metal coil, wound up and ready to spring into action'.[9] At the heart of their increasingly angry debate is an anonymous poem that Villa has published in his newspaper, *El Sureño*. As a longtime landowner, del Toro is cautious in wanting to court troubles with his Anglo neighbours. That the poem specifically names the Texas Rangers as the cause of the troubles further sets del Toro and Villa at odds. The poem to Villa is sardonic and ironic; to del Toro it serves as an act of sedition. Tensions only heighten when Joaquín (Romeo) confesses that he is the writer of the poem in question. At this point, whatever future plans Joaquín and Dulceña (Juliet) have are torn asunder and del Toro throws Villa out of his house. Though the poet's identity was unknown to Villa at the time of publication, Villa wholeheartedly supports the poem's exhortation that its readers, as *Tejanos*, as mestizos brought forth from conquistador and Nahua blood, respond in 'these dangerous times'.[10]

Much in keeping with the idea that what is past is prologue, *Shame the Stars* begins by articulating how the historical and cultural past is necessary for understanding the troubling issues at play in the present moment when the novel begins. In describing del Toro, for example, as light-haired and fair-skinned and Villa as darker and wiry, the novel foregrounds not only the history of Spanish conquest and colonialism in the Americas but also the significant ways in which the past informs current forms of colourism. As Laura Quiros and Beverly Araujo Dawson stress, 'colorism has its roots in the colonial ideology where lightness is associated with White Europeans and is therefore preferred and viewed as superior to darkness, which is associated with indigenous and Black African people'.[11] Further, currently 'within Latino/a communities, power and privilege are assigned to those who are closer to looking White, with some privilege assigned to individuals who are categorized in the intermediate shades of brown'.[12]

Racial hierarchies indeed play a pivotal role for the novel's characters. While at first glance, *Shame the Stars* seems merely to involve two Mexican American families whose contrasting politics are the driving force for their antagonism, an approach that employs intersectionality and Critical Race Theory allows us to see that the intersectionality of ethnic identity (the shared culture and set of common experiences of living along the US/Texas border) and racial identity (the privileges and disadvantages of lighter or darker skin) has constructed and maintained social experiences that are unequal. That is, in paying attention to colourism and its long history in Latinx communities, what is gained in our reading of the prologue are the vast ways in which conquest and colonialism of the past created racialized systems of privilege and disadvantage in the present. To wit, this history is emphasized in the figure of del Toro, a landowner, who 'has owned Las Moras since the times of the Spanish land grants. They are true *Tejanos*, original settlers of Texas'.[13] For this reason, as Joaquín notes, del Toro has 'always believed in cultivating friendships with local law enforcement and politicians'.[14] In this, racial privileges have allowed the del

Toro family long-standing affluence and influence. What is more, colourism means that del Toro, specifically because of his white privilege, can leverage wealth and status in his interactions with local political officials. Villa connects the ways colourism and safety go hand in hand when he states that the Texas Rangers 'would never hurt you. Your blond hair and green eyes guarantee you that much!'[15] From Villa's understanding, the visual signifiers of racial privilege afford del Toro safety, one that he (a person with darker skin) cannot count on.

This deep dive into *Tejano* history and culture enables us to see the complexity of Latinx ways of being and doing, specifically around issues that emanate at the intersection of race and ethnicity. This is to say that *Shame the Stars* has the potential to reconceptualize our understanding of *Romeo and Juliet*. In much the same way that Carla Della Gatta posits that the '*West Side Story* Effect' re-inscribed 'Shakespearean representations of difference of various kinds – class, locale, familial – as a cultural-linguistic difference',[16] I argue that *Shame the Stars* re-inscribes 'difference' in terms of Latinx race and ethnicity as a hallmark for understanding both *Romeo and Juliet* in America and Latinidad in the United States. In other words, just as productions of *West Side Story* have drawn attention to linguistic differences across the Latinx cultural spectrum, *Shame the Stars* can add to our understanding of the way colourism, race, and ethnicity intersect. *Shame the Stars*, in foregrounding the 'differences' between the two seemingly similar Latinx families, contributes substantially to our valuing of a Latinx Shakespeare that places race, ethnicity, and belonging at the centre of how we consume Shakespeare.[17]

Curing the historical silences, restoring identity and possibility

Shame the Stars, in presenting a little-known chapter in America's history, encourages readers to understand that, as Levins Morales explains, 'one of the first things a colonizing power, a new ruling class, or a repressive regime does is attack the sense of history of those they wish to dominate by attempting to take over and control their relationships to their own past'.[18] This is to say that given the ways the national imaginary has whitewashed Latinx history and controlled the relationship that Latinx people have with their past, novels such as *Shame the Stars* 'use history, not so much to document the past as to restore to the de-historicized a sense of identity and possibility'.[19] Understanding that most readers of *Shame the Stars* will only know the Texas Rangers as heroes, García McCall enlists Joaquín as the 'student' who has much to learn about the whitewashing of history.

As we begin the novel, Joaquín's educational trajectory becomes clear. Following the storyline from *Romeo and Juliet*, a letter inviting 'Romeo del Toro' to a masquerade ball to celebrate a *quinceañera* is hand-delivered to Joaquín by one of Dulceña's maids.[20] Much like the masque ball in *Romeo and Juliet*, the *quinceañera baile* allows the lovers to meet secretly. Once at the dance Joaquín approaches Dulceña by asking her, 'Are you my Julieta?', to which she responds, 'I don't know. . . . Are you my Romeo?'[21] However, instead of speaking of their mutual love, as perhaps Joaquín wishes, Dulceña wants to discuss the events preceding the *baile*, most notably the escalation of violence and disappearances. The Texas Rangers, Joaquín tells us, will deputize 'anyone willing to fight on their side and summarily killed Mexicans and *Tejanos* alike without bothering to bring them in to be tried in court for their crimes'.[22]

Further, in attempting to 'shed light on the plight of innocent *Tejanos* who had fallen victim to the Rangers',[23] Don Rodrigo's reporting in *El Sureño* has led to numerous threats and acts of vandalism to the print shop, so many in fact that Don Rodrigo withdraws Dulceña from school. Thus, the masque ball that is central to *Romeo and Juliet* meeting and falling in love at first sight, in *Shame the Stars*, becomes the necessary meeting point between Joaquín and Dulceña as they begin resisting the rule of the Texas Rangers and countering their violence in ways that are more productive to the social whole.

At this point in the novel, Joaquín believes that his father can handle the Rangers. To this, Dulceña pushes back by noting that Munro, the Texas Rangers captain, 'wouldn't think twice about arresting your father and shutting down Las Moras'.[24] She further counters his argument that his father and Munro are friends by stating, 'Munro has no friends, only allies and pawns. The minute he thinks your father is harbouring insurgents he will go after him with a vengeance'.[25] Even so, Joaquín remains doubtful.[26]

Joaquín has much to learn. His belief that the Texas Rangers are simply doing their duty mostly likely echoes the views of many readers of *Shame the Stars* who have grown up with the pop-culture image of the Rangers as valiant heroes. His realization and corresponding shift in perspective models for present-day readers this process of coming to understand how history has been whitewashed, for the benefits of white supremacy, and the process of engaging with the past for present-day social justice. In *Child-Sized History*, Sara Schwebel underscores the value of teaching historical literature, for it allows young students to wrestle with historical inquiry, to ponder that 'while the past itself is static, history – the interpretation of that past – continually evolves'.[27] In this educational process, historical fiction moves from a presentation of the 'objective truth of "what really happened"'[28] to active empathetic engagement with the text: 'historical novels paint three-dimensional historical figures (real and imagined) that enable students to relate to and care about people removed from them by time and space, and depending on the characters featured, by gender, class, race, and religion.'[29] Wrestling with the incongruities, juxtapositions, and varied perspectives from such historical reimagining allows young readers to gain an understanding 'about the constructed and contested nature of historical narrative'.[30] At the heart of Schwebel's project, therefore, is a deliberate movement away from 'heritage-based collective memory' inculcation that passes off itself as historical study and towards an understanding of the 'ongoing and at times contentious debate about the American past and its meaning in the present'.[31] *Shame the Stars*, similarly, leads us to an understanding 'that the past is knowable only through the lens of the present, a refracted vision always subject to change'.[32] By changing the lens of history from the perspective of the oppressive Texas Rangers to that of marginalized and yet resilient *Tejanos*, *Shame the Stars* allows young Latinx readers to cure the silence regarding their history and thus restores to them a sense of identity and possibility.

Finding voice and agency, funding communal solidarity

As the novel moves towards a resolution, Joaquín's mother, Doña Jovita, upon being discovered to be sympathizing with insurgents, is shot by a sheriff's deputy. When Tomás, Joaquín's brother (a Catholic priest), hits the deputy with the butt of a gun, Tomás is the one jailed: 'Whereas the deputy who shot my mother was not being brought up on charges, my brother, Tomás, was being charged with attempted capital murder for beating him up.'[33] The novel winds towards the end with Tomás headed for the gallows for his attempted capital murder.

The ingenuity of *Shame the Stars* is that, in this moment of injustice, Joaquín learns to channel his desires for vengeance and seek justice through the power of corridos, the popular narrative song or ballad of Mexican and Mexican American cultures.[34] As Dulceña tells Joaquín, 'words are important, and passion lends them power. I truly believe that. If we do this right, if we get the public's attention, we could very well force the governor's hand'.[35] In response to Dulceña's admonition, Joaquín writes 'The Martyr of Las Moras'. He tells us:

> I scribbled furiously, passionately, I thought about what A. V. Negra and all those other fearless journalists would say at a time like this. How would they *address* the problem? What angle would they take? What angle would my own beautiful wife, the brilliant A. V. Negrados, take? Mimicking her style, I started by quoting the laws of man and the laws of God. I referenced history both recent and past, from both sides of the border.[36]

With no way to seek justice and with his brother's life in the balance, Joaquín pens a corrido. For some readers of *Shame of Stars*, this may be a surprising way to solve the dilemma. Some may even find this a bit incredulous, that a song could commute a death sentence. And yet, here we see the novel deploying an art form with a long history as a symbolic expression of resistance in the Texas–Mexico border region.

As a counter-hegemonic mode, corridos function as vehicles for communal solidarity, an integral component in the social imaginary of the borderland community, which allow peoples on both sides of the border to imagine the nature of their communal belonging. Speaking of the corrido, *Los Sediciosos*, a ballad about the soldiers inspired to take up arms, Richard Flores, for example, argues that this corrido, specifically when it was first performed in 1915, served as a vehicle for an emergent consciousness revolving around what it means to be *Tejano* and Mexican American. As he notes, the corrido informs a collective consciousness of 'the corrido community's emerging ethnic identity, an identity incapable of being expressed by the authoritative discourse of the Mexican hero'.[37] The Mexican or *Tejano* hero, specifically for corridos from this time period in the Texas–Mexico border, is often contrasted with the *rinches*, the name given to Texas Rangers by the Spanish-speaking people of the area. The corrido strategically 'adapts various aspects of conflict so that they become battles between the "rinches" and the Mexican "heroes." And to the extent that conflict between Anglos and Mexicans on the Texas–Mexico border is due to cultural and national difference, the border *corrido* functions as an expression of resistance'.[38] To this, Joaquín notes that his corrido was 'an emotional piece – a story of faith and courage in the face of social injustice, subjugation, and prejudice. One which I hoped would make politicians and common men nod over in unison and clamor for answers'.[39]

Thus, with little legal recourse, Joaquín and Dulceña turn to corridos, to the power of the creative voice, as a way to signal the injustices before them. By invoking a 'local' form of addressing injustices, they recall other corridos, such as *Los Sediciosos*, that use the ballad form as a way of making themselves heard. In this way, they make use of the long-standing value of the corrido as a counter-storytelling resistive form. What is more, in the process, they create community. As the novel informs us, '"Free Tomás!" someone screamed, and suddenly, they were all chanting it, together, in unison. "Free Tomás! Free Tomás!" They kept screaming and chanting, getting louder and louder as more and more people joined us'.[40] Thus, while *Shame the Stars* began with discord between *Tejano* families, with the discord a by-product of age-old difference between those with Iberian roots and those who traced their descent from indigenous ones, by the end of the novel, the Mexican American community unites under the banner of social justice, in this case primarily through a form designed to give voice to social justice causes. By utilizing an art form with a long history of resistance and community formation in the Texas–Mexico borderlands, *Shame the Stars* artfully decolonizes the ending of its 'informing' text, Shakespeare's *Romeo and Juliet*.[41] Peace comes not from suicide but from active social engagement via the power of the voice – from writing poems and corridos, publishing and disseminating information, and a deep cultural dive into Latinx ways of being and doing.

Devouring Shakespeare, or the emergence of borderlands mirrors

In 2016, the publication year of *Shame the Stars*, the Cooperative Children's Book Center (CCBC), a library of the School of Education at the University of Wisconsin-Madison, committed to:

> Identifying excellent literature for children and adolescents and bringing this literature to the attention of those adults who have an academic, professional, or career interest in connecting young readers with books' received 3,400 children's and young adult books, from both small and large presses (the large majority of those published that year). Of those 3,400 books, 169 were written about Latinx peoples and cultures and of those 104 were written by Latinx authors and artists.[42]

Once again, if only because the numbers are so staggering, of the 3,400 books received by the CCBC only 104 were by Latinx authors and artists. At the same time, we know that Shakespeare's *Romeo and Juliet* is standard core reading in high schools throughout the United States. Renaissance.com, a learning analytics firm that tracks what children and young adult read in school curricula, for example, informs us in its 'What Are Kids Reading: 2020 Edition Report' that *Romeo and Juliet* is the third most-read work for ninth graders, right behind *To Kill a Mockingbird* and *Of Mice and Men*.

If we couple these two notions, the small number of Latinx books and the large number of students asked to read *Romeo and Juliet*, we arrive at a quandary: where can young Latinx readers see themselves and their culture represented? As Rudine Sims Bishop reminds us, 'literature transforms human experience and reflects it back to us, and in that reflection, we can see our own lives and experiences as part of the larger human experience. Reading, then, becomes a means to self-affirmation, and readers often seek their mirrors in books'.[43] Latinx readers should be able to find 'mirrors' of their 'own lives and experiences' as a means for self-affirmation. As the national literary movement, weneeddiversebooks.org has us envision 'a world in which all children can see themselves in the pages of a book'.

As I have argued in this chapter, a devoured Shakespeare provides nutrients for a cultural and literary product in *Shame the Stars* that seeks to heal a fractured social and national body. In this model, what and how we understand literary appropriation is recast, for it foregrounds the notion of 'a radical new relationship, concomitantly transforming themselves and each other' in which Shakespeare and Latinx culture 'become part of a mutually dependent and mutually empowering performative act'.[44] Even as the premise is simply that Shakespeare is devoured, and his works are absorbed, transformed, and incorporated into new elements, what materializes from this cannibalistic feast is the idea that young adult literary appropriations of Shakespeare illuminate in their transfigured appropriations the ways in which the taking and remaking of Shakespeare offers a lacuna wherein to imagine possible new versions of self, new forms of social identities, and new ways of cultural and national belonging. This is to say that as a literary appropriation of *Romeo and Juliet*, *Shame the Stars* emerges as a co-created product that invites young Latinx readers to find voice and agency as they engage with their history and as they contest oppression with counter-hegemonic artistic forms that emanate from culturally and regionally specific contexts. In this, the intermixing of Shakespeare and Latinx young literature provides young Latinx readers a mirror for seeing themselves in the text and for imagining heroes like them who live between and betwixt borders of language and cultures and who purposefully use those assets to thrive.

Notes

1 Aurora Levins Morales, *Medicine Stories: Essays for Radicals* (Durham: Duke University Press, 2019), 65.

2 Ibid., 61.

3 *Shame the Stars* is set in Texas during the Mexican Revolution, a time when the Texas Rangers openly and with impunity killed and lynched hundreds if not thousands of Mexicans and Mexican Americans. For more information see, Monica Muñoz. Martinez, *The Injustice Never Leaves You: Anti-Mexican Violence in Texas* (Cambridge: Harvard

University Press, 2018). See also William D. Carrigan and Clive Webb, *Forgotten Dead: Mob Violence against Mexicans in the United States, 1848–1928* (Oxford: Oxford University Press, 2013).

4 The place of the Texas Rangers in the collective memory of Texas and the United States is such that they have a Major League Baseball team named after them (The Texas Rangers) and numerous movies and books dedicated to them, specifically *The Lone Ranger* television series (1949–57), *Walker, Texas Ranger* television series (1993–2001), and the more recent film *The Lone Ranger* produced by Walt Disney Pictures in 2013.

5 Levins Morales, *Medicine Stories*, 62.

6 Anne Sophie Refskou, Vinicius Mariano de Carvalho, and Marcel Alvaro de Amorim. Introduction to *Eating Shakespeare: Cultural Anthropophagy as Global Methodology*, ed. Anne Sophie Refskou, Vinicius Mariano de Carvalho, and Marcel Alvaro de Amorim (London: Bloomsbury Publishing, 2019), 12.

7 In this respect, *curanderas/os* in Latinx communities are healers, and Levins Morales's turn from the healing of physical bodies to the healing of social bodies allows us to examine the medicinal uses of knowledge.

8 Guadalupe García McCall, *Shame the Stars* (New York: Tu Books, 2016), 7.

9 Ibid., 7. For a brief account of the Mexican Revolution, see Alan Knight, *The Mexican Revolution: A Very Short Introduction* (Oxford: Oxford University Press, 2016). For the ways the Mexican Revolution specifically impacted the *Tejano* communities, see Arnoldo De León, 'The Mexican Revolution's Impact on Tejano Communities: The Historiographic Record', in *War Along the Border: The Mexican Revolution and Tejano Communities*, ed. Arnoldo De León (College Station: Texas A&M University Press, 2012), 31–55.

10 García McCall, *Shame the Stars*, 1–4.

11 Laura Quiros and Beverly Araujo Dawson, 'The Color Paradigm: The Impact of Colorism on the Racial Identity and Identification of Latinas', *Journal of Human Behavior in the Social Environment* 23, no. 3 (2013): 288.

12 Ibid., 289.

13 García McCall, *Shame the Stars*, 143. For more information on the history of the early settlement (from the mid-eighteenth century onwards) of the Rio Grande Valley, see Armando Alonzo, *Tejano Legacy: Rancheros and Settlers in South Texas, 1734-1900* (Albuquerque: University of New Mexico Press, 1998).

14 García McCall, *Shame the Stars*, 143.

15 Ibid., 15.

16 Carla Della Gatta, 'From *West Side Story* to *Hamlet, Prince of Cuba*: Shakespeare and Latinidad in the United States', *Shakespeare Studies* 44 (2016): 152.

17 Two modern *Romeo and Juliet* performances that treat this Conquistador/Spanish and Indigenous paradigm are *Temple of the Souls . . . A Tale of Forbidden Love* by Anita Velez-Mitchell and *Kino and Teresa* by James Lujan. Both plays, much like *Shame the Stars*, engage with the history of and current forms of racial politics.

18 Levins Morales, *Medicine Stories*, 69.

19 Ibid., 70.

20 García McCall, *Shame the Stars*, 38.

21 Ibid., 46.

22 Ibid., 23–4.

23 Ibid., 24.

24 Ibid., 58.

25 Ibid., 58–9.

26 As her 'Author's Note' makes clear, García McCall was strongly influenced by Benjamin Heber Johnson, *Revolution in Texas: How a Forgotten Rebellion and Its Bloody Suppression Turned Mexicans into Americans* (New Haven: Yale University Press, 2003). While rich, land-owning *Tejanos* had been complicit or silent on many Anglo atrocities, the escalation of violence on the border meant that they now had reasons to fear the Rangers. Joaquín's education and evolution on the subject parallels those of his class and race.

27 Sara L. Schwebel, *Child-Sized History: Fictions of the Past in the U.S. Classroom* (Nashville: Vanderbilt University Press, 2011), 5.

28 Ibid., 6.

29 Ibid., 31.

30 Ibid., 33.

31 Ibid., 131.

32 Ibid., 134.

33 García McCall, *Shame the Stars*, 246.

34 For an overview of corridos, especially the agency of corridos in times of adversity, see Agustín Gurza, 'Strachwitz Frontera Collection: The Mexican Corrido: Ballads of Adversity and Rebellion', in *The Strachwitz Frontera Collection of Mexican and Mexican American*

Recordings, UCLA. Accessed 1 January 2020. For more sustained study on corridos, specifically those emanating from the Texas–Mexico borderlands, see Américo Paredes, *With a Pistol in His Hand: A Border Ballad and Its Hero* (Austin: University of Texas Press, 1958). A feminist account of corridos can be found in María Herrera-Sobek, *The Mexican Corrido: A Feminist Analysis* (Bloomington: Indiana University Press, 1990).

35 García McCall, *Shame the Stars*, 264.

36 Ibid., 267.

37 Richard R. Flores, 'The "Corrido" and the Emergence of Texas-Mexican Social Identity', *Journal of American Folklore* 105, no. 416 (1992): 177.

38 Ibid., 169.

39 García McCall, *Shame the Stars*, 267.

40 Ibid., 271–2.

41 For an example of contemporary corridos, specifically one that engages with Shakespeare, see Katherine Gillen and Adrianna M. Santos, 'Borderlands Shakespeare: The Decolonial Visions of James Lujan's *Kino and Teresa* and Seres Jaime Magaña's *The Tragic Corrido of Romeo and Lupe*', *Shakespeare Bulletin* 38, no. 4 (2020): 549–71.

42 Cooperative Children's Book Center, University of Wisconsin-Madison. https://ccbc.education.wisc.edu/default.asp (Accessed 7 March 2020). The numbers reflect 'Data on books by and about people of color and from First/Native Nations published for children and teens compiled by the Cooperative Children's Book Center, School of Education, University of Wisconsin-Madison'.

43 Rudine Sims Bishop, 'Mirrors, Windows, and Sliding Glass Doors', *Perspectives: Choosing and Using Books for the Classroom* 6, no. 3 (1990): ix.

44 Refskou, de Carvalho, and de Amorim, Introduction to *Eating Shakespeare*, 10.

6

The pattern of trauma in YA adaptations of Shakespeare

M. Tyler Sasser

Jacqueline West's *Dreamers Often Lie* begins seconds after a horrific skiing accident, where Jaye (the Juliet-like protagonist) lies bleeding with a fractured skull, believing she hears Romeo whispering 'Oh, speak again, bright angel!'[1] What follows is a hallucinatory romance about a teenager suffering from depression as a result of this skiing accident, the recent death of her father, and her conflicting love interests between Rob (Romeo) and Pierce (Paris). Jaye's world becomes further complicated by the dreamlike conversations she experiences with Shakespeare and several of his characters, all which compound Jaye's primary concern: returning to her school's production of *A Midsummer Night's Dream*. The play takes on a therapeutic quality for Jaye, as she becomes 'filled with light' and 'stronger [than she] had been in weeks' as well as feeling like 'someone new' during rehearsal.[2] Her performance as Titania eventually empowers her to confront her trippy visions of Shakespeare during a brain scan, when she challenges the playwright about his tragedies: 'Everybody's dead. The end . . . *Why?* Because somebody's just a few minutes early, or too late, or because somebody missed a message by leaving at exactly the wrong time? . . . It didn't have to turn out that way. You could have written a different ending. Let them make the right choices for once.'[3] In the climax of the novel, Jaye insists that henceforth she will take complete control of her life to avoid the tragedies of those Shakespearean characters who have haunted her throughout the novel.

This summary of *Dreamers Often Lie* introduces a common pattern in contemporary YA texts that appropriate Shakespeare: a young protagonist experiences a traumatic event – be it physical, emotional, sexual, mental, or psychological – and, in the wake of the event, undergoes a maturation via engagement with Shakespeare that mythologizes both the playwright and trauma. As Eric L. Tribunella observes, there exists 'a common narrative in twentieth-century American literature for youth', a 'striking pattern suggest[ing] that children's literature, and indeed American culture, relies on the contrived traumatization of children – both protagonists and readers – as a way of representing the process of becoming a mature adult'.[4] Tribunella demonstrates through a discussion of canonical books for young readers that trauma plays a fundamental role in the maturation of American youth or is at least frequently depicted as so doing. Building on Tribunella's claim, I demonstrate how adaptations of Shakespeare for young readers fit into this narrative, yet more specifically demand a Shakespeare-induced participation for maturation. Although ways in which such texts engage with Shakespeare vary – *Romiette and Julio* and *A Girl, a Ghost, and the Hollywood Hills* follow a Shakespearean plotline whereas *The Face in the Mirror* and *Exit, Pursued by a Bear* maintain a more thematic engagement – they collectively demand their protagonists and readers alike follow Shakespeare as a way to overcome trauma, in turn promoting an idealized image of trauma that can be overcome merely through engagement with Shakespeare. In so doing, they mythologize the ameliorating power of Shakespeare to such a degree as to suggest the naive, if not downright dangerous, notion that engagement with Shakespeare remedies tragedy into comedy.

Since Shakespeare's tragedies are so often taught in secondary education, it is not surprising to see plays such as *Romeo and Juliet* and *Hamlet* routinely adapted for young readers. Yet such texts often include a more hopeful alternative to tragedy, optimistically suggesting a way for young readers to overcome the trauma located in the original. For instance, Sharon M. Draper's *Romiette and Julio* follows the love story of Romiette Cappelle (Juliet), an African American teenager living in Cincinnati, Ohio, who falls in love with Julio Montague (Romeo), a Mexican American student recently transferred from Corpus Christi, Texas. The bullying from peers and family that Romiette and Julio experience updates the feuding families in *Romeo and Juliet* to reflect contemporary racial and class tensions. Draper considers the traumatic impact of racism, bullying, and violence on the protagonists to suggest engagement with Shakespeare as a remedy. Both sets of parents disapprove of the multiracial relationship. Mr Montague's deep-seated racism surfaces when he learns about Romiette, while her parents wrongly believe Julio has introduced their daughter to gang life, all of which climaxes with the couple's successful coercion of a gang towards violence with the intention of filming the violence for the local news. The families reconcile only when Captain Escaluski (Prince Escalus) suggests that neither youth is involved with gang life and that they have been targeted by the gangs as a result of their relationship.

Gang life particularly functions as a source of trauma for Julio. His family moved to Cincinnati primarily to escape the growing numbers of gangs, yet the new location fails to provide Julio with the trauma-free environment the Montagues envisioned. On his first day of class, a student degradingly calls Julio 'Chico' in passing: 'Anglos at home used that name as a put-down. And, at home, it was mostly the Anglo gang members who used it.'[5] Such racially motivated bullying continues, as Julio is eventually told that '[they] don't need no wetbacks movin' in here and takin' over [their] territory', all of which are damaging to Julio's mental and emotional health. Verbal threats transition into physical confrontations. Often in the cafeteria, members of the Devildogs approach Romiette and Julio 'just to stare at [them]' and eventually have Malaka, a former friend of Romiette, deliver a message:

> [T]hey don't like what you're doing. They wouldn't like it if you were eating with a white boy either. That's just the way they see things, . . . [and if Julio] doesn't learn the rules, he might have to be taught a lesson. . . . That Mexican ain't got a chance . . . We just don't need no foreigners around here mixing it up with the sisters.[6]

Such threats and the subsequent traumatization intensify when Terrell (Tybalt) pulls a gun on Julio while he and Romiette walk home one afternoon in London Woods and later when the

Devildogs kidnap both Romiette and Julio as part of the novel's rising action.

How Draper incorporates astrology and dreaming into her novel speaks to trauma theory's understanding of dreams while furthering the mythologization of Shakespeare in the text. Romiette's best friend Destiny spends much of the novel determining astrological connections between Romiette and Julio, particularly Romiette's fear of drowning and Julio's association with fire. Much more interesting is the novel's use of dreams and their connection. The word 'trauma' emerges from the Greek word *wound*, yet *traum* is also German for *dream*, and *dreams/dreaming* find significant engagement in psychoanalysis and trauma theory.[7] In *Unclaimed Experience*, Cathy Caruth locates a connective thread through dreams, psychoanalysis, and trauma theory: 'If Freud asks, *What does it mean to sleep?* Lacan discovers at the heart of this question another one, perhaps even more urgent: *What does it mean to awaken?*'[8] Thus, for Caruth, the etymology of *traum* speaks to the possibility of dreams playing an important role in coping with trauma, and such a connection helps readers to understand Draper's use of dreams and dreaming. As but one example, the novel's first two chapters depict Romiette's recurring nightmare of drowning, her deep fear of water based on previous traumatic events, and her attempt to 'find an answer to the terrible dreams'.[9] In her dreams, she hears a voice attempting to save her, which anticipates how Julio (a competitive swimmer) later saves her from drowning. In other words, the novel's constant engagement with dream analysis, particularly through the character fittingly named *Destiny*, positions Romiette's multiracial and Shakespeare-inspired relationship with Julio as treatment.

Ultimately, then, Draper suggests acknowledged engagement with *Romeo and Juliet* is a suitable anecdote for the trauma engendered by racism. In their first chatroom conversation, Julio's asks Romiette, 'you into Shakespeare?' and later the couple compares their name and situation to *West Side Story* and *Romeo and Juliet*.[10] This meta-reference to Shakespeare is the first of several, particularly in the final chapters as characters begin to recognize the traumatic impact of racism on Romiette and Julio through their understanding of Shakespeare's play. As but two examples, the local news headlines pose, 'Are Romiette and Julio lovers like the famous couple of old? . . . Were they desperate enough to consider suicide, as Shakespeare's characters did? Or are their lives in danger as they hid from the threat of gang violence?'[11] And once the teens are safely found and gang members are arrested, Romiette's mother, a news anchor, remarks, 'Once again, let me thank our new friends, the Montagues, and our many other friends who helped in the rescue effort. It shows what a community can do when it cares about its young people. And although I love Shakespeare, I sure am glad that this story of the Montagues and the Cappelles did not end as Shakespeare's tale did'.[12] Thus, whereas for Shakespeare the feuding between Capulets and Montagues is responsible for tragedy, for Draper, a community overcomes racism by partly engaging with the narrative, in turn suggesting that Shakespeare conveniently helps to reconcile complex issues such as racism, bullying, and trauma.

Similarly, in A Girl, a Ghost, and the Hollywood Hills, Lizabeth Zindel appropriates Hamlet by reimagining the play as the story of Holly (Hamlet), who returns home from boarding school for the holidays and for the first time since her mother died and her father Gardner (Gertrude) started dating Holly's aunt Claudia (Claudius). As Holly tells her best friend Felicia (Horatio), 'I don't know if I'm gonna survive winter break, let alone the rest of my life . . . I mean, now that my dad's locking lips with that psycho, I'm like an orphan'.[13] Feelings of abandonment, betrayal, and guilt engulf Holly as she attempts to navigate familial life after her mother's suicide. The novel parallels various narrative, thematic, and emotional aspects of Hamlet, particularly those most compellingly related to trauma. Most memorable is Holly's encounter with the ghost of her mother, whom she begins seeing at holiday parties, eventually leading to a conversation where the ghost informs Holly that Claudia poisoned her.[14] Since at least 1778, scholars have recognized in Hamlet a critical tradition that finds the ghost of King Hamlet to be a manifestation of Hamlet's trauma-induced mental illness, a tradition maintained in Zindel's novel.[15] Bennett Simon argues that Hamlet 'is severely traumatised by the Ghost's recollections, leaving him, as it were, both certain and uncertain that his father was killed by his uncle as well as of his mother's collusion with him or, at least, of her betrayal of the memory of her recently deceased husband'.[16] Likewise, Holly's immediate reaction communicates how she blames herself for her mother's death, previously thought a suicide, as well as the rage she now feels towards Claudia. Projecting this blame from herself onto

Claudia by way of the ghost is merely a distraction for Holly, as she then turns to revenge as an unhealthy way to manage the guilt she maintains for her mother's suicide.

These interactions (or hallucinations) with Kate's ghost further exacerbate Holly's trauma in ways also reminiscent of *Hamlet*. Immediately following this interaction, Holly struggles with the uncertainty of the situation and becomes so overwhelmed by the experience that she immediately is responsible for a violent car wreck. Then, she becomes obsessed with her father's sexual life. During dinner one night with Claudia, Holly asks how long they have been having sex, despite being 'so grossed out' by her aunt's explaining her physical attraction to Gardner, barraging her with questions about monogamy, and later listening to her father and aunt have sex.[17] Further, Holly reveals to Oliver (Ophelia) that her mother 'had depression for many years' and was 'diagnosed . . . [with a] bipolar disorder' that was common in her 'family history'.[18] Nevertheless, Holly begins searching for proof of Claudia's involvement in her mother's death. She regularly snoops through Claudia's personal belongings looking for incriminating evidence. Thus, though she is at first relieved of guilt when the ghost tells her it was Claudia, Holly continues to have difficulty accepting the truth; she begins wearing her mother's clothes, having convinced herself that doing so is part of her revenge.

The climax of the novel occurs when Holly, in *Mouse-Trap* fashion, produces a short movie suggesting Gardner and Claudia's involvement in her mother's death. Zindel's version signals a long-awaited confrontation between Gardner and his daughter. In these final moments of the novel, Holly tells Gardner that she believes Claudia killed her mother but is then shocked to discover that at the time of her mother's death, Gardner and Claudia were elsewhere. Gardner explains that Holly's mother previously asked for a divorce, was suffering from severe depression, and that the romantic relationship between Claudia and himself only began after Kate's overdose. Holly recognizes that no one in the family is to blame, including herself: 'it wasn't my fault, either. It wasn't even Claudia's fault, as much as I had wanted to blame her.'[19] When Holly returns to her psychologist, she acknowledges that 'the ghost wasn't real'. As Dr Arbuckle explains, 'you subconsciously came up with this ghost of your mother to help you through', an acceptance that eventually brings Holly peace as she returns to her positive relationship with Oliver, Gardner, and even Claudia.[20] Thus, unlike Hamlet's traumatic experiences, for Holly the narrative of *Hamlet* is the vehicle for a healthy, even peaceful, conclusion in Holly's story, no longer suffering from the guilt that she has placed on herself by way of the ghost.

Whereas these two novels find in Shakespeare's narratives a way to undergo and overcome traumatic experiences, other appropriations engage with Shakespeare's text beyond plot. In Jennifer S. Tolan's *The Face in the Mirror*, it is through performance that one overpowers trauma. *Richard III*, a play rarely taught in secondary education, seems an unlikely candidate for appropriation. Yet Tolan finds the well-known familial trauma experienced throughout the play – between brothers, between uncles and nephews, and so on – a source for considering the impact of abandonment on its protagonist. The novel begins shortly after Jared's grandfather, his primary caregiver, suffers from a stroke, and *Richard III*'s famous opening lines resonate with the teen:

> 'Now is the winter of our discontent / Made glorious summer . . .'
>
> That's how Shakespeare's *The Tragedy of King Richard the Third* begins. It's a play I knew pretty well by June the year my grandfather had his stroke. The 'winter of our discontent' was not a bad description of the winter I'd just had. . . . I'd read *Richard III* (as it's usually called) on the bus for what must have been the tenth time . . . because Pop was determined that I was going to be just what he is – a survivor. And Shakespeare, starting with *Richard*, was going to be the admission ticket to the summer, and just maybe the whole rest of my life. . . . Pop's voice was clear in my head . . . *Survive, guy. Survive!*[21]

The novel's opening furthers this pattern of situating a contemporary teen protagonist in a narrative comparable to a Shakespearean play in that since his grandfather's illness, Jared has been learning how to survive via interactions with Shakespeare's work. More specifically, after suffering through the difficulty of several familial conflicts – his grandfather's illness, orphaned by his mother, has never met his father – in addition to being bullied, Jared is now going to live with Phillip (his father), Julia (his stepmother), and Tad (his stepbrother). Further, the family's last name, *Kingsley*, suggests the royal implications of the central conflict of the novel: Jared's rivalry with his stepbrother.

Thus, *The Face in the Mirror* again uses Shakespeare as an inversion of Jared's own life, in turn suggesting how readers might mitigate trauma through callow engagement with Shakespeare. The Kingsleys operate the New World Shakespeare Company in Michigan, and when Jared arrives, they are deep into pre-production of *Richard III*. Jared is cast alongside Tad as Richard's nephews, princes Edward and the Duke of York. Not surprisingly, Phillip performs as Richard III, thus linking the familiar conflict between Richard and his nephews to Phillip and his sons. Jared, too, recognizes the comparison: 'I could hardly believe the difference between what I knew of Phillip Kingsley the man and the character he was playing. There was a physical difference – a slight limp, a tiny change in posture, a different tone in the voice. But the effect was a lot more than that. . . . There was something dark underneath, like a shadow.'[22] Such association, along with numerous conflicts with Tad, deepens Jared's depression, and midway through the novel, hoping to break away from the pressures of his new family life, Jared finds himself in the trap room beneath the floor of the main stage where the novel becomes supernatural. As Sue Misheff explains of those fantastical places commonly depicted in children's literature, 'Children, who control little else in their lives, have always been drawn to the concept of a place of their own'.[23] Jared originally discovers the room while trying to hide from Tad, but he begins spending more time there studying the script: 'My hiding place, dark and shadowy before, had become a snug, cozy little room. I settled into the big comfortable chair with my *Richard* script.'[24] The trap room, along with performing in *Richard III*, becomes Jared's safe space.

The healing power of Shakespeare, now juxtaposed with Jared's safe place, is immediately apparent. Despite the paralleled conflict between Jared's family and the play's characters, performing Prince Edward comes with a healing component: 'First there had been that sense of becoming somebody else. Not like pretending, but as if I had really quit being me for a while. I liked it. More than liked it. For just that little while, Jared Kingsley and all the junk of Jared Kingsley's real life had disappeared.'[25] In other words, performing Shakespeare becomes therapeutic: 'All of a sudden, I realized for the first time since I'd come to Addison, Michigan, I wasn't just surviving. I felt good. I felt wonderful!'[26] Such emotional and psychological growth occurs simultaneously with Jared becoming absorbed with a particular object in the trap room: a mirror.

Tolan's metaphorical use of this mirror signals the psychological growth experienced by Jared as it represents the repressed anger the boy feels towards life, particularly his new family. The initial instance where Tolan uses a mirror as such occurs when Jared sees his father and thinks, 'I kept looking for something in his face that I recognized from looking in a mirror', thereby looking for a physical resemblance between himself and his biological father.[27] Although Jacques Lacan's theory of 'The Mirror Stage' focuses on a toddler's cognitive ability to understand an 'I' separate from the body he sees in the mirror, this theory also serves as a useful way to witness Jared's post-traumatic growth as depicted in the novel. Like Jared's first interaction with his father and stepbrother, a toddler's initial confrontation with his *self* via a mirror is often traumatic.[28] For Jared, the recognition that he physically resembles his father serves as a *gestalt* now requiring Jared to confront those familial relationships he has repressed. According to Lacan, the child 'precipitously moves from insufficiency to anticipation' as he moves 'from a fragmented image of the body to [a] form of its totality'.[29] For Jared, this move occurs vis-à-vis his performance as Prince Edward in *Richard III*. Lacan argues that the child who has not been adequately parented often will re-enact traumatic moments in solitude, which Jared does as he performs *Richard III* and is in confrontation with his stepbrother-as-York and father-as-Richard. Thus, Lacan helps readers to observe how Jared's traumatic homelife (i.e. grandfather's illness, bullying, abandonment, a new family environment) couples with his participation in *Richard III* to become his story of maturation.

Further, just as the mirror symbolically forces Jared to confront his past, so does it likewise function as a wormhole bringing forth moments from 1858, specifically the time Garrick Marsden performed as Richard III and now haunts the theatre as a ghost. Thus, the second half of the novel addresses this additional conflict for Jared, though earlier he overheard members of the troupe debating whether their theatre was haunted. Some members are delighted by the possibility – 'Theatre ghosts are always good ones. . . . They bring luck' – while others are less optimistic: 'You'll change your tune when you meet up with it'.[30] At first, Jared finds comfort in this spirit from the past, since it helps him play harmless practical jokes on Tad. The ghost appears friendly, helpful, and it even tells Jared that he 'reminds [him] of himself' because of the 'abandonment that is a wound to the heart'.[31] But such affability turns violent when Jared realizes Marsden is out for 'sweet revenge'.[32] The ghost suggests, after attempting to kill Tad, that they 'make an excellent team . . . Like Richard of Gloucester and Buckingham'.[33] Further, Jared discovers that Marsden haunts the theatre and plans to kill some of the actors in response to bad reviews he received during his 1858 production of *Richard III*. Marsden and his travels through the mirror tellingly reflect Jared's own initial vengeful feelings towards his stepfamily, and throughout the remainder of the novel, he must confront these suppressed feelings. As Marsden's pranking becomes increasingly destructive, to the point that the production might fail, Jared understands 'suddenly that [he] care[s] about that stage over [his] head and the play [they] were doing – as much or, maybe more than, [he'd] cared about anything else in [his] whole life'.[34] Eventually, the successful combination of his performance in *Richard III* with his emotional growth with his new family and his outwitting Marsden causes the ghost and all that the ghost represents to disappear, thus signalling a transcendence through his own Lacanian mirror stage of maturation.

As with *The Face in the Mirror*, E. K. Johnston's *Exit, Pursued by a Bear* follows less the narrative of a particular play in favour of appropriating ideas from it, in this case *The Winter's Tale*. The novel follows Hermione Winters, who is raped at cheerleading camp and spends her senior year undergoing the aftermath of the assault and subsequent abortion. Thus, only very loosely does *Exit* follow *The Winter's Tale*: there is a gendered assault on a protagonist named Hermione, who in turn finds solace in a homosocial peer group led by her best friend Polly (Paulina). Yet unlike Shakespeare's play, *Exit* is without magical resolution, though Hermione's ability to collect a DNA sample from her attacker through a disregarded water bottle at a school dance at the very least requires some suspension of belief. Indeed, the novel ends with the overtly optimistic chance for some form of resolution and/or justice, as Hermione thinks to herself, 'I have danced before and I will dance tomorrow'.[35]

Through various connections with *The Winter's Tale*, Hermione addresses her trauma. While her first name echoes the Sicilian queen, Hermione's last name, 'Winters', is in conversation with the play, as she is called 'Winters' by her boyfriend, Leo (Leontes), in the opening pages, an insult meant to convey what Leo considers to be her cold, uncompromising attitudes towards sex.[36] Further, Leo taunts Hermione, when he sneaks several condoms into her luggage at camp, aiming to both embarrass her and aggressively express his intentions. According to Hermione, Leo 'always looks at me like he has expectations that I never meet the way he wants', and when he places his arm around her, 'instead of being sweet it feels possessive'.[37] In Leontes-like fashion, Leo exacerbates her trauma; he pressures Hermione about sex, cheerleading, and college applications, and he later resorts to victim blaming. Further, Paulina informs Johnston's depiction of Polly. As Hermione affectionately says of Polly in the opening pages, 'they are almost ideal complements of each other', 'a great team', and 'years in the making'.[38] Polly is beside Hermione in the hospital when she learns she was drugged and raped, during the subsequent abortion and numerous medical check-ups, and throughout the investigation. Johnston explains in an interview that *The Winter's Tale* is 'about the friendship between two *women*: Hermione and Paulina, who loved one another more than they loved their husbands (with good reason)'.[39]

Thus, Johnston finds inspiration for Polly in the tradition of Shakespearean scholarship that locates Hermione and Paulina's homosocial, if not somewhat romantic, relationship as a positive, affirming, and life-giving one that counters the play's depiction of violent heterosexuality. As Hermione explains during her first visit with a male gynaecologist, 'It dawns on [her], for the first time, that having Polly for a best friend is about to become more important than it ever was before'.[40] Johnston reinforces the connections when Polly begins a healthy, romantic relationship with Amy, as well as through the investigation officer being a woman named *Plummer*, which maintains an alliterative connection with Paulina and Polly. Polly is perhaps even associated positively with the novel's title, when in the final pages Hermione remarks that she 'looks completely harmless, except when her teeth are bared. In her heart, she's always been a bear'. Moments earlier, when Hermione recognizes her assailant, she fantasizes about revealing him to her entire support network, Polly first and foremost, to 'see how he runs when pursued by a sleuth of bears', a metaphor enhanced by her school's mascot, the Fighting Golden Bears.[41] Such details locate the possibility of healing through such varied associations with

Shakespeare, and just as readers and scholars generally identify the comedic ending of *The Winter's Tale* as problematic, so too might readers find moments of tragedy in *Exit*'s ending.

These adaptations represent a pattern in contemporary young adult fiction whereby Shakespeare's plays are called upon first to induce and then maturate through trauma for its protagonists.[42] In other words, as Judith Herman explains in *Trauma and Recovery*, 'The conflict between the will to deny horrible events and the will to proclaim them aloud is the central dialectic of psychological trauma. . . . When the truth is finally recognised, survivors can begin their recovery'.[43] The novelists find in Shakespeare not only ways to explore the trauma caused from sporting accidents, racism, bullying, fluctuating family dynamics, hospitalization, suicide, and sexual assault but also ways its heroes and presumably some of its readers might also cope. Although Herman literally argues that storytelling might offer survivors the possibility of healing by sharing their experiences with an audience, a potentially harmful pattern consequently emerges when such sharing is juxtaposed with Shakespeare.

With each such adaptation of Shakespeare, authors further mythologize the playwright and his texts, and when such adaptations address trauma, they in turn run the risk of mythologizing trauma as well as the playwright. As Kalí Tal remarks, 'Mythologization works by reducing a traumatic event to a set of standardized narratives (twice- and thrice-told tales that come to represent "the story" of trauma) turning it from a frightening and controllable event into a contained and predictable narrative'.[44] In appropriating trauma in Shakespeare – often away from tragedy and towards the much more optimistic and comedic resolution discussed in this chapter – these novels trivialize the very difficulties they aim to address. These texts may collectively aim to provide readers who identify with the characters the understanding and perhaps even the voice to work through similar experiences, yet in so doing, they also risk patterning the public perception of trauma under the name of 'Shakespeare'. This chapter maps the interplay between Shakespeare and the patterns of trauma in its disparate forms while also casting a light on how YA authors, however unintentionally, turn to Shakespeare to prescribe treatment for traumatic experiences. Flourishing throughout each of these texts, and only amplified when taken together, is a reflection on the ways YA authors turn to Shakespeare to model and mythologize trauma, as if to suggest the Bard not only now provides cultural capital but mental health care as well. If such texts are intentionally being used in such a way in classrooms, libraries, or homes, it is important for those people publishing and purchasing such books to tread carefully when introducing such material to young readers, who might conclude that their own trauma always will end as happily as catalogued in YA adaptations of Shakespeare.

Notes

1 Jacqueline West, *Dreamers Often Lie* (New York: Dial, 2016), 2.

2 Ibid., 88.

3 Ibid., 308.

4 Eric L. Tribunella, *Melancholia and Maturation: The Use of Trauma in Children's Literature* (Knoxville: Tennessee University Press, 2010), xi.

5 Sharon M. Draper, *Romiette and Julio*, 1999 (New York: Simon Pulse, 2001), 25.

6 Ibid., 92, 136–7.

7 "Trauma." *Oxford English Dictionary*. Accessed 21 November 2021.

8 Quoted in Kenneth Kidd, '"A" is for Auschwitz: Psychoanalysis, Trauma Theory, and the 'Children's Literature of Atrocity', *Children's Literature* 33 (2005): 126.

9 Draper, *Romiette and Julio*, 1, 3, 92.

10 Ibid., 43, 106.

11 Ibid., 284.

12 Ibid., 316.

13 Lizabeth Zindel, *A Girl, a Ghost, and the Hollywood Hills* (New York: Viking, 2010), 5.

14 Ibid., 83.

15 Bennett Simon, '*Hamlet* and the Trauma Doctors: An Essay at Interpretation', *American Imago* 58, no. 3 (2001): 707.

16 Ibid., 714.

17 Zindel, *A Girl, a Ghost, and the Hollywood Hills*, 159–61, 164–7.

18 Ibid., 131.

19 Ibid., 288.

20 Ibid., 295.

21 Stephanie S. Tolan, *The Face in the Mirror*, 1998 (New York: Harper Trophy, 2000), 1, 2, 6.

22 Ibid., 49.

23 Sue Misheff, 'Beneath the Web and Over the Stream: The Search for Safe Places in *Charlotte's Web* and *Bridge to Terabithia*', *Children's Literature in Education* 29, no. 3 (1998): 131.

24 Tolan, *The Face in the Mirror*, 73.

25 Ibid., 90.

26 Ibid., 91.

27 Ibid., 5.

28 Jacques Lacan, 'The Mirror Stage as Formative of the Function of the I as Revealed in Psychoanalytic Experience', in *Ecrits*, translated and edited by B. Fink (New York: Norton, 1949), 78.

29 Ibid., 28.

30 Tolan, *The Face in the Mirror*, 13.

31 Ibid., 106.

32 Ibid., 127.

33 Ibid., 133.

34 Ibid., 172.

35 E. K. Johnston, *Exit, Pursued by a Bear* (New York: Speak, 2016), 243.

36 For more analysis on how Hermione Winters's name and nickname 'The Ice Queen' are associated with her identity, see the following: Amber Moore, 'Traumatic Geographies: Mapping the Violent Landscapes Driving YA Rape Survivors Indoors in Laurie Halse Anderson's *Speak*, Elizabeth Scott's *Living Dead Girl*, and E. K. Johnston's *Exit, Pursued by a Bear*', *Jeunesse: Young People, Texts, Cultures* 10, no. 1 (2018): 58–84.

37 Johnston, *Exit, Pursued by a Bear*, 19, 32–3.

38 Ibid., 13.

39 Amy Allen Clark, 'Sundays with Writers: *Exit, Pursued by a Bear* by E. K. Johnston', Momadvice.com. https://www.momadvice.com/post/sundays-with-writers-exit-pursued-by-a-bear-by-e-k-johnston (Accessed 20 November 2021).

40 Johnston, *Exit, Pursued by a Bear*, 68.

41 Ibid., 240, 241.

42 Such a pattern exists also in Gary Schmidt's *The Wednesday Wars* (2007), E. Lockhart's *We Were Liars* (2014), and Healey's *The Ophelia Girls* (2021).

43 Judith Herman, *Trauma and Recovery*. 1992 (New York: Basic Books, 1997), 1.

44 Kalí Tal, *Worlds of Hurt: Reading the Literatures of Trauma* (Cambridge: Cambridge University Press, 1996), 6.

SECTION II

Empowerment
and education

7

Ophelia

A new hope

Natalie Loper

The last *Star Wars* trilogy, released between 2015 and 2019, focuses on the rise of a new Jedi warrior. Whereas the first trilogy focused on Anakin Skywalker and the second featured his son Luke, the third trilogy's protagonist is Rey, a tough young woman gifted with the power of the Force used by Jedi including Anakin and Luke Skywalker. Rey, played by Daisy Ridley, eventually learns to channel her tremendous strength to lead a diverse group of people in their fight against the evil First Order, which enslaves and oppresses people all over the universe.[1] The films are part of a broader cultural movement that privileges women's stories and perspectives, including adaptations of Shakespeare. Lisa Klein's 2008 YA novel *Ophelia* retells *Hamlet* from Ophelia's perspective.[2] The 2018 film adaptation of the novel, directed by Claire McCarthy with a screenplay by Sami Chellas, features *Star Wars*'s Daisy Ridley as Ophelia.[3] Focusing on women's survival in a violent patriarchal world, the book and film attempt to interpret *Hamlet* from a contemporary feminist perspective, in which some women move beyond male violence and authority through literacy, female alliances, and a tenacious hope in a better future. The novel follows

Ophelia to a Catholic convent in France, where a community of women gives her the time and space to grieve for all she has lost in Denmark and helps her heal from trauma. She gradually uses her expertise in herbal remedies to become a well-respected healer and influences other women to tell their stories. The film radically cuts this ending and focuses more on Ophelia's last-ditch effort to get Hamlet to choose her over vengeance, followed by a brutal massacre of the entire Danish court. Whereas Klein's novel shows how Ophelia and other women process their trauma, the film presents limited options: bitter vengeance, death, or an escape to an idyllic but unrealistic new life.

In his afterword to *Shakespeare/Not Shakespeare*, Douglas Lanier describes the move away from fidelity criticism, which measures an adaptation's value based on its proximity to the Shakespearean 'original', a move that has allowed for serious consideration of a seemingly endless assortment of material and cultural artefacts that can be considered 'Shakespeare'. Lanier's theory of Shakespearean rhizomatics usefully describes this proliferation. All Shakespearean adaptations, productions, performances, editions, and references become part of a vast network – the Shakespeare rhizome – with new works 'tapping into multiple notes in that network'.[4] Sometimes things are intentionally 'Shakespeare', but other times memes, echoes, themes, and remediations become 'Shakespeare' when they are labelled as such, regardless of authorial intent. Lanier suggests that adaptation critics have swung so far away from questions of fidelity that 'we run the risk of making all cultural production a form of Shakespeare adaptation', which 'radically overestimates the cultural centrality of Shakespeare, but more crucially it obliterates the very discursive differences that criticism has sought to articulate and respect for the past thirty years'.[5] He poses a challenge to adaptation scholars: 'we need . . . more precise articulations of how Shakespearean adaptors have conceptualized and deployed the "spirit of Shakespeare" in their works, with the proviso that Shakespearean texts cannot serve as privileged standards or ultimate sources for the category of "Shakespeare."'[6] Decentring Shakespeare can privilege different stories, which in turn advance difficult conversations and highlight under-represented voices. People might initially approach adaptations because of their proximity to Shakespeare, but the ever-expanding Shakespeare rhizome allows for new ways of looking at contemporary problems.

By centring the story on the experiences of young people, YA novels and teen Shakespeare films can shape their source texts into stories that resonate in the late twentieth and early twenty-first centuries. In *Shakespeare and Girls' Studies*, Ariane M. Balizet invokes the Shakespeare rhizome to examine how girls are interpreted in young adult adaptations of Shakespeare in films, television, young adult novels, and web series. She uses the critical lens of Girls' Studies 'to demonstrate how the construction of girlhood within and through Shakespearean adaptation has cultural meaning that is useful in advancing the rights of and opportunities for girls'.[7] This requires examining both the Shakespearean and non-Shakespearean parts of these adaptations, especially since characters like Ophelia have expanded far beyond Shakespeare's plays.

Both the novel and film versions of *Ophelia* update Shakespeare's *Hamlet* for a twenty-first-century audience by drawing on adaptations and interpretations of the character Ophelia that have proliferated over the past two centuries. Ophelia's presence in popular culture is well documented.[8] Indeed, cultural appropriations of the character are as ubiquitous as Hamlet holding Yorick's skull. From John Everett Millais's pre-Raphaelite painting to the recently revised and updated book *Reviving Ophelia* by Mary Pipher and her daughter Sara Pipher Gilliam (2019), discussions and cultural appropriations of Ophelia typically focus on her sexuality, her madness or mental illness, and her watery death.[9] In online communities, adolescent girls channel Ophelia to represent their pain, including in groups created by and for those who live with eating disorders and psychological distress.[10] Ophelia represents suffering, particularly at the hands of a repressive patriarchal society.

Whereas many of these depictions focus on the tragic nature of Ophelia's downfall and death, some authors reclaim Ophelia and give her a hopeful, if not entirely happy, ending. Klein's *Ophelia* and McCarthy's adaptation both depict a challenging and oppressive world and imagine an escape from Denmark: Ophelia begins a new life in France, where she gives birth to Hamlet's child away from the prying eyes of the rotten court. The adaptations differ, sometimes radically, in their use of source materials and history, particularly in how they choose to end their stories. Whereas the final third of Klein's novel focuses on Ophelia's new life as a guest at a convent in France, where the sexual politics of court life are replaced by the equally dramatic world of cloistered nuns, McCarthy's film focuses instead on Queen Gertrude and her sister Mechtild, who was forced to leave Elsinore after she was impregnated by Claudius and nearly burned as a witch. The sex of Ophelia's child also differs in the two versions. In Klein's novel, Ophelia names her son Hamlet and acknowledges that he will have to contend with his birthright one day. The film's child is a girl, whom Ophelia will ostensibly raise as a strong woman who will forge her own path in life. Mothers and virgins, servants and queens, nuns and witches: these stories showcase the roles women are cast into and how women must constantly adapt within a culture that seeks to pigeonhole them. As these texts become new shoots of the Shakespeare rhizome, they show how his plays continue to be sites of discussion about gender roles, social structures, and human possibility.

Klein's *Ophelia* has been marketed towards young adults, their teachers, and librarians in publications such as *Writing*, in which it appears in an online issue 'all about revision' and *Young Adult Library Services*, within an article about fan fiction.[11] Abigail Rokison cites the book in her discussion of 'adaptations and re-workings of *Hamlet* for young people of secondary school age', including film and television adaptations, picture books, short stories, plays, and novels.[12] She pairs Klein's adaptation with Lisa Fiedler's *Dating Hamlet* (2002) and calls them 'feminist' novels; Klein's Ophelia is 'well-read and intelligent, defiant towards Laertes and deliberately deceptive of her father'.[13] Other scholarly discussions of the novel analyse it alongside other YA adaptations that recast Ophelia as the central character, including Fiedler's novel and Michelle Ray's *Falling for Hamlet* (2011). Erica Hateley argues that these three novels 'offer adolescent readers an Ophelia who engages critically and creatively with her context, and model a Shakespearean subjectivity which values intellectual and emotional engagement with *Hamlet*'.[14] Discussing Klein's novel, she too focuses on Ophelia's 'maturity being indexed by literacy' and the character's journey from reader to author.[15] Jennifer Flaherty also focuses on *Dating Hamlet* and *Ophelia* and argues, 'by revising Ophelia and creating newer, more assertive versions in their novels, Fiedler and Klein subvert the critical tradition of Hamlet and invert the popular perception of Ophelia in an effort to create "relatable" (recognizable and accessible) role-models for their young readers.'[16] In contrast to the 'relatable' connection between Ophelia and mental illness described by Perni, Pipher, and others, these novels seek to forge a new, anti-tragic path for both the character and their readers: 'These novelizations grant Ophelia a form of agency that is impossible for her to achieve in the Shakespearean source text, an agency that challenges the expectations of both her readers and her fellow characters.'[17] Ophelia's 'mad scene' in which she distributes flowers becomes in both novels a conscious act in which Ophelia demonstrates her knowledge of plants (she is 'part botanist and part apothecary' in both novels) and uses this knowledge to indict Gertrude and Claudius.[18] She concocts a potion to fake her own death, à la Juliet, but instead of death by suicide she lives to tell her tale.

While these YA adaptations are admirable in offering hope to adolescent girls who may relate to them, the notion of a rational Ophelia who fakes mental illness to escape her situation smacks of ableism and does not fully address the myriad pressures faced by teen girls today. For many girls, there is no escape from the pressures of perfection that permeate social media and popular culture. As rates of anxiety and depression skyrocket, especially in the wake of the Covid-19 pandemic, it can be difficult for girls to feel hopeful. The book suggests that adversity can be overcome. Klein's Ophelia makes a perilous journey from Denmark to France. Her flight is more than madness (real or feigned) or the desire to start over; she is afraid that Claudius has sent Edmund, who has been the epitome of male sexual violence throughout the novel, to kill her.[19] After realizing that Hamlet is bent on revenge and does not wish to denounce his claim to the throne in order to start a new life with her, Ophelia decides to leave him and set out on her own. She drinks a poison she concocted from stolen mandrake root and other herbs and must rely on Horatio and Mechtild, the healer/witch who lives in the forest, to save her life and the life of her unborn child, whom she conceived with her secret husband Hamlet.

Ophelia's journey to France is not easy, nor is her slow recovery, pregnancy, and assimilation into the all-female community of St Emilion. In this place of refuge, Mother Ermentrude is subject to the authority of the bishop and the convent's wealthy and judgemental benefactor, Sister Marguerite is as hard to please as some of the courtiers, and the other sisters vie for attention and blessings. Most are suspicious of Ophelia, some are scandalized by her pregnancy, and few offer to help her. On the one hand, the novel demonstrates that the journey to wellness is far from straightforward and may come with serious losses; on the other hand, only those with inner fortitude and proper credentials are able to move beyond their pain. Klein depicts the convent as a space for women to grow into who they are apart from the expectations of arranged marriage, clandestine affairs, and potential ruin at the hands of men, but her inclusive space is plagued by some of the same challenges that marginalized girls face today.

Critics tend to focus on the first two-thirds of Klein's novel, which offers a clearer adaptation of Shakespeare's *Hamlet*, and gloss over this section. Balizet sees the novel's ending as problematic, and she analyses it within the tendency of YA Shakespeare novels to present heroines who choose when and with whom to have sex, but whose sexual choices mean that they 'articulate their worth in terms of sexual purity, echoing not early modern standards of chastity so much as the modern pro-abstinence rhetoric' that dominated sexual education in the 1990s.[20] As she points out, Ophelia's decision to have sex with Hamlet is framed 'within the rhetoric of marriage', and indeed they are married soon after.[21] Ophelia can prove that her child is the legitimate heir of Hamlet, Prince of Denmark, and this proof allows her protection and freedom. Ophelia also escapes an attempted rape, but Sister Marguerite, who does not escape her rapist Fortinbras, is 'doom[ed] . . . to life as a nun'.[22] Sexual assault, then, can determine whether a character is accepted by her society and allowed agency over her future. The novel presents a problematic view of sex, but despite these shortcomings it does depict some of the complicated reasons women sought refuge or were placed in convents and it showcases the roles women played in the life of the church. Women in religious orders could be scholars and writers and pursue a way of life that did not rely on them marrying for political alliances, on giving up their bodies without their consent, and on producing heirs.[23] Religious communities were (and are) critiqued for many valid reasons, but for some women, cloistered life offered a level of fulfilment beyond what the secular world could offer.

Much has been written about Catholic echoes in *Hamlet*, and Klein's novel imagines what Ophelia might encounter on the European continent. In her study of female adolescence in early modern England, Caroline Bicks builds on the work of critics such as Alison Shell and Alison A. Chapman to argue that Catholic references in Ophelia's songs identify her with recusant Catholic girls in post-Reformation England, many of whom went abroad to study their faith in convents.[24] According to Bicks, 'Catholic daughters sent to be educated in convents overseas, or to enter them as novices, formed populations of adolescent English girls that both represented and enabled the future of their faith back home'.[25] Klein's Ophelia is ambivalent about her own faith. She witnesses the religious fervour of others, but she does not always understand it and sees how it can cause great harm, and even death.

Ophelia's afterlife in the French convent does not imagine a future spreading Catholicism in England but rather friendship with a young woman named Therese, who is modelled on several Catholic saints. Therese, a physically disabled servant who does the laundry, is ridiculed by some of the sisters for her bizarre devotion to Christ. She subsists on only communion bread and water, claims to have visions of the Christ child nursing at her breast, and says her hands bleed like the wounds of Jesus. Ophelia alone helps Therese with her chores and tries to save her from starvation, but she cannot save her life. As the woman lies dying, Ophelia holds up her infant son and Therese responds by cradling the baby in her arms and exclaiming, "'It is my salvation! . . . He smells of honey and roses and milk", she murmurs, a look of ecstasy on her face.'[26] Therese's death is seen as a miracle when her palms begin to bleed as soon as she dies. Known as the stigmata, these bleeding wounds recall other religious figures such as Saint Francis of Assisi and Servant of God Therese Neumann von Konnersreuth, a German woman who died in 1962 after allegedly subsiding on the eucharist alone for thirty-six years.[27] Klein's character also recalls two other famous saints: Teresa of Avila (1515–82), a mystic who wrote about her intense visions of Christ, and Thérèse of Lisieux (1873–97), who took the name Therese of the Child Jesus and the Holy Face but is known more commonly as the Little Flower. The latter wrote about how her 'Little Way' of daily devotions and small gestures was enough to bring her close to Jesus. Both saints were named Doctors of the Catholic Church, one of the highest honours the church bestows.[28]

Why is this story inserted into Ophelia's? It demonstrates the levels of difficulty faced by women, including those who are revered for their goodness and devotion. Even saints faced ridicule and abuse from their contemporaries, secular and religious alike. They experienced terrible suffering, but they saw their pain in connection to Jesus, who suffered and died at the hands of his critics. The all-

female community of St Emilion is not a utopian escape; it is subject
to external male control and the same sort of pettiness that divides
the women at court. But, inspired in part by Ophelia, the women
learn that treating each other with kindness and respect leads to a
renewed life and sense of purpose. Marguerite uses the experience
to move beyond the trauma of being raped by Fortinbras, to whom
she was engaged. Whereas she had masked her pain by looking
down on the other women of her community, Ophelia's kindness
and Therese's death inspire Marguerite to use her education for a
greater purpose – to provide a voice for unrecognized women and
thus to inspire others.

In addition to writing her story and encouraging others to
tell theirs, Ophelia becomes an apothecary and healer. Beginning
with her study of plants in Denmark, she creates herbal remedies
that help heal other women; they call on her rather than the male
doctor in many cases. Her life is peaceful, but she knows this may
be temporary. Ophelia names her son Hamlet and reveals his
parentage to those around her. She anticipates a future where she
will have to tell her son about 'the foul crimes of Denmark, the
revenge unleashed there, and its tragic ending. When I tell him of
his father's madness, his mother's grief and their unfortunate love,
what will he make of this true but unbelievable tale?'[29] For now,
she can suspend this dark future. Her story ends with romance.
Horatio, who has shown his devotion to Ophelia throughout the
book, journeys to her, tells of how he managed to get Hamlet and
Laertes to forgive each other (a promise he made to Ophelia), of
how Denmark is oppressed under Fortinbras, and of how he came
to France to find her. Despite this romantic ending, which Hateley
calls 'a deus ex machina',[30] the book leaves open the possibility of
future struggle, as the young prince must decide whether and how
to claim Denmark's throne. In this novel, Ophelia takes seriously
the call to action in Shakespeare's play: the ghost's 'Remember me'
and Hamlet's plea to 'tell my story'.[31] Ophelia's story becomes more
than just one of murder and deception, greed and power, threat and
trauma. Ophelia's story is one of strength, healing, and hope.

McCarthy's film adaptation radically cuts Klein's ending and
central message of healing from trauma. Ophelia's voice and story
bookend the film, which begins visually with a tribute to Millais's
painting. Ophelia floats on her back in greenish-brown water, arms
outstretched, surrounded by water lilies and clutching a handful of

FIGURE 7.1 *Daisy Ridley as Ophelia.* Ophelia, *directed by Claire McCarthy (2018).*

purple and white flowers (see Figure 7.1). Her extra-diegetic voice narrates the opening sequence: 'I have seen more of heaven and hell than most people dream of. But I was always a wilful girl and followed my heart and spoke my mind. And it is high time that I should tell you my story myself.' Like Klein's novel and other Shakespearean teen adaptations, this Ophelia controls her outcome rather than becoming a tragic victim. The movie ends with Ophelia at the French convent, her voiceover resuming:

> You may think you know my story. You've heard it ends in madness, hearts broken, blood spilled, a kingdom lost. That is a story. But it is not mine. I did not lose my way. I did not lose myself to vengeance. Instead, I found my way to hope that one day I would tell my own story. As one day you, my love, you will tell yours.

These words play over Ophelia being taken in by the habited nuns, followed by a jump cut to her as a mother: smiling, Ophelia watches her daughter run towards her through the long grass and wildflowers, toy sword in hand, laughing as she falls into her mother's loving embrace. Ophelia is determined to move beyond her trauma and grief, towards a new life of love and possibility, but the film fails to show how she gets there.

Although McCarthy's Ophelia's story ends with hope, her journey is problematic. Instead of leaving for France immediately from Mechtild's cottage, where she recovers from the deathlike potion, Ophelia wears her man's disguise to court, finds Hamlet, and asks him to go with her. Klein's Ophelia chooses to leave Hamlet much earlier, when she recognizes that their goals are no longer aligned. In the film, Ophelia foolishly risks discovery on the slim chance that she will get to have a romantic ending with her beloved. Only after he refuses does she make the journey alone. In France, Ophelia gives birth to a girl, not a boy. Horatio does not join her. The final third of the book is condensed into just a few minutes, long enough for Ophelia's final voiceover. There is no Therese or Marguerite, no focus on this community of women who heal each other and find a way to live separate from the man's world of sexual assault and revenge, no male heir who may someday have to reclaim his rightful title in Denmark. Instead, Ophelia and her daughter make a *Sound of Music*-type journey over sunlit mountains.

The book's careful construction of female alliances devolves in the film into mistrust and revenge. Whereas the novel depicts two communities of women – the ladies at court and in the convent – the movie depicts a different sort of sisterhood. *Ophelia* transfers Hamlet's revenge to the hands of Gertrude and her beautiful sister Mechtild, who is a recluse rather than the wizened old herbalist of Klein's novel. This Mechtild fell in love at nineteen with Claudius, but after he impregnated her and refused to acknowledge the child, she was nearly burned at the stake as a witch. She escaped by drinking a potion that made the mob believe she was dead and revived herself with a remedy after they threw her body into the woods. Her son did not survive. She now lives removed from society, concocting potions in her cabin. Ophelia serves as a bridge between the sisters at the end of the film. She tells each one separately that Claudius was the one who ruined Mechtild's reputation, and they both enact their revenge. Hamlet and Laertes fatally wound each other in their duel, but Hamlet does not kill the king. Instead, after witnessing her son's death, Gertrude grabs the heavy sword and stabs Claudius through the torso, the bloody weapon emerging from the other side of his throne. Mechtild, meanwhile, joins the invading Norwegian army and leads them into Elsinore, bursting in just as Claudius dies. Understanding that all is lost, Gertrude drinks poison while everyone around her is violently slaughtered by the unnamed Fortinbras and his men. Amid the destruction, the sisters reunite, the warrior-witch cradling the dead queen's body. Indifferent to the bloody takeover of the Danish throne, Mechtild's isolation is complete: everyone she loved is dead, and unlike Ophelia, her child did not survive to keep her company or journey to a new life abroad. Whereas both adaptations focus on women's trauma, the film depicts their isolation, violent revenge, miscommunication and potential regret rather than the healing, social support, and agency of Klein's novel.

Klein's *Ophelia* strives towards a restorative justice in which women work through trauma to reclaim their lives and their stories. In casting Daisy Ridley as its heroine, the film could have drawn on her *Star Wars* character, Rey, to imagine a character able to do more than beg Hamlet to leave Denmark so that she could have a happy ending. Rey is incredibly gifted in the Force, but she must learn to balance the good side of the Force with the fear, anger, and thirst for revenge represented by the Dark Side. In the end, Rey overcomes evil by refusing to participate in a cycle of revenge, and her courage inspires creatures everywhere to fight oppression and experience true freedom. She chooses the love and comradery of the oppressed over the power to rule an empire. Like Rey, Daisy Ridley's Ophelia could have lifted a sword to fight for justice, done more to help Gertrude and Mechtild, or shown how the journey to healing and self-knowledge is more than driving a team of horses across a serene valley or strolling to the crest of a light-dappled mountain. Courage is facing one's fears and working to heal from trauma. If Shakespeare's girls are to truly inspire twenty-first-century women, they need to do more than escape – they need to grow. By turning Ophelia into a bland wife whose tragedy is that she could not convince Hamlet to follow through on his promises to her, the film missed out on an opportunity to show how a woman with a strong mind and fierce heart could walk away from her lover precisely because he could not match the imaginative vision she has for herself and the world she wishes to embody. By using the nineteenth-century imagery of Millais rather than the cinematic language of Rey, McCarthy's film ensures that its female characters are locked in a fantasy world where they might escape trauma but are never able to truly reconcile and overcome it.

Notes

1 *Star Wars: Episode VII – The Force Awakens* (Lucasfilm, 2015); *Star Wars: Episode VIII – The Last Jedi* (Walt Disney Pictures, 2017); *Star Wars: Episode IX – The Rise of Skywalker* (Walt Disney Pictures, 2019).

2 Lisa Klein, *Ophelia* (New York: Bloomsbury, 2006).

3 *Ophelia*, directed by Claire McCarthy (Covert Media, 2018).

4 Douglas Lanier, 'Afterword', in *Shakespeare/Not Shakespeare*, ed. Christy Desmet, Natalie Loper, and Jim Casey (New York: Palgrave Macmillan, 2017), 297. See also Douglas Lanier, 'Shakespearean Rhizomatics: Adaptation, Ethics, Value', in *Shakespeare and the Ethics of Appropriation*, ed. Alexa Huang and Elizabeth Rivlin (New York: Palgrave Macmillan, 2014), 21–40.

5 Lanier, 'Afterword', 302.

6 Ibid., 302–3.

7 Ariane M. Balizet, *Shakespeare and Girls' Studies* (New York: Routledge, 2020), 18.

8 See, for example, *The Afterlife of Ophelia*, ed. Kaara L. Peterson and Deanne Williams (New York: Palgrave Macmillan, 2012); Elaine Showalter, 'Representing Ophelia: Women, Madness, and the Responsibilities of Feminist Criticism', in *Shakespeare and the Question of Theory*, ed. Patricia Parker and Geoffrey H. Hartman (New York: Methuen, 1985); and Alan Young, *Hamlet and the Visual Arts, 1709-1900* (London: Associated University Presses, 1984).

9 Mary Pipher and Sara Pipher Gilliam, *Reviving Ophelia: Saving the Selves of Adolescent Girls* (New York: Riverhead Books, 2019). The book, originally published in 1994, was revised and updated in 2019 to include a discussion of social media and other challenges faced by adolescent girls in the twenty-first century. Balizet opens her book with an epigraph from Pipher and situates her study within its context: 'The argument that girls can and should be "saved" from the dangers of adolescence became a powerful (but not unproblematic) driving force in some quarters of Girls' Studies. In appropriating the story of Ophelia, Pipher ensured that the public attention paid to girls in the wake of her book would be authorized, at least partly, by its association with Shakespeare's *Hamlet*', 5.

10 Remedios Perni, 'Ana and Mia: Ophelia on the Web', *Shakespeare Quarterly* 67, no. 4 (2017): 503–14. Perni focuses on these 'pro-Ana (anorexia) and pro-Mia (bulimia)' communities, 504.

11 'Ophelia The Next Generation', *Writing* 29, iss. 3 (November/ December 2006): 4; and Robin Brenner, 'Teen Literature and Fan Culture', *Young Adult Library Services* 11, iss. 4 (2013): 33–6.

12 Abigail Rokison, '"Our Scene is Alter'd": Adaptations and Re-Workings of Hamlet for Young People', *Literature Compass* 7, iss. 9 (2010): 786.

13 Ibid., 791.

14 Erica Hateley, 'Sink or Swim?: Revising Ophelia in Contemporary Young Adult Fiction', *Children's Literature Association Quarterly* 14, no. 4 (2013): 435.

15 Ibid., 443–4.

16 Jennifer Flaherty, 'Reviving Ophelia: Reaching Adolescent Girls through Shakespeare's Doomed Heroine', *Borrowers and Lenders: A Journal of Shakespeare and Appropriation* 9, no. 1 (2014): n.p.

17 Ibid., n.p. Balizet also devotes a chapter to these novels, plus YA fiction adaptations of *Romeo and Juliet*, *The Winter's Tale*, *Macbeth*, and others. She identifies two common themes: the main characters' pursuit of education, most commonly as healers, and the constant threat of sexual assault. See Balizet, *Shakespeare and Girls' Studies*, 93–129.

18 Flaherty, 'Reviving Ophelia', n.p.

19 For a discussion of sex, sexual assault, and rape culture in YA Shakespeare novels, see Balizet 113–28.

20 Balizet, *Shakespeare and Girls' Studies*, 114.

21 Ibid., 117.

22 Ibid., 125.

23 Although the notion of consent may seem anachronistic, especially as it has been articulated in the #metoo era, I would point to the many women saints who chose disfigurement, torture, and even death over sex and/or marriage to men who tried to lay claim to their bodies.

24 Caroline Bicks, *Cognition and Girlhood in Shakespeare's World: Rethinking Female Adolescence* (Cambridge: Cambridge University Press, 2021), 155–8.

25 Ibid., 157.

26 Klein, *Ophelia*, 308.

27 For the latter, see Otto Seidl, 'Stigmatisation and Absence of Nutrition in the Case of Therese Neumann (1898-1962)', *Nervenarzt* 79, no. 7 (2008), 836–44 and Johannes Steiner, *Therese Neumann; A Portrait*

Based on Authentic Accounts, Journals, and Documents (New York: Alba House, 1967).

28 Of the thirty-six Doctors of the Church, only four are women. See Mary T. Malone, *Four Women Doctors of the Church: Hildegard of Bingen, Catherine of Siena, Teresa of Avila, and Therese of Lisieux* (New York: Orbis Books, 2017). Teresa of Avila founded the Discalced Carmelites, a reform movement that stresses austerity. Thérèse of Lisieux belonged to the same order. Mechtild, a significant character in Klein's Denmark, is also associated with Catholic women authors. Mechthild of Madgeburg was a thirteenth-century mystic who wrote *The Flowing Light of Divinity*. Mechthild of Hackeborn was a thirteenth-century mystic who wrote *The Book of Special Grace*.

29 Klein, *Ophelia*, 321–2.

30 Hateley, 'Sink or Swim?', 443.

31 William Shakespeare, *Hamlet*, ed. R. A. Foakes, in *The Arden Shakespeare, Third Series, Complete Works* (London, New York, Oxford, New Delhi, and Sydney: Bloomsbury, 2020). All references to Shakespeare's works are to this edition (5.2.304).

8

'You should be women'

The figure of the witch in Young Adult adaptations of Shakespeare's *Macbeth*

Melissa Johnson

'You should be women / And yet your beards forbid me to interpret / That you are so' (1.3.46–8).[1] In Shakespeare's *Macbeth*, Banquo's remark regarding the gender indeterminacy of the witches speaks to their fringe position in the world of the play; because they do not adhere to the role women are expected to inhabit, they are marginalized by the other characters and their power goes unnoticed or underestimated by all but Macbeth. Shakespeare's witches are iconic characters, the word 'Macbeth' often conjuring images of them positioned around a boiling cauldron and the lines of their speeches frequently reprinted on commercial products from Halloween decorations to T-shirts to drinkware and candles.[2] Theories abound about the witches, but early modern English laws, primarily those enacted by James I himself, condemned anyone even remotely connected to the idea of witchcraft. James, who had ascended the throne of England by the time Shakespeare composed

Macbeth, spoke out vehemently against witches and witchcraft. His 1604 'Act against Conjuration, Witchcraft, and dealing with evil and wicked spirits' established witchcraft as a felony under common law and penalized any ostensible practice of witchcraft, no matter the perceived result, with death. Katherine Howe describes the early modern conception of witchcraft as 'a legitimate, but dangerous, category for explaining reality'.[3] Today, however, many women have reclaimed the term 'witch' and the connotations around it as symbolic of feminine power and resistance.

In many ways indicative of early modern attitudes towards female power and agency, adaptive representations of Shakespeare's witches today also reflect attitudes towards the power structures that limit young women's voices and autonomy. Authors of young adult adaptations of *Macbeth* within the last twenty years have latched onto these new perceptions when shaping the heroines of their novels. Rebecca Reisert's 2001 *The Third Witch* and Lisa Klein's 2009 *Lady Macbeth's Daughter* both follow rejected daughters of Lady Macbeth who eventually take on identities as witches to challenge Macbeth's tyranny. Hannah Capin's 2020 *Foul Is Fair* resets the storyline of *Macbeth* in a more contemporary environment, exploring today's gendered power structures among young adults and imbuing the play's female characters with the power to challenge these dynamics. These novelists use Shakespeare to further the feminist reclamation of witches while challenging previous interpretations of the weird sisters as marginal or singularly malicious.

Shakespeare wrote *Macbeth* in the early seventeenth century, shortly after the death of Elizabeth I and the ascension of James I to the throne of England. James's attitudes towards witches were already well known; he published his famous work on witches and witchcraft, *Demonology*, in 1597. Shakespeare's characterization of his weird sisters appears to align with the more sinister portrayal of witches propagated by James. In the first book of James's work, structured as a dialogue between two men, Epistemon tells Philomathes that 'Yea, he [the devil] will make his scholars to creep in credit with princes, by foretelling them many great things, part true, part false, for if all were false he would lose credit at all hands; but always doubtsome, as his oracles were'.[4] Many familiar with *Macbeth* would argue that this description of witches' prophecies mirrors those that Shakespeare's weird sisters deliver to the title character. James also describes witches as having the ability to make themselves invisible ('And in this transporting, they say to themselves that they are invisible to any other, except among themselves; which may also be possible in my opinion'[5]). Shakespeare portrays this ability of witches in *Macbeth* when Banquo and Macbeth note that the weird sisters 'vanished . . . into the air, and what seemed corporal melted /As breath into the wind'(1.3.80–2). James's claim that 'they can raise storms and tempests in the air, either upon sea or land'[6] is also borne out by Shakespeare's witches: 'Though his bark cannot be lost/Yet it shall be tempest tossed' (1.3.24–5). In his history of one particular seventeenth-century English witch hunt, Malcolm Gaskill notes that 'sailors were notoriously afraid of witchcraft',[7] and lines like these appear to indicate why. Such historical references, coupled with the language of the witches in the play, demonstrate how Shakespeare's weird sisters clearly adhere to an early modern understanding of witches.

James's, and by extension, Shakespeare's, conception of witches did not exist in a vacuum. Mythology around witches circulated prior to *Demonology* and *Macbeth*, and it influenced the ideas of witches depicted within each text. Other early modern dramatists, such as Thomas Middleton (who is often credited with adapting and inserting passages into Shakespeare's *Macbeth*), William Rowley, and Thomas Dekker, also reflect these attitudes in their work. Many of these attitudes continued into the nineteenth century and beyond. Charles Lamb described both Shakespeare and Middleton's witches as 'rais[ing] jars, jealousies, strifes, like a thick scurf o'er life'.[8] In the 1930s George Wilson Knight delineated the evil components of Shakespeare's Macbeth, noting 'in particular storms, blood and animals'[9] – all of which the witches mention in their scenes. Various bleak perceptions of *Macbeth*'s witches still hold sway, including grotesque representations of them in film and graphic novel adaptations of the play.[10] The image of the malevolent witch in well-known and frequently adapted fairy tales such as 'Hansel and Gretel' and 'Snow White' also still persists, colouring our collective ideas of witches. L. Frank Baum's Wicked Witch of the West is the major villain of the classic *The Wizard of Oz*, often overshadowing her benevolent counterparts, the Witch of the North and Glinda, the Witch of the South (conflated in the film). And other children's authors, such as Roald Dahl and C. S. Lewis, cast witches in villainous roles, pitting them as evil women who wield trickery and malevolent magic against the young protagonists they confront. The idea of witches as villains embodying female guile is a prevalent one and difficult to shake. And all of these perceptions play into our evolving view of Shakespeare's witches.

The cultural perception of witches, however, is shifting, allowing for the Glindas to take centre stage, even if the nature of their abilities is more ambiguous than Baum's straightforward characterizations. As Mikaella Clements notes in her article, 'The Brief History of the Tumblr Witch':

> It's safe to say that witches are having a socio-pop culture moment. We love witches in all their permutations, strengths, spells, and darkness. After centuries of persecution, distrust, and disdain, witches are even being viewed positively, in a cloak of mysterious light. This isn't always the case – the witch as a festering image of cruelty, synonymous with controlling, enigmatic, or needy women, is still everywhere – but slowly, surely, some of us are beginning to embrace them. The witch is becoming a hero as much as an outcast – she is even a hero *as* she is an outcast.[11]

Authors, screenwriters, and artists are gradually populating pop culture with witch protagonists and redeemed witches from familiar stories, and YA authors and adapters are leading the way. Beginning in the mid- to late 1990s, female, teenage or young adult witches became increasingly prevalent in media. *Buffy the Vampire Slayer*'s Willow Rosenberg (played by Alyson Hannigan) stands out through her impressive skill in witchcraft and essential assistance in defeating the many villains Buffy faces. The *Harry Potter* series' Hermione Granger, referred to as 'the cleverest witch of [her] age',[12] also plays a pivotal role in the outcome of Harry's story. Since the introduction of these characters in the 1990s, many more have graced film, television, and the pages of books.

Today, YA authors continue to tap into this trend in their books; those who adapt Shakespeare for their readers are no different. Two of these authors, Rebecca Reisert and Lisa Klein, allow the heroines in their adaptations of *Macbeth* to take on the roles of witches at critical moments within their stories, leading to beneficial resolutions for them and for other characters. A third author, Hannah Capin, casts her heroine, Jade, as Lady Macbeth, but Jade's actions often align with those of Capin's witch characters, blurring their identities and creating an interpretation of Lady Macbeth in which she shares and even somewhat controls the witches' power, and echoing critical interpretations of her role like that of Dympna Callaghan, who states that 'by seventeenth-century standards . . . Lady Macbeth is a witch'.[13] This power allows Capin's characters to confront the culture of toxic masculinity that surrounds them and enact revenge on the young men who engage in this culture by committing acts of violence against them. These resolutions, in turn, convey the message that identifying as a witch is liberating and empowering, aligning with the changing idea of the witch in response to the frequent dismissal of young women's voices in our current society.

Reisert's *The Third Witch* follows Gilly, the daughter of Lady Macbeth and her first husband. After Macbeth murders her father and marries her mother, usurping the throne in a plot more reminiscent of *Hamlet*, Gilly flees, surviving by living and scavenging in the woods with two peculiar older women. A number of events and references connect these women to Shakespeare's weird sisters; the mention of Graymalkin,[14] their use of 'second sight'[15] to predict the future, similar to the prophesying alluded to by both Shakespeare and James I, and their existence in the woods, outside of organized society, all connote predominant ideas of witches and witchcraft. Gilly vows revenge on Macbeth and convinces her companions to help her, relying on their witchcraft to carry out her plans. Gilly disguises herself as a boy and secures a place as a servant in Dunsinane castle, gathering intel and slipping subtle suggestions to Macbeth before returning to the other women to complete her plans. Once she reunites with the women who raised her, Gilly steps into the role of witch and exercises the power she now has over Macbeth:

> Nettle and Mad Helga wait silently. I must say something. 'Macbeth, Macbeth – beware – ' *What, what can I say?* Suddenly I recall His conversation with His wife back at the castle. *Frighten Him. Name an enemy.* . . . 'Beware Macduff!' I croak in my best Mad Helga voice. 'Beware the Thane of Fife. Dismiss me. Enough!'[16]

At this moment, Gilly assumes a leadership position among her fellow witches and drives much of the action of the scene. While her prophecies are not magical or supernatural, merely supplied by the knowledge she has surreptitiously garnered about Macbeth's own fears, they have power over him nonetheless. Reisert thus formulates Macbeth's downfall as an event brought about by Gilly, shifting Shakespearean witch into protagonist and emphasizing her prophecies as a tool for restoring order rather than causing chaos.

Klein's *Lady Macbeth's Daughter* centres on Albia, who, as the title suggests and like Gilly, is also the daughter of Lady Macbeth. Because her child is a girl and born with a noticeable leg deformity, Lady Macbeth orders Albia's death, yet Rhuven, one of Klein's Wyrd Sisters, rescues her and hides her in the woods with the other two witches. From this point, Albia's journey is similar to Gilly's. After becoming the ward of Banquo and learning of his death at the orders of Macbeth, Albia vows revenge and travels to Macbeth's castle in an attempt to carry this vengeance out. Her plans eventually return her to the Wyrd Sisters, where, taking the place of one of the sisters who has died, she joins them and delivers the prophecies that mislead Macbeth about Macduff and Birnam Wood:

> I remember overhearing Fiona say that Macduff was born unnaturally, torn from the womb before his time. This bit of truth will be my bait. . . . 'Be bloody, bold, and resolute!' I shout. 'Scorn the power of men, for none of woman born shall harm Macbeth.'[17]

Unlike Gilly, Albia does experience prophetic dreams, leading to some of the images she passes to Macbeth. But, similarly to Gilly, she is clear that some of her words to him are supplied by the fears she already knows he possesses. Both Gilly and Albia use intellect to overcome Shakespeare's tragic hero, indicating a privileging of this trait for young female readers. The idea of witches possessing sharp intelligence is not new. Joss Whedon connected the image of witches with the quality of intelligence in his aforementioned television show, *Buffy the Vampire Slayer*, and J. K. Rowling's hugely popular *Harry Potter* series also features a highly intelligent witch in the character of Hermione Granger. By emphasizing intelligence and quick thinking in their lead characters, YA adapters of Shakespeare's *Macbeth* lean into the current portrayal of witches in pop culture to reform the images of those Shakespeare created. Simultaneously, they figure these traits as a kind of power, one that gives the young women who possess it a power akin to supernatural magic.

Gender is one of the most important factors influencing these characters' actions and experiences. Just as Macbeth calls the weird sisters' genders into question in the first act of Shakespeare's play, Gilly and Albia challenge the expectations assigned to them as young women: 'I feel the broken-edged dagger in my hand. *I will not be a girl, I will not be a woman, I will be a thing, a sexless thing, a thing with short hair, as short as leaves. I will be more tree or rock than woman.*'[18] Not only does Gilly's rejection of her feminine identity mark her with the perceived masculinity of early modern witches, it mirrors one of Shakespeare's Lady Macbeth's most famous speeches: 'Come, you spirits / That tend on mortal thoughts, unsex me here, / And fill me, from the crown to the toe, top full / Of direst cruelty!' (1.5.40–3). Albia steps outside the bounds of traditional femininity as well, learning combat and horsemanship, and joining the final battle that concludes Shakespeare's *Macbeth*. Both heroines' quests for vengeance also link them to masculinity, as revenge is a task typically given to male characters. These gender subversions signal the heroines' connections to early modern perceptions of witches, yet also convey a broader range of possible paths for today's young women to YA readers. Both girls combine the strength and cunning commonly associated with the masculine with feminine modes of being at the conclusion of their stories. Albia develops a romantic relationship with Fleance, and Klein hints at a happily-ever-after ending for them at the close of her book: '"Albia, my fate is bound with yours", he whispers. The words of my own dream startle me, coming from Fleance's mouth. "I know", I breathe back. "You and I share a single future."'[19] While Gilly does not enter into a romantic relationship, she vows to take on a more nurturing role moving forward: 'more important than killing a king is making the world safe for all abandoned children, and now I have a place and the money and power to make a safe world within this world for those I love to learn and grow.'[20] Embracing the identity of 'witch' gives both characters the autonomy to make choices and progressive change – autonomy they would not have outside of this more fringe position.

Hannah Capin further blurs the line between moving forward and taking revenge in *Foul Is Fair*. Capin's *Macbeth* retelling exemplifies Ariane Balizet's assertion in *Shakespeare and Girls'*

Studies that 'to be a girl is to . . . experience suffering in a particular way' and that 'girlhood is a powerful animating force in contemporary Shakespearean adaptation'.[21] Capin's protagonist, Jade, experiences a gang rape at a party and vows revenge against the boys responsible. These heightened stakes reflect the very real traumas many young women face in today's world, and the feelings of powerlessness that they often experience as a result, feelings that Jade enlists the help of her friends and the practice of witchcraft to combat: 'There on the screen Summer's holding, I see the boys we're going to ruin. . . . My nails are long and silver. Ten little daggers, sharp enough to tear throats open. . . . Today I choose who dies and I choose who kills.'[22] Jade's revenge takes the form of a murder plot for which she enlists her three best friends, whom she calls her 'coven'. Jade forms a relationship with Mack, a friend and lacrosse teammate of the boys she plots against, to advance her scheme. In the Lady Macbeth role, Jade dictates the actions of her coven and attempts to manipulate Mack and the boys who raped her into betraying and killing each other: '"Killing hurts worse if somebody you love is holding the knife", I say. "So make one of them do it?" Summer asks. . . . Jenny smiles her pink-heart smile and says: *Fair is foul, and foul is fair* – another spell.'[23]

Jade's power over her coven and the many references from the source play that Capin weaves into her text align with the interpretation that Lady Macbeth is connected to the witches, possibly even a kind of fourth witch herself, through her own invocation of dark spirits and symbolic unsexing. Erica Hateley states that 'the play symbolically aligns Lady Macbeth with the witches on a continuum of feminine power'[24] while Marguerite A. Tassi raises another connection, noting that the witches 'are frightening spectres of feminine vengefulness, which subliminally fuse with Lady Macbeth when she calls upon malign spirits and then persuades her husband to kill for worldly acquisition'.[25] Jade quite literally calls on her coven of friends to carry out her plot and directs both their and Mack's actions in pursuit of her revenge. Jade acknowledges that her plans would not be possible without her friends, saying: 'A spell from my three witch sisters . . . I open my eyes – now, this morning, here in my coven with Jenny and Summer and Mads – and they've done magic again.'[26] Jade's profound love and connection towards her coven are tied up with her desire for revenge. For Jade, her coven represents the empowerment of true female friendship, embodying the idea of female connection encompassed in many recent portrayals of witches in popular media, from the sisterly connection shared by the three heroines of the television show, *Charmed*, to the friendship and eventual romantic love that blossoms between Willow and fellow witch Tara as they learn their craft on *Buffy the Vampire Slayer* – a groundbreaking portrayal of a lesbian couple at a time when such relationships on television were not explicit or common.[27] While Shakespeare's *Macbeth*, as Jennifer Flaherty notes, 'has no existing social spaces for young, unmarried female characters'.[28] YA adaptors of the play borrow the communal nature of witchcraft as it is represented in pop culture to create these spaces in their own texts.

Though these empowering relationships are an important part of Capin's story, the packaging of the book focuses on the idea of revenge. The cover features an illustration of a girl, presumably Jade, her face rendered in sharp angles and her red lips and black hair harsh against the green and yellow background. Unlike Klein and Reisert's texts, Capin's book does not include an author's note explicitly connecting the text to Shakespeare, just a content warning at the beginning of the text and an acknowledgements page at the end, both addressing the themes of gender, sexuality, and rape present in the novel: 'To all who survive, every day, in spite of everything: those who forgive and those who fight, those who seek justice and those who seek revenge, those who have stood up with the whole world watching and those whose stories will never be told. You are strength and you are power.'[29] This focus places a stronger emphasis on the thematic content of the book and the psyches of the characters than any connection to Shakespeare. One might question, then, why Capin chose Shakespearean adaptation to tell her story in the first place. One answer is that our cultural perception of witches is inherently linked to Shakespeare's *Macbeth*. While Shakespeare may have drawn images such as the use of a cauldron for mixing magical ingredients and the calling of animal familiars from popular early modern beliefs about witches, his translation of these images onto the stage remains the primary conduit of these ideas to the general public, as evidenced by the numerous memes and other pop cultural references playing on the lines of *Macbeth*'s weird sisters, specifically, as a kind of shorthand for immediately identifying their characters as witches. For YA adaptors of *Macbeth*, witchcraft itself serves as a metaphor for female coming of age.

For many creators of modern media geared towards young adult women, discovery of and experimentation with witchcraft parallels their adolescent female characters' maturation and exploration of adulthood. Often, heroines of these stories inherit or begin to manifest latent magical powers when they reach a certain age, such as Lena and Ridley Duchannes of Kami Garcia and Margaret Stohl's *Beautiful Creatures* series, who come into magical powers and are 'claimed' by either light or dark magic on their sixteenth birthdays,[30] or Sabrina Spellman, better known as Sabrina the Teenage Witch, who in most versions of her story also inherits her powers and the identity of witch upon turning sixteen years old.[31] Nell Scovell, a writer for the television series *Sabrina the Teenage Witch* stated in a 2020 interview that 'magic was a metaphor for a young girl learning to control her desires and emotions'.[32] The acquisition of supernatural powers and the choices and responsibility that come with that acquisition stand as a metaphor for growing up and obtaining adult responsibilities and freedoms. Thus, it is reasonable for the ability to wield magic or witchcraft to be a source of empowerment as well, as it signifies experience, wisdom, and respect, as well as new possibilities for the young female characters who possess such a talent.

The profusion of witch heroines demonstrates this empowerment and the broadening of possible paths for young women. Emotional expression, often denied to or looked down on in teenage girls, becomes permissible through embodiment of the witch: 'Inside you have these feelings, like anger, but you don't want to say them because if you did, people mightn't like you. But, being a witch . . . you can say those feelings.'[33] Confidence is also often either a cause or a result of the witch persona. Quoting Lisa Simpson in the article, 'The Simpsons, Gender Roles, and Witchcraft: The Witch in Modern Popular Culture', Sarah Antinora takes note of how modern popular culture interrogates the dominant conception of witches: 'why is it that when a woman is confident and powerful, they call her a witch?'[34] Clements figures witches as a feminist response to a social and political climate that causes women, especially young women, to feel under attack. 'And she makes sense to me as something we can embrace, some way to justify the boring, upsetting, desperate, tired ways we live. . . . She lets us turn away from cat-callers with a strained smile and tweets – *all men are already toads, the magic is in revealing it.*[35] Janet Adelman illuminates the mechanisms within Shakespeare's *Macbeth* that construct a solution to 'the problem of masculinity by eliminating the female'.[36] Reisert and Klein, by positioning their main characters as witches, allow them the power to thwart Shakespeare's ending, thereby rejecting these mechanisms. When the final battle is lost and won, Albia turns that power towards reconciliation and renewal: 'I see myself taking both her wounded hands in my own. . . . With my fingertips, I stroke the skin of her hands until the bloody spots begin to fade, then disappear.'[37] Gilly plans to reverse the societal systems that placed her in the position of a witch in the first place: 'I am a wealthy woman. I have lands and money of my own . . . and now I have a place and the money and power to make a safe world within this world for those I love to learn and grow.'[38] While Jade's mission ends with significant destruction, her motivation for her actions throughout remains preventing the brutal sexual assault that happened to her from happening to another girl in the future: 'For every girl who wants revenge. I think of the four boys in the white-sheets room. Walking out. Stalking proud through the halls of St Andrew's with everyone knowing exactly what they did that night and every other night. But never again.'[39] Becoming a witch allows each heroine the power to rewrite her own story and avert the tragic end that awaits Shakespeare's characters in *Macbeth*.

In her introduction to a 2012 special edition of *The Upstart Crow* focusing on Shakespeare's female icons, Francesca T. Royster states,

> from Lady Macbeth to Ophelia . . . Shakespeare's female icons have become useful shorthand for exploring highly recognized, highly charged images of femininity in the contemporary moment. . . . Icons fascinate in the ways that they tap into the desires and anxieties of the culture that worships them and in the ways that they reflect a changing culture.[40]

If the witches of Shakespeare and James I are demonstrative of malevolence, the witches of those YA authors who adapt *Macbeth* are demonstrative of a way to harness these perceptions and turn them towards a productive resolution. This possibility sends a powerful message to young women everywhere and further expands and complicates our understanding of and engagement with Shakespeare's *Macbeth*.

Notes

1 William Shakespeare, *Macbeth*, ed. Sandra Clark and Pamela Mason, in *The Arden Shakespeare, Third Series, Complete Works* (London, New York, Oxford, New Delhi, and Sydney: Bloomsbury, 2020). All references to Shakespeare's works are to this edition.

2 At the time of writing, a search for 'Macbeth witches' on the 'global marketplace' Etsy.com netted over 450 results, including the aforementioned products.

3 Katherine Howe, *The Penguin Book of Witches* (New York: Penguin Books, 2014), xii, 84, 226.

4 King James I, *The Demonology of King James I*, ed. Donald Tyson (Woodbury: Llewellyn, 2011), 91.

5 Ibid., 122.

6 Ibid., 130.

7 Malcolm Gaskill, *Witchfinders* (Cambridge, MA: Harvard University Press, 2005), 68.

8 Quoted in Sandra Clark, 'The Critical Backstory', in *Macbeth: A Critical Reader*, ed. John Drakakis and Dale Townshend (London: Bloomsbury Arden Shakespeare, 2013), 35.

9 Ibid., 42.

10 See Lauren Shohet, '*Macbeth*: The State of the Art', in *Macbeth: A Critical Reader*, ed. John Drakakis and Dale Townshend (London: Bloomsbury Arden Shakespeare, 2013), 118.

11 Mikaella Clements, 'The Brief History of the Tumblr Witch', *The Establishment*, 10 July 2016. https://medium.com/the-establishment/a -brief-history-of-the-tumblr-witch-8f30657849f.

12 J. K. Rowling, *Harry Potter and the Prisoner of Azkaban* (New York: Scholastic, 1999), 346.

13 Dympna Callaghan, 'Wicked Women in Macbeth: A Study of Power, Ideology, and the Production of Motherhood', in *Reconsidering the Renaissance: Papers from the Twenty-First Annual Conference*, ed. Mario A. Di Cesare (Binghamton: Medieval & Renaissance Texts & Studies, 1992), 355–6. Quoted in *Shakespearean Criticism*, ed. Michelle Lee, Vol. 100 (Detroit: Gale, 2006). *Gale Literature Resource Center*.

https://link.gale.com/apps (accessed 27 July 2022). *Shakespearean Criticism* 100 (2006): 358–9. https://go.exlibris.link/Rtv1hkq9.

14 Rebecca Reisert, *The Third Witch* (New York: Washington Square Press, 2001), 24.

15 Ibid., 21.

16 Ibid., 243.

17 Klein, *Ophelia*, 72–3.

18 Reisert, *The Third Witch,* 9, emphasis Reisert.

19 Klein, *Ophelia*, 269–70.

20 Reisert, *The Third Witch*, 307.

21 Ariane Balizet, *Shakespeare and Girls' Studies* (New York: Routledge, 2020), 1, 4.

22 Hannah Capin, *Foul is Fair* (New York: Wednesday Books, 2020), 7–8.

23 Ibid., 8, emphasis Capin.

24 Erica Hateley, *Shakespeare in Children's Literature: Gender and Cultural Capital* (New York and London: Routledge, 2009), 86.

25 Tassi Marguerite, *Women and Revenge in Shakespeare: Gender, Genre, and Ethics* (Cranbury: Associated University Press, 2011), 62–3.

26 Capin, *Foul is Fair*, 5.

27 *Buffy the Vampire Slayer*, created by Joss Whedon, 20th Century Fox, 1997–2003.

28 Jennifer Flaherty, 'How Many Daughters Had Lady Macbeth?' in *Shakespeare and Millennial Fiction*, ed. Andrew James Hartley (Cambridge: Cambridge University Press, 2018), 104–5.

29 Capin, *Foul is Fair*, 326.

30 Kami Garcia and Margaret Stohl, *Beautiful Creatures* (New York: Little, Brown and Company, 2009), 189.

31 See *Chilling Adventures of Sabrina*. Roberto Aguirre-Sacasa, creator. Netflix (2018–2020). and *Sabrina the Teenage Witch* (1996–2003).

32 'The 90s Witch Craze', *History of the 90s*, narrated by Kathy Kenzora, season 1, episode 35, Curiouscast, 27 October 2020. https://curiouscast.ca/podcast/466/history-of-the-90s/.

33 Hateley, *Shakespeare in Children's Literature*, 83.

34 *The Simpsons*, 'Treehouse of Horror XIX', (2008), quoted in Sarah Antinora, 'The Simpsons, Gender Roles, and Witchcraft: The Witch in Modern Popular Culture', *452° F*, Issue 3 (01 July 2010): 115–30

35 Clements, 'Tumblr Witch', emphasis Clements.

36 Janet Adelman, *Suffocating Mothers: Fantasies of Maternal Origin in Shakespeare's Plays,* Hamlet *to* The Tempest (New York: Routledge, 1992), 146.

37 Klein, *Ophelia,* 286.

38 Reisert, *The Third Witch,* 306–7.

39 Capin, *Foul is Fair,* 323.

40 Francesca T. Royster, 'Introduction to "Shakespeare's Female Icons": Sorcerers, Celebrities, Aliens, and Upstarts', *Upstart Crow: A Shakespeare Journal* XXXI (2012): 5.

9

Adaptation and intersectionality in Aoibheann Sweeney's *Among Other Things, I've Taken Up Smoking*

Lawrence Manley

The game of chess played between Miranda and Ferdinand at the end of *The Tempest* aptly characterizes the unusual degree to which this play's cast of characters, and the encounters among them, creates multiple possibilities of sympathy, identification, and interaction. Interpretations and adaptations of *The Tempest* have demonstrated, over centuries, that it can be framed not only as Prospero's play or Miranda's and Ferdinand's but also as Ariel's, or (in Auden's *The Sea and the Mirror*) as Alonso's, Sebastian's, and Antonio's, or even (in H. D.'s *By Avon River*) as the unseen Claribel's. While early adaptations by the first generation of (mostly male) postcolonial writers developed new possibilities by interpreting the play from Caliban's perspective as colonial subject, more recent adaptations like Michelle Cliff's *No Telephone to Heaven* (1987), Dev Virahsawmy's *Toufann* (1991) and Marina Warner's *Indigo* (1992) have added to these possibilities through further recombination, developing, between Caliban and Miranda, unexpected intersectional alliances that can only have belonged to the unconscious of *The Tempest* but that matter profoundly to multicultural modernity.

Revisioning along these lines has been slow to emerge, however, in the recent wave of adaptations of Shakespeare in novels for young adults. As Ariane Balizet demonstrates in *Shakespeare and Girls' Studies*, contemporary mass-market adaptations of Shakespeare use girlhood 'as a vehicle – a time machine to make Shakespeare relevant to contemporary popular culture' by importing contemporary concerns to the historical settings of Shakespeare's plays or by retailoring Shakespeare's works to fit contemporary settings.[1] In doing so, Balizet argues, the post-2000 wave of Shakespeare-oriented fiction for young adult readers, following the example of popular youth-oriented film adaptations in the 1990s, has embraced 'a postfeminist ideation of girlhood that appeals to Shakespeare's cultural capital to resist an intersectional understanding of girls and girlhood'.[2] While contributing to the 'elevation of a postfeminist, neoliberal girl subject', the heteronormative 'Girlpower' paradigm prevalent in these adaptations has often been 'exclusionary along lines of race, ethnicity, sexuality, gender identity, class, size, and ability'.[3] Serving both for market promotion and as cultural authority, the Shakespeare being adapted for adolescent consumers has often failed to yield the scope and inclusionary potential produced elsewhere in the field of cultural adaptation.

In light of Balizet's attempt 'to broaden the reach of adaptation studies to animate the intersectional reach of girls' friendships, community, creative potential and education', the purpose of this chapter is to introduce a recent *Tempest* adaptation that answers Balizet's call for 'intersectional reach'.[4] Aoibheann Sweeney's *Among Other Things, I've Taken Up Smoking* (2007) is a coming-of-age novel that draws on *The Tempest* to frame a young woman's exploration of her emerging sexuality and of the mysteries of her parents' marriage, her mother's disappearance, and her father's troubled isolation. Summarized in this way, Sweeney's version of Miranda's plight in *The Tempest* sounds written for teenagers, and this impression is reinforced by Sweeney's comments about her work as a 'first novel': 'What would happen if you could have somebody who has just hatched out of the egg, just fresh – what do they see in the world? I think a lot of first novels are about just trying to see what's there to a new mind.'[5]

Among Other Things, I've Taken Up Smoking has not, however, been marketed or reviewed as young adult fiction. Rated for 'ages 18 years and up',[6] it belongs, with Salinger's *The Catcher in the Rye* or Alison Bechdel's *Fun Home*, to that class of novels that can profitably be read by adolescents as well as adults. More in keeping, perhaps, with the historical Shakespeare, who has been said not to know the modern Western adolescent or 'teenager' and to recognize only the two categories children and 'youths' who are beginning to experience the challenges and realities of adult life,[7] Sweeney's novel is comparatively resistant to the 'post-feminist ideal of girlhood' that Balizet attributes to 'contemporary popular culture'.[8] The novel is among other things a deft literary adaptation in which Ovid's *Metamorphoses*, with its treatment of changing bodies, becomes a powerful metaphor for Sweeney's exploration of sexuality and identity while supporting Sweeney's method of adapting Shakespeare by way of *contaminatio*, the mingling of literary sources. *Among Other Things* follows *The Tempest* in a deliberately distant and attenuated manner, resisting the suspense of the play's political intrigue, straightforward adoption of its main roles, or market promotion by way of Shakespeare. These resistances contribute to a metamorphic strategy that deliberately holds open questions of identity and relationship, both as they apply to the novel's characters and as they apply to Shakespeare's influence over this adaptation. In the manner of adult postcolonial adaptations of the play, the novel brings racial considerations into its development of *The Tempest*, exploring the intersectionality of race with sexuality, gender, class and nationality in the shaping of identity and the bonding of humans across difference. As it does so, the novel rewrites the quest for happiness in *The Tempest* and in its young adult fiction progeny by seeking happiness in unexpected places, in the spaces of what the novel calls 'never belonging'.

'Of bodies changed into different bodies'

As indicated by the first sentence of the novel – 'Among other things I've taken up smoking' – Miranda Donnal, raised on an island off the coast of Maine by her widowed and reclusive father, tells her story in retrospect, from the standpoint of an ending that also represents a coming-of-age beginning. Her narrative encompasses key childhood memories and episodes, beginning before her third birthday, when, shortly after the family's move to Crab Island, her mother took the family boat into the fog and disappeared; her body was found washed up three days later. Miranda is raised in a seemingly neglectful manner by her Irish father, who trained for the Catholic priesthood before becoming briefly a university professor of Latin in Boston and then a translator of classics and a collaborator with a wealthy older friend, Arthur Mitchell, in founding a Manhattan-based institute of classical studies and building its collection of rare books. Like her Shakespearean namesake, Sweeney's Miranda grows up in solitude, ignorant of her past, of her family's move to the remote island, of her mother's disappearance and death and her father's brooding silence about his Ovid-like exile and his solitary task of translating Ovid's *Metamorphoses*. What *The Tempest* charts out in the long backstory of 3.2, Sweeney's Miranda must discover for herself in the course of growing up and writing her narrative.

Miranda's upbringing is left mostly to an all-capable local fisherman, Jonas Blackwell, whose descent from a Passamaquoddy mother along with his dark skin, blue almond-shaped eyes and derogatory nickname 'Blackie' mark him as a version of Caliban (though it emerges he doubles as an Ariel). Serving in all the offices that profit the Donnals, Mr Blackwell sees to Miranda's education, ferries her to school on the mainland and teaches her, while she is still in elementary school, to pilot the family dory by herself and to care for both her own and her negligent father's daily needs. For knowledge of her mother, Miranda has only odd hints from Mr Blackwell about her shyness and a few photographs in which her mother always 'looked distant, as if she had stepped into a fog to lose herself just before the shutter snapped'.[9] From her father, affectionate but depressed, inattentive and increasingly alcoholic, Miranda receives only such clues she can extract from the Ovidian tales he reads to her, 'tales of bodies changed into different bodies'.[10] As she learns to read the past and her own situation and experiences, Miranda draws on Ovid to negotiate among categories of narrative that her father insists on keeping separate: 'imaginary' myth, 'unverifiable' legend, and 'actual' history.[11] Miranda's traversal of all three categories lends a remarkable degree of openness and flexibility to the novel's handling of adolescent questions about sexuality, identity, and relationship.

Not to be found in the foreground of Sweeney's novel are the mysteries of puberty and the attendant biological developments – the periods, budding breasts, and erections – that in a teen-oriented adaptation like Jacqueline Carey's *Miranda and Caliban* (2017) cause the vexed Miranda to remark: 'I should like to know how this whole business works'.[12] Neither is there found anything like Carey's close adherence to the Shakespearean masterscript such that Carey's Miranda must have her bodice torn by Caliban in the course of consensual experiments with sex before passively yielding to a forced marriage with Ferdinand. Gently handled sex scenes do find their place in *Among Other Things* but with a primary view to the ways in which sexual orientation figures into the broader shaping of a life of intellectual and social maturity.

Told against the background of Ovid's four ages and organized into sections named after The Age of Silver (which begins with Jupiter's usurpation of his brother Saturn's reign), The Age of Bronze, and The Age of Iron, Miranda's story is keyed to several myths from Ovid's pre- and post-diluvian worlds. Myths that play a crucial role in Sweeney's initial discussion of the four ages are those of Proserpina and her mother Ceres, giver of grain in the Silver Age (Miranda ponders what would have happened if Prosperpina were motherless and had no reason to leave her confinement in Pluto's kingdom), and the new beginning that follows the deluged Age of Iron, when the stones cast by Pyrrha and Deucalion are shaped into humans, 'women in the hands of female sculptors, and men in the hands of male sculptors'.[13] From this sharply bifurcated gendering of stone-derived humanity comes Ovid's sense of 'the hardness of our race. . . . We give proof from what origin we are sprung'.[14]

Motherless Miranda's hard existence in the first section of the novel is profoundly changed by the day when she and her friend Julie Peabody return from school to the island unexpectedly early and discover Mr Blackwell's boat at the dock and Mr Blackwell sleeping barefoot on the sofa before Miranda's tipsy father intervenes and whisks the girls away. Miranda has in effect discovered, as no one in Shakespeare's play ever does, Prospero's secret relationship to his 'tricksy spirit' Ariel. Mr Blackwell's visits become less friendly and less frequent after this awkward incident, and, following a quarrel over Miranda's welfare, the friendship between the two men all but ends. Lacking the pretty dresses, doll-filled bookshelves, and boyfriends – the conventional shaping experiences – of her female schoolmates, and tied to serving her father's needs and typing his translations, Miranda paces the island's paths wondering whether her mother had done the same while longing to escape. Increasingly isolated during her adolescence, Miranda spends the day of her college admissions exam at a local bar, where a quiz show featuring the answer 'ALTERNATIVE ROUTES' plays on the television. Illegally served by Susie, a girl not much older than herself, and then persuaded by Susie to join a cold and clumsy sexual encounter with two crewmen from an oil tanker, Miranda comes away from her initiation numb in feeling but with the astonishingly outward-looking impression that in Susie, whose half Native American mother is living on a reservation in Arizona, she has 'finally met someone who was more lonely than me'.[15]

Miranda's lack of postgraduation plans and Peter's parental jealousy of Mr Blackwell's influence lead her father to arrange a job for her at the classical institute in Manhattan, where she is assigned the menial task of typing a computerized version of the library catalogue. Miranda's own subliminally guilty reading of her banishment emerges in her version of Ovid's Cinyras and Myrrha, where the daughter, having (in Miranda's mind) seen the world through her father's eyes and fallen under his spell, then met with his rebuff and 'fled, wandering across the earth'.[16] Miranda's journey into Manhattan exile is marked by a storm, and she turns up at the institute bedraggled 'like a shipwrecked sailor'.[17] Meeting the institute's director, Walter (successor to Peter Donnal's old friend Arthur Mitchell) and Walter's slightly younger companion Robert, she soon surmises that they are lovers (or in the denigrating words of their handsome young assistant Nate Stoddard, 'two queens'[18]).

If Walter's succession to the directorship marks him as the usurping Sebastian to the Alonso figured in Peter's once-beloved friend and patron Arthur, then the jealous Robert, as the backstory unfolds, becomes the Antonio who long ago profited by Peter's exile to Maine. Cool in his memories of Miranda's father and resentful of Miranda's sudden presence, Robert is wary that Peter may reassert a claim to the institute. From Walter and Robert Miranda learns the further information that Arthur 'drove your father crazy'[19] with the parties he used to hold in the library, that her father had once loved Manhattan more than the island in Maine, and that no one had known of the existence of Peter's wife, an obscure secretary, until he moved away with her. While Miranda takes in the vibrant gay life of the West Village, 'Not once did I think my father might actually have been in love sometime, anytime in his life, with anyone but me'.[20]

In the Age of Iron

Most of Miranda's discoveries about the past are withheld until the final section of the novel, 'The Age of Iron', named for the time when 'jealousy and hatred take root and flourish between lovers and friends'.[21] Miranda's journey into this dark backward and abysm of time is through two love affairs of her own, one with Nate Stoddard, a university student of classics and a privileged WASP (a version of Ferdinand, as confirmed by the impending wedding of his Claribel-like sister Liz), and one with Adonis-like Ana Mones, an attractively muscular streetcart coffee vendor and part-time business student whose independent spirit, Dominican immigrant background, queer sexuality and air of confidence link her with Mr Blackwell. Through her coffee business, Ana is bound up with Miranda's first introduction to coffee by Mr Blackwell, and Miranda mentally connects Ana's skilful handling of her van and cart with Mr Blackwell's adept piloting of his boat. As Miranda ponders her attraction to Nate and to Ana – not missing the roll of Robert's eyes when he describes Nate as 'very pretty but dumb as a post' (105) – she compares the myth of Galatea with that of Salmacis and Hermaphroditus. With Nate, Miranda reflects, 'I was Galatea',[22] more shaped to Nate's desires (in his gifts of clothing, for example) than shaping of her own. With Ana, Miranda becomes instead Salmacis, pressing against the body of Hermaphroditus: 'their bodies begin to condense, her soft breasts melting into his hard chest, their legs twining together, until Hermaphroditus cries out, surrendering, and they are one boy, neither man nor woman'.[23] In this Hermaphroditic mutual shaping – desire for which is first broached in Miranda's adolescent crush on Rebecca Hemmings, when a touch between the girls is misunderstood – Miranda finds herself yielding to reciprocated desire: Ana's 'mouth was so soft that I could feel my own mouth too, perfectly soft'.[24]

The novel's crisis arrives when Miranda is a guest of Nate's family at their Connecticut shoreline estate for the wedding of Nate's sister. The wealthy and pretentious Stoddards, like the family of Julie Peabody back in Yvesport, are a seemingly perfect nuclear family, bound to each other in a life of striving for advantage amid constant mutual slights and aggressions. In pointed contrast to the worn dories piloted so skilfully by Mr Blackwell and Miranda, the identical white hulls of the sailboats at the Stoddards' yacht club are neatly stacked unused near the parking lot. Nate's insensitivity to the Stoddards' cool treatment of Miranda, the family's disapproval of her shocking red dress and a wedding guest's injurious judgement that Miranda is 'a real keeper' ('like a fish',[25] Miranda thinks) send Miranda fleeing into a second tempest and back to the arms of Ana.

The novel's final turn towards Ana, who has taught Miranda to smoke cigarettes and 'to stop with the good girl/bad girl stuff',[26] coincides with two others. The first involves Miranda's evolving understanding of the past. When Ana suggests that pregnancy was possibly the reason for the marriage of Miranda's parents, Miranda begins to understand the mysterious sadness on her mother's face in the photo of her parents' wedding day. 'Maybe she never wanted to get married or – whatever – have a kid', Ana suggests: 'Women have to do what other people want all the time'.[27] A further discovery occurs during a conversation with the increasingly sympathetic Robert when Miranda discovers at the institute a photo of her father as a young man in a swimsuit, looking boyish, handsome, and 'the happiest I had ever seen him'.[28] Robert explains how Arthur fell in love with the 'ridiculously good-looking' Peter; how Arthur sickened, died, and left the island in Maine to Peter; and how Peter suddenly 'disappeared, with that secretary or whatever she was, and never said a word to us'.[29] Left unsaid is that in the time scheme of the novel Arthur Mitchell died in the later 1980s, during the AIDS epidemic. Enough of Peter Donnal's past and of Miranda's mother has been unveiled for Miranda to begin thinking of her parents with love and sympathy and to see, despite their being so mismatched and unhappy, how much she has in common with each of them.

A second major turn comes through Miranda's encounters with art and visual abstraction. As a child, Miranda was always most absorbed when drawing plants and flowers. In New York galleries and museums, she discovers Franz Kline and then, in a MoMA retrospective, Mondrian's progress from works like *Willow Grove* to the abstraction of *Flowering Trees* to the grids and colour blocks of the 'Composition' series and the visual rhythm and activity of the 'Boogie Woogie' paintings, completed during Mondrian's own wartime exile in New York City. Mondrian's progress towards abstraction, which Miranda thinks of as a process of representational loss, helps to gloss Sweeney's own distanced and attenuated manner of adapting *The Tempest*, which drops most details of the plot while rearranging the relationships of its characters. But in Miranda's mind, abstraction by 'loss' describes the way that personal lives and identities actually take shape. Thinking of the defining elements that remain in later Mondrian – 'the lines without design, the colors without context' – Miranda also thinks of the careful, realistic drawings of flowers in her girlhood sketchbook and 'of my whole careful life. What was I afraid of losing anyway? There was no regret, nothing but hope in the obstinate boxes of color. It seemed easy, all of a sudden, to change everything. . . . I could do anything I wanted'.[30]

'That superior kind of beauty that never belongs'

In the wake of the novel's second deluge, Miranda returns by car with Ana to Maine, and while Ana waits on the mainland, Miranda does an unexpected thing: she borrows Mr Blackwell's tiny dinghy – whose oars are never locked because no one would ever hazard rowing in it – and performs the feat that only Mr Blackwood has previously accomplished, rowing the tiny craft all the way to Crab Island. In a moving reunion scene, father and daughter share for the first time their common love of New York, and Peter answers Miranda's announcement of wanting to attend art school by nodding suggestively: 'I would imagine you'd have quite a few choices in the city.' Peter's silence in response to Miranda's equally suggestive observation that 'Robert was pretty jealous of you and Arthur' leads father and daughter, finally in process of coming out to each other, into a long-suppressed expression of mutual love. For the first time, Miranda perceives in her father the beautiful young man in the photograph, 'the man he had been all his life: that superior kind of beauty that never belongs'.[31]

The 'choices' imagined by and for Miranda in connection with both her artistic aspirations and the opportunities of Manhattan speak to the possibilities of metamorphic change. But the still-abiding physical beauty now visible to Miranda in her ageing father speaks instead of things that do not, and perhaps cannot, change. The most crucial perceptions of the novel are not found in Miranda's touching reunion with her father; they are found, rather, in the conversation that immediately proceeds Miranda's solo voyage to the island, her dialogue with her lover Ana in the parked car on the dockside. Being raised on Ovid, Miranda explains, left her feeling throughout childhood that some marvellous change was ever imminent; but in the unhappiness of Ovid's tales and in her imminent return to her father's island, she has come to recognize 'they're really about people who can't change, like my father'.[32] Ovid's stories, she hazards while lighting a cigarette, 'aren't really about what it's like to be changed. They're about how hard it is before you change'. 'But isn't that kind of like being in love?'[33] Ana asks. In the de-mythologized world of the novel, which does not know Ovidian physical metamorphosis, transformation comes with recognizing love for another as a commitment that cannot be changed or willed otherwise. For Miranda, who can no more than her father change herself in order to please others, the problem of identity – *who* she is – is no longer a matter of *what* she is but of *whom* she loves.

With this sense of miraculous discovery – in keeping with the closing mood of *The Tempest* – goes also a reckoning with reality: the unchanged beauty of Peter is that superior kind that 'never belongs'.[34] That 'each of us also had our own particular way of not fitting in'[35] with mainland Yvesport society is evident from the beginning of Miranda's narrative, when she reflects on the Native American identity that isolates Mr Blackwell from the local community and when she comments on the factors that separate both her and her father – as New Yorkers, as an unconventional family unit, as emotional solitaries – from the townspeople of Yvesport. In the course of the novel Miranda comes to perceive how, despite Mr Blackwell's sexual affair with her father, the race and class of the loyal fisherman have subjected him to her father's rude and ungrateful mistreatment. As a motherless and neglected child, she is personally pained by the disapproval of the Peabodys, the hyper-normal family of her friend Julie. On the day that Miranda and her father are invited to an awkward outing on the Peabodys' shiny white boat, she feels as well, in Peter's reciprocal contempt for the Peabodys' provinciality, the self-isolating effects of his elitism and closeted sexuality. In her unhappy first sexual encounter,

Miranda experiences some measure of what the barmaid Susie's poverty and gender routinely inflict on her. At the institute, in the condescension of Walter and Robert towards her, her mother, and her father's marriage, Miranda experiences the force of gender bias coming from gay men. Among the prep school boys in blazers who are tutored in Latin at the institute, and by comparison to Nate's accomplishments in the language, Latinless Miranda perceives how much her father has short-changed her (Miranda's account of the Echo and Narcissus myth seems to gloss her passive role of merely typing up her father's self-absorbed Ovid project). She explains to a guest at the Stoddard wedding that hers is a menial secretarial position at the institute, just as her mother had been some kind of secretary in Robert's recollection. Among the heckling male vendors at the depot where Ana takes her coffee cart for cleaning, and again in the taunts of the young men gathered on the street outside the Washington Heights apartment of Ana's family, Miranda witnesses male abuse of Ana's gender and sexuality. In the extreme caution Ana must exercise with her Catholic Dominican family when it comes to her queer sexuality, Miranda encounters the cultural and familial sources of repression, just as she encounters the cultural inflection of gender oppression in the family's straitened circumstances, a consequence of the father's remaining in the Dominican with his mistresses. Such is the stony hardness of a world resistant to change.

But as they take her across differences in race, class, gender, and sexuality, Miranda's hard experiences suggest that while such categories and their intersections marginalize or oppress those who do not 'belong', none is insurmountable or exclusively defining of identity or character. Miranda's identity is 'multiply positioned', processual, and open-ended: her encounters, intersectional in nature, are multiple in their effects and implications.[36] In keeping with the principles outlined in Olena Hankivsky's primer, 'Intersectionality 101', Sweeney's novel is also 'multi-leveled' in its perspectives on these encounters.[37] All of Miranda's personal feelings and experiences, summarized above, are framed by structures that can be seen to operate not just personally but also at the institutional level – especially in the school, in the family, and in the effects of economics and social class – and at the global level in natters like the historical Passamaquoddy of the maritime northeast, the reservations of the American Southwest, the colonization of the Caribbean, and postcolonial migration to New York. The novel's intersectionality is 'reflexive'[38] in the sense that while Miranda finds common ground in her relations with Mr Blackwell, the barmaid Susie and the Dominican Ana Mones, she never mistakes her own plight for theirs. The novel's drift – exemplified in Ana's counsel to Miranda about resilience[39] – is that in the face of marginalization, alliance with others across the boundaries of difference can be powerful and empowering. Miranda's travels – from Crab Island to Yvesport, from Maine to New York, and from Washington Heights to the Connecticut gold coast – demonstrate that through change of setting what might have seemed confining can become liberating.[40]

This point about mobility and intersectionality may be another lesson of Miranda's transformative visit to the Mondrian exhibition at MoMA. Her account begins, like the exhibition itself, with Mondrian's early experiments in abstraction, where 'brown, black, grays, and pinks intersected'.[41] Though Miranda does not mention by name Mondrian's last completed work, *Broadway Boogie-Woogie*, she clearly experiences something like it on her walk back downtown that night, as she passes the blinking lights and signs of Forty-second Street and arrives at her little room to watch 'the windows of the city light up, yellow, red, a grid of constellations – busy, alive, and all my own'.[42] Mondrian's play with Manhattan intersections and traffic in the painting is an apt model for the way that Sweeney's way of adapting Shakespeare yields a complex social vision that speaks to the present.

The novel's spirit of creative recombination, in other words, is not just an attribute of its abstract way of adapting Shakespeare's *Tempest*; it is essential also to the novel's open-ended treatment of sexuality and identity formation. Ron Charles, in a *Washington Post* review, has written eloquently of the novel's 'reticence':

The gay relationships in this novel never become the subject of a scandal, are never a source of pride, are never 'accepted' in the face of oppressive straight culture. *Among Other Things* isn't interested in looking at homosexuality as a socially constructed lifestyle or a biological orientation; in fact, though almost all the characters are gay, the novel doesn't seem interested in looking at homosexuality as a distinct and defining characteristic at all. Instead, Sweeney completely subsumes sexuality in a larger process of self-discovery, and with that subtle shift she has moved from 'gay fiction' to 'post-gay fiction'.[43]

If the purposes of a proper 'queer pedagogy' are to rethink 'the unthought of normalcy', to 'attend to the proliferations of one's identificatory possibilities' and to suggest that identity is never essential, fixed, or exclusively individual but a matter of communities, relations, and alliances, then *Among Other Things* can serve young adult readers in just these pedagogical ways.[44] In its concluding emphasis on 'that superior kind of beauty that never belongs', *Among Other Things, I've Taken Up Smoking* invites readers – in the manner of Bechdel's *Fun Home*, an exactly contemporary novel that it much resembles[45] – 'to approach sexuality as an open question rather than a container for identity'.[46] In its opening of such important questions, *Among Other Things, I've Taken Up Smoking* is Shakespeare-inspired reading for adults of all ages.

Notes

1 Ariane Balizet, *Shakespeare and Girls' Studies* (New York, Routledge, 2020), 125.

2 Ibid., 2.

3 Ibid., 8.

4 Ibid., 2.

5 Karen Rota, 'Among Other Things: An Interview with Aoibheann Sweeney', *Irish America Magazine*, October/November 2008, https://www.irishamerica.com/2008/10/among-other-things-an-interview-with-aoibheann-sweeney/.

6 https://www.amazon.com/Among-Other-Things-Taken-Smoking/dp/1594201307/ref=sr_1_1?keywords=among+other+things+i%27ve+taken+up+smoking&qid=1632425180&sr=8-1.

7 Kevin J. Wetmore, 'Shakespeare and Teenagers', in *The Edinburgh Companion to Shakespeare and the Arts*, ed. Mark Thornton Burnett and Adrian Steele (Edinburgh: Edinburgh University Press, 2011), published to Edinburgh Scholarship Online (2012), 1–2; see also Paul Griffiths, *Youth and Authority: Formative Experience in England 1560-1640* (Oxford: Clarendon Press, 1996), ch. 1.

8 Balizet, *Shakespeare and Girls' Studies*, 94, 125.

9 Aoibheann Sweeney, *Among Other Things, I've Taken Up Smoking* (New York: Penguin, 2007), 19.

10 Ibid., 10.

11 Ibid., 128.

12 Jaqueline Carey, *Miranda and Caliban* (New York: Tor Books, 2017), 179.

13 Sweeney, *Among Other Things*, 4.

14 Ibid., 14.

15 Ibid., 70.

16 Ibid., 171.

17 Ibid., 102.

18 Ibid., 117.

19 Ibid., 154.

20 Ibid., 161.

21 Ibid., 12.

22 Ibid., 168.

23 Ibid., 46.

24 Ibid., 189.

25 Ibid., 227.

26 Ibid., 3.

27 Ibid., 187.

28 Ibid., 244.

29 Ibid., 245–6.

30 Ibid., 178.

31 Ibid., 257.

32 Ibid., 250.

33 Ibid.

34 Ibid., 257.

35 Ibid., 22.

36 For this 'constructivist' model of intersectionality, see Baukje Prins, 'Narrative Accounts of Origins: A Blind Spot in the Intersectional Approach', *European Journal of Women's Studies* 13, no 13 (2006): 277–90; Jennifer C. Nashe, 'Re-Thinking Intersectionality', *Feminist Review* 89 (2008): 1–15; Kathy Davis, 'Intersectionality as Critical Methodology', in *Writing Academic Texts Differently: Intersectional Feminist Methodologies and the Playful Art of Writing*, ed. Nina Lykke (New York: Routledge, 2014), 17–29; and Kaisa Ilmonen, *Queer Rebellion in the Novels of Michelle Cliff: Intersectionality*

and Sexual Modernity (Newcastle upon Tyne: Cambridge Scholars Publishing, 2017), 27–36.

37 Olena Hankivsky, *Intersectionality 101* (Simon Fraser University: Institute for Intersectionality Research and Policy, 2014), 9. http:// vawforum-cwr.ca/sites/default/files/attachments/intersectionallity_101 .pdf.

38 Ibid., 10.

39 Sweeney, *Among Other Things*, 182–6.

40 Hankivsky, *Intersectionality 101*, 10.

41 Sweeney, *Among Other Things*, 177.

42 Ibid.

43 'Island in the Storm', Washington Post, Sunday, 29 July 2007. https:// www.washingtonpost.com/wp-dyn/content/article/2007/07/26/ AR2007072601645.html.

44 D. Britzman, 'Queer Pedagogy and Its Strange Techniques', *Counterpoints: Vol. 367, Sexualities in Education: A Reader* (2012): 292–308.

45 The 2007 paperback edition of *Among Other Things* includes a front-cover blurb by Bechdel.

46 Anne Stebbins, 'Fun Home: Questions of Sexuality and Identity', *Journal of LGBT Youth* 8 (2011): 285–8.

10

'Hello, people of the internet!'

Nothing Much to Do and the young adult creators and communities of vlog-Shakespeare

Jane Wanninger

From its opening scene, the 2014 YouTube web series *Nothing Much to Do* establishes a tone and aesthetic that would have been immediately familiar to its social media-literate young audience.[1] The series begins in a whimsically curated teenage girl's bedroom, the walls adorned with fairy lights, a map, a poster of Benedict Cumberbatch, and a gallery of quirky illustrations that a former student once confidently described to me as 'total 2014 Tumblr girl aesthetic': a floral pot of tea, a girl holding a cat, a typewriter and so on (see Figure 10.1). A smiling blond teen waves and issues a self-consciously jaunty greeting to her viewers: 'Hello, people of the internet!'[2] This opening line, simultaneously grandiose and self-deprecating, underscores and ironizes the public potential of a YouTube video, even as the chatty tone reinforces the intimate

FIGURE 10.1 *Harriett Maire as Beatrice.* Nothing Much to Do, *produced by The Candle Wasters (2014).*

interactivity implied by the first-person narration. The speaker introduces herself as Beatrice and goes on to cheerfully describe the video as the start of a vlog (video blog), a project that she hopes will be a 'productive use of time when there's nothing much to do',[3] situating the series as a quotidian creative outlet – a standard activity in the face of high school boredom. It is clear, based on her framing of the endeavour, that Beatrice as a vlogger is self-reflexively participating in an existing mode of social and aesthetic engagement, a form of digital self-publication with recognizable generic features and rooted in a spirit of interactive familiarity. The Shakespeare-savvy viewer will immediately experience another kind of familiarity: this cheerful vlogger is in fact a character from *Much Ado about Nothing*, reimagined out of seventeenth-century Messina and into twenty-first-century Auckland, New Zealand.

The series goes on to unspool over multiple YouTube channels, and its world is built out across different social media platforms: Tumblr, Twitter, Instagram. In plot and characterization, it hews fairly closely to its source text, even as this situates it in a contemporary vernacular. The soccer pitch becomes the space of 'battle' for the male characters, and a student council election cements Pedro's relative status in the social hierarchy. It is Beatrice, however, who provides the guiding perspective of *Nothing Much to Do*, which takes Shakespeare's famously outspoken and wilful heroine and situates her as both the protagonist and primary artistic creator of the production. This focus on Beatrice reflects Ariane Balizet's assertion that 'girls are always already at the centre of Shakespearean adaptation in popular culture', something Balizet notes is particularly true of the literary-inspired web series (LIW), in which their 'prominences . . . would be nearly impossible to overlook'.[4] This prominence likewise reflected off-screen as *Nothing Much to Do* was the creation of four real-life teenage vlog-producers: Sally Bollinger, Elsie Bollinger, Minnie Grace, and Claris Jacobs, working under the collective name The Candle Wasters.

Nothing Much to Do mines the contemporary resonance of the gender dynamics of *Much Ado about Nothing*, offering an intertextual interrogation of the misogynist structures that underlie Shakespeare's plot – and many contemporary gender norms. Jennifer Flaherty describes the liberatory potential of such 'creatively critical' adaptive approaches to Shakespeare, which leverage his cultural familiarity and prestige to inspire similar kinds of agency in their young female audiences.[5] This liberatory potential has a special resonance in the world of the LIW, an adaptive mode that centres a type of creative production familiar to its target audience, and draws on a transmedia storytelling apparatus that emphasizes the interactive spirit of the adaptation. The agency of teenage girls is not only thematically central to the content of *Nothing Much to Do*, it is also vital to the series' adaptive strategy itself, encompassing not only the authorial agency of the series' young creators but also feeding into the ways in which the interactive, transmedia elements of vlog storytelling situate the series as a locus of agential, creative community among its largely young, female audience. Freed from the strictures of institutional or canonical understandings of what constitutes the Shakespearean text, the web series models dynamic engagement with Shakespeare's play as an intertext offering diverse and layered avenues for authorial agency. The play here is a site for, well, play – in a digital landscape that encourages collaborative creative participation in a familiar canonical work, among a cohort of digital natives engaging in (to extend the metaphor) a native form of social media self-publication.

Nothing Much to Do and the LIW world

YouTube was launched in 2005, and the site, both a massive archive of digital video content and a social media platform, quickly became not just a repository for existing content but also a spur to new creative forms. This has proven particularly true for young users; a 2018 Pew Research Study reported that 85 per cent of teenagers at that time used the platform.[6] YouTube was vital to the proliferation of a then-emergent media mode: that of the vlog, which in Stephen Pihlaja's words 'blends traditional film-making techniques, the text-based genre of blogging, the selfie and reality television' in an interactive, narrative mode.[7] As a curated projection of personal experience, the vlog form involves a constant negotiation of authenticity and artifice, and central to the form is the rhetorical construction of the relationship between vlogger and viewer: 'the address of the audience as "you" creates a position for the viewer . . . as a character' in the vlog's world.[8] Genre conventions quickly evolved: episodic first-person addresses to the camera, often set in a bedroom or other familiar domestic space, sometimes interspersed with themed posts, including Q&As, room tours, product demonstrations and so on. The filming style embraces face-on medium close-ups, with jump cuts splicing together individual shots, sometimes for comedic/ironic effect. Reaction shots and captions can further the form's meta-cinematographic qualities. Real-life vlogs became popular in YouTube's first decade, and as a 2008 study suggested, female users found a particular niche in cultivating personal, participatory vlogs.[9]

Once established as a genre for real-world self-publication on the internet, some content creators began to seize on the formal potential of the vlog as a vehicle for intertextual play. In particular, it emerged in the early 2010s as a popular medium for reimagining works of classic literature. The emblematic example of the emergent LIW genre is *The Lizzie Bennet Diaries*, a popular and acclaimed 2012–13 series created by Hank Green and Bernie Su reimagining Jane Austen's *Pride and Prejudice*.[10] While Lizzie's vlog anchors the narrative, the series extends beyond YouTube, the narrative playing out over a larger transmedia storytelling apparatus in which characters engage on platforms such as Twitter and Tumblr in real time with the vlog posts. The formal template established with *The Lizzie Bennet Diaries* would go on to inspire a host of LIW transporting canonical classics into contemporary contexts through fictional vlogs centring young female characters. Shakespeare quickly emerged as popular fodder for LIW adaptation; *Nothing Much to Do* (hereafter *NMtD*) was among the early entries into this canon, with dozens of additional series appearing alongside it and in its wake.[11]

NMtD was posted in regular short instalments to YouTube from July to November 2014. While the official 'story' on YouTube allows the viewer to watch all of the seventy-nine mostly two-to-five-minute episodes in order, the drama is actually spread out over three channels: the primary vlog featuring Beatrice, with assists from Hero; Benedick's vlog; and a third channel split between Ursula, positioned here as an arts student who occasionally posts fly-on-the-wall style footage of the group of friends, and 'The Watch', the socially awkward, Sherlock-aping Dogberry and Verges. *NMtD* also extended its storytelling across social media platforms; for instance, Beatrice posted throughout the series on Twitter, while Hero maintained an Instagram. This leveraging of the complementary affordances of a range of social media platforms not only helps the LIW expand its narrative frame, it also reinforces the immersive quality to these stories generated first by the episodic, diaristic nature of the vlog itself; the line between the 'real world' and the world of the story blurs when viewers can interact with characters by liking, retweeting, or commenting on posts.

The LIW characters' participation in a genre that already balances a cultivated authenticity with self-reflexive engagement with a set of recognizable formal conventions feeds into what Douglas Lanier calls a 'reality effect'. The term refers to 'the sense that we are seeing "real" teen lives filtered through a Shakespearean narrative rather than watching the Shakespearean narrative being updated to an artificially heightened representation of teen culture'.[12] The appeal of the LIW derives in no small part from the way the reality effect is animated by a meta-awareness of adaptation, from the tension between an audience member's familiarity with plot points and character arcs and their sense that they can interact with characters who feel like peers occupying a lived-in world. My former student, Coco Marcil, who initially drew my attention to the series, reinforced the importance of the interplay of reality effect and adaptive meta-cognition for her own engagement with and appreciation for *NMtD*.[13] Coco watched the series during its initial run when she was fourteen or fifteen and was drawn into its fandom, she said, because it offered a more authentic representation of her own teenage emotional experience than other texts she encountered – it was both affectively and formally relatable. She was also a Shakespeare fan, and she knew the play, and as a fellow teenager occupying the same online world of pop-culture referents, vlogs, and Tumblrs as the creators and characters, she knew the world in which his plot and characters had found themselves.[14]

At its core, the web series reflects what Henry Jenkins has termed 'convergence culture', a cultural field in which both content and audiences flow across media platforms in which 'the power of the media producer and the power of the media consumer interact in unpredictable ways' with all participants invested in the 'work – and play – of engagement in a media landscape'.[15] When the characters, creators, and consumers of a series are already engaging in the same kinds of online activity, the presumed boundaries between artist and audience can be difficult to discern, even when one of the artists is Shakespeare. Media consumption and media creation are, in this landscape, inextricably linked such that adaptation becomes a regenerative act that prompts ongoing, collaborative, and expansive forms of creative engagement. The Candle Wasters were themselves directly inspired to create their own LIW by their avid fandom of *The Lizzie Bennet Diaries*. While that series was helmed by two men with significant professional experience, the four teenage girls who formed The Candle Wasters were amateurs, and they were demographically and culturally connected to both the characters they were imagining and to the audience they were targeting – in this case, a literary, feminist/queer-friendly corner of the microblogging platform Tumblr. In a personal interview, co-creators Elsie and Sally Bollinger described the ways in which their own subject position as fans and fellow teens guided their approach. They recognized that in tackling a LIW, the familiar beats of the source text would be integral to engaging the audience, but they also wanted, they said, to amplify the realism of the world they were building around and through the Shakespearean plot through their engagement with the medium. In both formal strategies and in their scripts, they wanted to make a world that felt real and lived in; it helped that, as Sally put it, 'we were writing characters our own age'.[16]

'Sincerely, Beatrice Duke'

The world of *NMtD* is populated exclusively by teens – the first episode establishes that Hero's mothers are on a six-month European honeymoon, and Beatrice's parents have relocated to Australia for her own mom's promotion; Leonato's parental authority is displaced onto Leo, Hero's older brother.[17] Against this canvas, the series works to illuminate and critique *Much Ado about Nothing*'s preoccupations with female agency and chastity with a contemporary feminist spin – a goal that the Bollinger sisters said the group approached intentionally. Beatrice, in her orientation towards the creative and interactive affordances of the vlog, is the character most consistently and clearly foregrounded as a creator, as well as a character. In one early episode on Ursula's channel ('The Game Is Afoot(ball)'), for instance, the fly-on-the-wall footage captures Beatrice in the background, busily setting up a camera and tripod next to her friends; another episode, posted to Beatrice's channel ('Football Antics: Part One'), features the scene she was depicted setting up. The finished episode includes varying camera angles and captions to frame the action; these markers of Beatrice's work as a cinematographer and editor reinforce for the audience the sense that the vlogs she posts are constructions shaped by her creative acumen. Throughout, Beatrice and Hero both demonstrate savvy awareness of the vlogs' formal and interactive qualities; within the diegetic frame of the series, this reflects their self-avowed status as consumers of other vlogs, as well as stars of their own: in the comments for the episode 'Q&A', for instance, Beatrice mentions a question from Tumblr about her and Hero's favourite YouTubers and links to a list of real vlogs.

The distinct vlog feeds that comprise the series reinforce the ways in which Beatrice (with Hero) and Benedick exact, within the world of the story, editorial control over the narrative, and the juxtaposition of those two feeds in particular reinforces the way gendered spaces structure Shakespeare's narrative. Vlogger Beatrice is afforded a public platform from which to critique the misogyny that percolates through the plot in a way play Beatrice never can; though the latter is famously outspoken, Shakespeare doesn't give her a platform to directly critique the men responsible for Hero's traumatic humiliation. In contrast, vlog-Beatrice responds to Leo's offering of his 'blessing' for Hero's fledgling romance with Claudio with a side-eye and wry 'honey, she doesn't need it'.[18] Later, when Leo sides with the boys in slut-shaming Hero, Beatrice lambasts him as a 'misogynistic bastard'.[19] The vlog format reinforces her authority here: Leo is appearing on *her* channel.

Hero's sixteenth birthday (the reimagined wedding scene) makes the violence of privilege and misogyny vividly clear with Claudio's bitter accusation, 'You put on this cute little face, but underneath, you're just a f-cking slut.'[20] As Christy Desmet notes, this modernized distillation of Claudio's attack is 'striking in its cruelty and directness'.[21] Visible throughout Claudio's verbal attack are numerous party guests recording the exchange on their cell phones, and the episode 'Evidence' includes the jerky and chaotic footage that results. The repetition of this pivotal exchange in the series playlist reinforces the trauma with which it is associated; in fact, the birthday episode is prefaced by a trigger warning for verbal abuse. The inclusion of the cell phone video reflects the power of virality in modern digital culture; Hero's trauma reverberates in footage over which she has no control, evoking the secondary trauma of social media slut-shaming familiar to modern girls and women.

The final third of the series foregrounds Beatrice and Hero's efforts to regain their sense of narrative control and linguistic agency. In 'Idiots', Beatrice's first post after the party, she tells Leo, in reference to her filming for the vlog: 'this is better than being passive.'[22] The act of posting is itself an assertion of narrative agency as Beatrice demands to be heard and understood. In Shakespeare's play, Hero's clear denial: 'I talked with no man at that hour'[23] falls on deaf ears to her accusers; correspondingly in the series, both girls – and especially Hero – speak repeatedly about their desire to be listened to. Beatrice demonstrates a frustrated, heartsick fury that clearly evokes Shakespeare's depiction of the character in 4.1, with one notable difference. Shakespeare's Beatrice famously demands that Benedick kill Claudio, and he reluctantly assents. In the series, however, Benedick explicitly signals his public support for Beatrice by having her on his vlog. After he attempts to cheer her up, Beatrice rhetorically asks Benedick, 'you'll kill him for me, won't you?'[24] But that is a mere wind-up to her looking directly into the camera and saying with conviction: 'watch your back, fuckface, I am coming for you. Sincerely, Beatrice Duke'.[25] The vlog gives

Beatrice's righteous anger a platform and a direction, and the series consistently foregrounds her sense of agency.

The web series likewise gives Hero a voice that resonates for her modern-day contemporaries. Hero disappears from the vlog for a full month after her disastrous birthday party – Beatrice tells people that Hero's pre-existing health issues have gotten worse and she is in the hospital. When she finally reappears in the episode 'Hello Again', she explains, 'I needed a break, from everything, from the world, and I needed people to *listen* to me'.[26] Like play Hero's symbolic death, vlog Hero's illness helps spark a shift in public feeling about her, but Hero also underscores that the break was about *her* needs. Hero's emphasis on being *listened* to signals the importance of a reciprocal responsibility between speaker and auditor; she wants to be recognized as a speaking subject in her own right – not as an interchangeable bride, as in the play. Hero's sense of agency upon her return emerges, unsurprisingly, in a different vein than does Beatrice's: Hero appears in this episode with Claudio, who expresses contrition for his stupidity, and Hero forgives him. She does not, however, get back together with him romantically. The play's arc of reconciliation is satisfied but in a way that reinforces Hero's independence. The series ends with the announcement that the girls are stepping away from the vlog for a while, having decided that 'face to face communication is key'.[27]

#NMTD: Participant-creators

For participants in the initial run of the series, a powerful sense of affinity and ownership emerged through engagement in a version of the play that so thoroughly blurred the boundaries between the real world and Shakespeare's plot. The two- to three-hour stage time of *Much Ado about Nothing* is in the web series extended over months, its posts knitting into the rhythms of real high school life. The duration of the web series was integral to the development of the fan community that formed around it; the series ran long enough that viewers could join in and catch up as it went along. Tumblr was their hub, and as viewers began to share reaction posts or show related media with the tag #NMTD or #NothingMuchToDo, other users would get interested in the new tag. As Elsie put it, 'Literally, through word of mouth, we had this community form . . . you could search the hashtag and immediately get a sense of how the fandom was reacting, who was watching, and how they were perceiving it'.[28] In the comments and on Tumblr, viewers could feed off one another's anticipation about how the adaptation would unfold. This culminated, Elsie said, as the pivotal moment of Hero's birthday party loomed and 'excitement accumulated in the tag'. After the blow-up at the party, she continues, 'we went cold turkey and just stopped, we didn't post anything', keeping all their YouTube channels and social media feeds dark – a metatextual reaction that reinforces the trauma associated with Claudio's abusive eruption at the party. Amid the silence from the series' official channels, there was a flurry of fan engagement on Tumblr, leading to a spike in viewership for the cathartic return of the series when Beatrice finally posted.[29] Reflecting on the interactive dynamics of this mode of Shakespearean adaptation, Sally pointed to the ways in which the online accessibility of The Candle Wasters and their demographic/ cultural connection to their characters and audience heightened the fandom's sense of agency and engagement: 'we were releasing stuff online, they were online – how were we any different from the characters who were also posting stuff online?'

The web series creators, actors, and the characters themselves all engage members of the same digital communities as their audiences, drawing those viewers/participants into the LIW world and creating community among them. The Candle Wasters were already avid Tumblr users when the series came out, and it was through leveraging their existing fandom communities on the site that they marketed NMtD. In the early 2010s, Tumblr was particularly associated with a young, female/queer-friendly user base, and it was a hub for nerd culture and online fan communities around series such as Sherlock, Dr. Who, and Harry Potter, all of which are knit into the referential culture of the characters within NMtD.[30] The structure of Tumblr, which emphasizes 're-blogging' or sharing posts to one's own feed with added content, is one that 'emphasizes ever-shifting collective authorship and diverse communities over individual originality and idea ownership'.[31]

In the interactive online culture of vlog-Shakespeare, The Candle Wasters quartet, Beatrice and her fictional compatriots, and viewers of the series are all united in being participant-creators, examples of what Louisa Stein calls the 'ideal cultural participant, one who merges cultural engagement with community participation, readership with authorship, and emotional investment with critical literacy'.[32] Fans of the series collaborated in the creative process, sharing fan art, memes, collages, and fan-fic that became part of the series' online corpus. Just as The Candle Wasters were inspired to create their series by their appreciation for another, *NMtD* would also help inspire the next wave of amateur LIW creators.[33] This interplay exemplifies the dynamic modes of creative agency that are animated by – but extend beyond – the plot of Shakespeare's text in this mode of adaptation. Shakespeare's characters, plot, and language diffuse seamlessly into the 'real' world occupied by the online community playing with his text; meanwhile, the 'text' of *Nothing Much to Do* extends beyond the boundaries of the series itself, encompassing not just the transmedia elements added by the creators but also the array of fan-created media related to the series.

This collaborative, multi-modal paratext around *NMtD* is both integral to a full understanding of the power of LIW as a platform for active engagement with Shakespeare and totally ephemeral. As in any social media experience, users come and go, content disappears, and social media site interfaces can make older posts difficult to find. Individual Tumblr feeds update constantly, it is impossible to replicate the immersive experience of interacting with the show in real time. More recent posts on the tag #NMTD reflect the effects of temporality in their own way; posters commenting after the initial run speak to re-watches and wax nostalgic about the show as a past artifact. A contemporary viewer of the series can watch all seventy-nine episodes of the series in sequence, YouTube's autoplay feature making the process effortless. For the audience engaging with the series during its original airing, however, their experience was much different, with posts spaced out over days and weeks, and carefully timed to reflect a realistic sense of when, down to the time of day, a specific character might release a specific video, furthering the series' crucial reality effect. In this, the transmedia web series bears an unexpected but powerful similarity to live theatre. The former expands its narrative to fit the rhythms of everyday life, whereas the latter is condensed into, per *Romeo and Juliet*, two hours' traffic, but both produce a communal – but fleeting – storytelling experience. This dynamic is particularly apt, perhaps, for the LIW, a mode of creative production so closely tied to adolescence, which is itself characterized by both its intensity and evanescence.

The immersive experience of initial viewership may have been fleeting, but the creatively participatory fandom was not, and even a present-day search for posts tagged #NMTD reveals a robust archive of creative fan engagement: memes, text posts, gifs, mood boards, and fan art abound. More recent posts regarding the show make explicit the effects of temporality, as posters speak to re-watches or wax nostalgic about the show as a past artefact. The Candle Wasters would follow up *NMtD* with a sequel of sorts, *Lovely Little Losers*, based on *Love's Labor's Lost*, featuring the same core cast and allowing viewers to stay engaged with the characters of *NMtD* beyond the five-act arc afforded by Shakespeare's play.[34] The Tumblr archive associated with these works demonstrates the deeply personal attachment that fans felt and feel to the story and characters, as well as to the virtual community that came together around the show. For series fans, The Candle Wasters themselves became characters, interpellated into the transmedia narrative of the adaptation. Sally recalled fans put together a Tumblr account to celebrate the show's final episodes, which included fan fiction imagining the filming of the final episode. She paraphrased: 'Sally calls cut and looks at Elsie for confirmation. "Are we good?" They had just finished filming the final episode in Auckland, New Zealand.'[35] The relative youth of The Candle Wasters and the affinities they shared with their characters and fans alike helped to draw the process of their adaptation into the broader online story of the series, and identification flows freely among creators, characters, and audiences, with Shakespeare's story acting as the conduit.

The participatory social media culture that subtends the vlog as a narrative form facilitates an insistently de-hierarchized engagement with Shakespeare. In their inherently self-reflexive and interactive approach to the project of adaptation, the Shakespearean LIW in general, and *Nothing Much to Do* in particular, foster dynamic, agential engagement with Shakespeare among young adult audiences. In relating the web series to the play, we can see an intertextual relationship that flows both ways, as Shakespeare's play provides the scaffolding and lifeblood for the adaptation, while the series both illuminates and revises the gender dynamics of its source play in ways that are directly tied to its formal strategies. Beyond merely demonstrating the effects of translating Shakespeare's play to contemporary vlog, though, analysis of the trans-modal storytelling/community-building apparatus around *Nothing Much to Do* reveals the ways in which interactive affordances of the internet can create new and ongoing opportunities for engagement and collaboration, opportunities that can productively decentre traditional understandings of authority and the nature of the text.

Notes

1 Candle Wasters (Elsie Bollinger, Sally Bollinger, Minnie Grace, and Claris Jacobs), *Nothing Much to Do,* 2014, web series. https://www .youtube.com/user/nothingmuchtodovlog/videos.

2 Ibid., Episode 1.

3 Ibid.

4 Ariane M. Balizet, *Shakespeare and Girls' Studies* (New York: Routledge, 2019), 132.

5 Jennifer Flaherty, 'Reviving Ophelia: Reaching Adolescent Girls through Shakespeare's Doomed Heroine,' *Borrowers and Lenders: The Journal of Shakespeare and Appropriation* 9, no. 1 (1 May 2014): 2–3. https://openjournals.libs.uga.edu/borrowers/article/view/2295.

6 Monica Anderson and Jingjing Jiang, 'Teens, Social Media & Technology 2018', *Pew Research Center: Internet, Science & Tech*, 31 May 2018. https://www.pewresearch.org/internet/2018/05/31/teens -social-media-technology-2018/.

7 Stephen Pihlaja, '"Hey YouTube": Positioning the Viewer in Vlogs', in *Rethinking Language, Text and Context: Interdisciplinary Research in Stylistics in Honour of Michael Toolan*, ed. Ruth Page, Beatrix Busse, and Nina Nørgaard (New York: Routledge, 2018), 257.

8 Ibid., 259. This relationship might be affective, but it is also practical, manifesting in the clicks, comments, and channel subscriptions that fuel the YouTube algorithm.

9 A 2008 study suggested that while at that point in time they recorded more male vloggers than female vloggers, female vloggers were 'more likely to vlog about personal matters than male vloggers . . . and more women created vlogs that interacted with the YouTube community'. See Heather Molyneaux, Susan O'Donnell, Kerri Gibson and Janice Singer, 'Exploring the Gender Divide on YouTube: An Analysis of the Creation and Reception of Vlogs', *American Communication Journal* 10, no. 1 (Spring 2008): 5.

10 Bernie Su and Hank Green, *The Lizzie Bennet Diaries*, 2012, web series. https://www.youtube.com/user/LizzieBennet.

11 For a comprehensive study of the broader constellation of Shakespeareana on YouTube, see Stephen O'Neill, *Shakespeare and YouTube: New Media Forms of the Bard* (London: Bloomsbury Publishing, 2014). For more background and analysis of the Shakespearean subgenre of vlog series, as well as the conventional tropes that characterize the LIW itself, see Douglas M. Lanier, 'Vlogging the Bard: Serialization, Social Media, Shakespeare', in *Broadcast Your Shakespeare: Continuity and Change Across Media*, ed. Stephen O'Neill (London: Bloomsbury Publishing, 2017). Lanier helpfully includes a comprehensive list of Shakespearean LIW through 2017 (202–6).

12 Lanier, 'Vlogging the Bard', 199–200.

13 Coco Marcil, Personal Interview, November 2019.

14 See Jules Piggot 'Emotion, Empathy, and the Internet: Transforming Shakespeare for Contemporary Teens' in this volume.

15 Henry Jenkins, *Convergence Culture: Where Old and New Media Collide* (New York: New York University Press, 2008), 2–3.

16 Elsie Bollinger and Bollinger, Sally, Personal Interview, October 2020.

17 These framing devices reflect a class privilege generally reflected in the series. The characters are also almost exclusively white (which may be influenced in part by the demographics of New Zealand). This generally reflects the broader world of LIW and their typical audiences, which tend to share a white, middle-class perspective. At the same time, from the early reference to Hero's two moms onwards, the series maintains a queer-friendly ethos.

18 Candle Wasters, *Nothing Much to Do*, 'Preparing for Pedro's Party'.

19 Ibid., 'Idiots'.

20 Ibid., 'Hero's Birthday'.

21 Christy Desmet, 'New Directions: Much Ado About Nothing and Social Media,' in *Much Ado About Nothing: A Critical Reader*, ed. Deborah Cartmell and Peter J. Smith (London: Bloomsbury Publishing, 2018), 167.

22 Candle Wasters, *Nothing Much to Do*, 'Idiots'.

23 William Shakespeare, *Much Ado about Nothing*, ed. Claire McEachern, in *The Arden Shakespeare, Third Series, Complete Works* (London, New York, Oxford, New Delhi, and Sydney: Bloomsbury, 2020). All references to the play are to this edition (4.1.88).

24 Candle Wasters, *Nothing Much to Do*, 'Words'.

25 Ibid., 'Words'.

26 Ibid., 'Hello Again'.

27 Ibid., 'Nothing Much to Do'.

28 Elsie and Sally Bollinger, personal interview with the author, October 2020.

29 Elsie said that the tension created by this silence among the fandom was to the extent that there were frantic questions among posters about whether an earthquake had struck New Zealand.

30 Emma Sarappo, 'How Tumblr Taught Social Justice to a Generation of Teenagers', *Pacific Standard*, 13 December 2018. https://psmag.com /social-justice/how-tumblr-taught-social-justice-to-a-generation-of -teenagers.

31 Alexander Cho, Indira N. Hoch, Allison McCracken and Louisa Stein, 'You Must Be New Here: An Introduction', in *A Tumblr Book: Platform and Cultures* (Ann Arbor: University of Michigan Press, 2020), 6.

32 Louisa Stein, 'The Digital Literary Fangirl Network: Representing Fannishness in the Transmedia Web Series', in *Seeing Fans: Representations of Fandom in Media and Popular Culture*, ed. Lucy Bennett and Paul Booth (New York: Bloomsbury Publishing USA, 2016), 170.

33 The Bollingers noted that by the time the third wave of LIWs came out, the fictional LIW itself was entrenched as a generic form with an intertextual currency of its own, as The Candle Wasters realized when they started to see Shakespearean LIW modelled on their own approach. One notable example is *Call Me Katie* (2015), an Australian web series adaptation of *The Taming of the Shrew*, whose creators have explicitly cited the inspiration provided by *Nothing Much to Do*.

34 The Candle Wasters (Elsie Bollinger, Sally Bollinger, Minnie Grace, and Claris Jacobs), *Lovely Little Losers*, 2015. https://www.youtube .com/user/pedrodonaldson/featured.

35 Bollinger, personal interview.

11

Emotion, empathy, and the internet

Transforming Shakespeare for contemporary teens

Jules Pigott

I discovered Shakespeare web series in 2014. I was fifteen years old and had just spent my freshman year of high school being tutored and homeschooled after multiple panic attacks caused my parents and me to decide I needed a break from the world. It is now eight years later; I have a BA in film and media studies as well as eight fully produced web series under my belt. The first of those two are Shakespeare adaptations: *Like, As It Is*,[1] based on *As You Like It*, and *Twelfth Grade (or Whatever)*,[2] based on *Twelfth Night*. While the production of *Like, As It Is* was mostly a learning experience, I found my footing with *Twelfth Grade (or Whatever)*, and I'm incredibly proud of it. Without Shakespeare-inspired web series, I don't think I would have had the confidence to work on my own creative writing and directing skills and share them with the world.

In my year of Countess Olivia-esque isolation, I read one of my favourite books (Dostoevsky's *Crime and Punishment*) and my least favourite book (Hesse's *Narcissus and Goldmund*), and I watched as many television shows as I could. In the summer of 2014, I emerged to attend a day camp at the New York Film Academy. I'd always been interested in storytelling, and a filmmaking camp seemed like a great way to learn about a new medium, as well as to slowly get myself used to a classroom environment again. It didn't turn out as I'd hoped; I had to drop out of the programme about a week in. In that one week, however, I did manage to become friends with a girl my age named Simona who shared a lot of interests and fandoms with me. We quickly followed each other on Tumblr and kept in contact even after I left. By following her, I learnt about a web series she was really into at that time. It was called *Nothing Much to Do*,[3] a modern adaptation of Shakespeare's *Much Ado about Nothing* made by a group of young adults from New Zealand.

At that point in my life, I wouldn't have called myself a huge Shakespeare fan. I'd read a couple of plays in middle school English class and seen one or two stage productions that my parents brought my brother and me to. I thought Shakespeare was interesting, but the language always made the stories seem like they took place in a reality I couldn't quite understand. However, the quotes and images from *Nothing Much to Do* that my friend posted looked fun. A few years earlier, I'd enjoyed *The Lizzie Bennet Diaries*,[4] a similarly-conceived web series based on *Pride and Prejudice*. Both series were told in a 'vlog' format, with the protagonists of the series portrayed as making YouTube videos about their lives in-universe (in *Nothing Much to Do*'s case, Beatrice and Benedick posted videos to separate channels). I was a big fan of, as Jane Wanninger describes, 'the sense of an intimate and interactive engagement with characters who feel like peers operating a lived-in world'.[5] At the time, I lacked intimate relationships with real-world peers. I began to watch *Nothing Much to Do* not just out of a desire to relate to the characters on-screen but also to keep up conversation with Simona, who I hoped could become a friend if we had enough things to talk about.

One thing that grabbed me right away about *Nothing Much to Do* was that everyone involved in the production was about my age – not just the characters and the actors but also the writers and directors. They were fellow teenagers and young adults, and this in part is what made the characters of *Nothing Much to Do* feel so authentic. Beatrice was an angry feminist into nerdy television shows. I found the intensity of her emotions relatable and her ability to express her thoughts and feelings aspirational. Her cousin Hero was sweet and kind, and it was easy to tell why Beatrice loved her so much. Benedick was, like Beatrice, nerdy and a bit awkward. As I got to know the characters over the course of the series, it became clear that Beatrice and Benedick would be a great romantic match if they could just get over their respective egos. I caught up on *Nothing Much to Do* episodes about three-fourths of the way through the series' airing, and watching the rest of it live was incredibly fun. I talked about it on my own Tumblr and made friends with fellow users who were into the show as we theorized about how different plot points would be adapted and made jokes about the characters and relationships. I'm still friends with most of them. Recently I found an exchange on Tumblr from 2014 between my friend Hazel and me during *Nothing Much to Do*'s original release (see Figure 11.1).[6]

A few weeks before *Nothing Much to Do* ended, I had a sudden thought: I could make my own web series. I still had a camera from my half-hearted attempts to become a vlogger back in 2012. My love for *Nothing Much to Do* inspired me to read the source text, as well as quite a few other Shakespeare plays. I'd both found a few I really enjoyed and gained a new appreciation for the ones I had read in school. I'd realized, for example, that Juliet and Romeo weren't just lovestruck fools – they were kids, just like me, trying

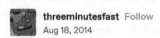

threeminutesfast Follow
Aug 18, 2014   Aug 18, 2014

caught up with nmtd
oh god heros lung condition I get what they're gonna do
when was the party? there's been no word since I know that

greatestvoyageinhistoryofplastic
Aug 18, 2014

The early evening of the 16th O.O

#nmtd

FIGURE 11.1 *Tumblr post by Jules Pigott, posting as threeminutesfast (2014).*

to find love in a world that was built to prevent it. In fact, most Shakespeare plays were about young people making bad decisions; adapting them as modern-day high schoolers just made sense. I could even ask some of the friends I'd made if they wanted to help me write the show. The creators of *Nothing Much to Do* weren't *that* much older than me. I could certainly try.

Shakespeare's characters, much like teenagers, are overflowing with passion, whether it be for their friends, lovers, families, or enemies. At that age, everything that happens to you feels like the most important thing that will *ever* happen, and the over-the-top situations in Shakespeare plays are relatable, if you're able to understand what you're reading. Even though Shakespeare wrote about the nobility of his day or earlier, the basic emotions and motivations of his characters continue to be relevant. In the twenty-first century, a child is unlikely to be born into a feud between noble families, but they can still inherit biases and prejudices that their parents teach them from birth. The moment in *Much Ado about Nothing*, where Benedick believes vulnerable women over his male friends who hurt them, is a powerful feminist statement whether he's a soldier in Messina or a high schooler in Auckland, New Zealand. I felt confident that I could translate Shakespearean characters to modern day; all I needed to do was pick a play.

I decided on *As You Like It*, which, at the time, was the only Shakespeare play I had actually seen live, and the one I still consider my favourite. I describe it as the midpoint between *Twelfth Night* and *A Midsummer Night's Dream*. Unlike *Midsummer*, there's no magic to explain the terrible decisions that characters make, which I found fascinating. I made a post on Tumblr asking if anybody wanted to write with me, and when two girls my age responded, we got to work. By the end of 2014, we had a fifty-episode script for *Like, As It Is*. Because I lived in New York City (and would therefore have the biggest pool of potential actors), I volunteered to produce the show myself.

Filming took up the first six months of 2015. Between wrapping the shoot and actually beginning to post episodes of the show that August, I decided I could do better. In retrospect, *As You Like It* was a difficult play to adapt. The characters, like in *Much Ado about Nothing*, are young and foolish, but while I've often seen *Much Ado* placed as both a drama and comedy, *As You Like It* is a more straightforward comedy. Terrible things happen, but they are framed as part of the comedy, rather than a tragic disruption. At fifteen, I was not skilled enough as a writer to adapt emotional stakes that I didn't fully understand.

As an example, in *As You Like It* the strained relationship between brothers Orlando and Oliver is healed after Oliver is attacked in the French woods by a geographically misplaced lion. It's a lighter situation than my choice to have Oliver and Orlando get into a car crash. While both events result in reconciliation of the two brothers, my desire for *Like, As It Is* to feel grounded in reality clashed with the more comedic elements in the original play. While I was proud of putting together a racially diverse and queer cast of characters, I wanted to prove to myself that I could improve as a screenwriter. And so, with *Like, As It Is* not taking off among literary-inspired web series fans, I started writing *Twelfth Grade (or Whatever)*.

Adapting *Twelfth Night*'s story to modern day came easily as other parts of myself found their way into other characters. To me the obvious characters to tell the story through videos were Viola and Liv, with Viola vlogging out of a desire to express herself even when in her male disguise and Liv being encouraged to make personal videos by a well-meaning therapist after years of agoraphobic isolation (see Figure 11.2). I wasn't arbitrarily

FIGURE 11.2 *Sarah E. Taylor as Viola/Sam Messing and Kristen Vaganos as Liv Belcik*. Twelfth Grade (or Whatever) *(2016)*.

tacking on my personality to Shakespeare's characters. The strong-willed, cross-dressing Viola had outspoken feelings about historical accuracy in movies and a complex relationship with her gender. That my personal thoughts on how Viola identifies often mirrored how I feel about my own gender at the moment is not coincidental. Both Orsino and Oren romanticized the people they cared about and became troubled when their views were challenged. Where Sir Andrew Aguecheek can come across as Sir Toby's comical lackey, Drew Aguecheek always felt like the least important part of any friend group he was in.

Reading *Twelfth Night*, I found myself identifying with Olivia. While my own anxiety was not the result of a family tragedy as Olivia's was, we both tried to limit our social lives as much as possible in order to protect ourselves from a world we'd grown afraid of. A countess can afford to never leave her castle, but a teenage girl cannot, and I wanted to show how much Liv's anxiety held her back. More important, I wanted her to find the strength to push through and live her life to the fullest, even though at the time, I was struggling to find that courage for myself. Liv ends the show by conveying a lesson I'd finally learnt, 'The world is big, and you can't control it. It's not mine to control'.[7]

In *Twelfth Grade (or Whatever)*, many of the new aspects of Liv Belcik's character were pulled completely from my own life; she went on angry rants about Marie Antoinette, her favourite incarnation of *Doctor Who* was the ninth, and she tended to pre-emptively apologize if she was worried she'd made someone upset. She was a lonely girl who tried to hold on to any tentative personal connection she made, much like I had done when I watched *Nothing Much to Do* to keep up with Simona. And because I had been successful in forming bonds with Simona (she helped out with production for a few days on the set of *Twelfth Grade (or Whatever)*) and others on Tumblr, writing Liv's own journey of re-entering the world was cathartic.

The connections I made between *Twelfth Night* and my own life illustrate why I think the work of modernizing Shakespeare for young people is so important. I knew William Shakespeare was a 'great writer', the kind that Western scholars and educators like to push as an essential part of literary canon. The problem with teaching Shakespeare as a master of his craft is it can give young students the idea that Shakespeare's plays are perfect and therefore boring. The fact that a lot of high schoolers need to consult a glossary every few minutes while reading in order to understand just the basic events of the story doesn't make the prospect of reading Shakespeare any more exciting. I didn't realize how much his stories could appeal to me until I saw them through a more relatable framing in shows like *Nothing Much to Do*, where the characters say all the same things, but they speak like me. I hope that my own work has helped other kids see themselves in Shakespeare as well.

Notes

1 Quip Modest Productions, *Like, As It Is,* 2015, web series. https://www.youtube.com/playlist?list=PL7Aos6cZ-mUw3t3B9LyKlfXK7-dY6wMwM.

2 Quip Modest Productions, *Twelfth Grade (or Whatever),* 2016, web series. https://www.youtube.com/watch?v=csp35NipXEU&list=PL7Aos6cZ-mUxgWreHGvC1S5dY5IHq3Am6.

3 Candle Wasters (Elsie Bollinger, Sally Bollinger, Minnie Grace, and Claris Jacobs), *Nothing Much to Do,* 2014, web series. https://www.youtube.com/user/nothingmuchtodovlog/videos.

4 Bernie Su and Hank Green, *The Lizzie Bennet Diaries,* 2012, web series. https://www.youtube.com/user/LizzieBennet.

5 See Jane Wanninger, '"Hello, people of the Internet!": *Nothing Much to Do* and the Young Adult Creators and Communities of Vlog-Shakespeare' in this volume.

6 greatestvoyageinhistoryofplastic. Tumblr, 'threeminutesfast: caught up with nmtd oh god . . .' 18 August 2014. https://greatestvoyageinhistoryofplastic.tumblr.com/post/95088349573/threeminutesfast-caught-up-with-nmtd-oh-god.

7 Quip Modest, *Twelfth Grade (or Whatever),* 'Response'.

12

Promoting companion texts for reading Shakespeare plays

Future teachers, Young Adult literature, and connecting adolescents to *Romeo and Juliet*

Laura Turchi

In a teacher education programme in Houston, my students remember high school days where they felt seen only as test scores: they felt unknown by most teachers. They aspire to become the exception, become like the teacher who made them feel they mattered, who was aware of their out-of-school identities, interests, and dreams. It's not surprising that this teacher was often an English language arts teacher, as that is what these students are in training to become. These pre-service teachers (PSTs) imagine themselves teaching interesting books and nurturing young writers. More than anything else, their goal is connecting with their students. Most of these PSTs love reading and some love writing: some of them even love Shakespeare, my own pedagogical passion. But as future teachers they are unsure how to make a connection between what the state says they must teach and how they most want students to feel about learning. To become 'their kind' of teacher, I recommend what Arnetha F. Ball calls generative learning, where teachers seek to understand the lives of students and then use that knowledge for 'pedagogical problem solving'.[1] The problem new teachers want to solve: their students won't necessarily love reading, or literary analysis, and they may not appreciate opportunities to become fluent writers or more ambitious readers. What will connect their lives and the texts?

Future teachers need to learn how to design for equity and success in English language arts classrooms: my goal is to make Shakespeare part of their solutions. The most advanced high school students often study multiple Shakespeare plays through innovative and creative activities; teachers who work with less able readers and writers often choose to limit Shakespeare study to translations, like *NoFear Shakespeare*, or film watching. New English language arts teachers need to believe all their students are capable of making sense of a Shakespeare scene and that even struggling readers can have a play resonate in their lives.

One approach replaces traditional lectures with student-centred reading/writing workshop models. Fundamentally, the purpose of a workshop model is to reduce the amount of time teachers spend explaining texts and to increase the meaningful reading and writing that adolescents do. Reading/writing workshop models support increased learner independence: the ELA teacher serves as a guide and mentor rather than a transmitter of information. School systems around the country promote workshop models through investing in classroom libraries, providing more books for students to read and discuss independently, often Young Adult literature titles. I want PSTs to aspire to ELA classrooms full of students reading and writing, and not just listening, even when they are working on Shakespeare plays. I try to solve this pedagogical problem by asking future teachers to experiment with the activities of a workshop – in the case of this chapter, a 'book talk' on a Young Adult novel that can be a companion text for *Romeo and Juliet*. They must imagine teaching *Romeo and Juliet* and connecting to their students' lives through their selection of a text.

In the coursework analysed in this chapter, the reading/writing workshop model is from Kelly Gallagher and Penny Kittle's *180 Days: Two Teachers and the Quest to Engage and Empower*

Adolescents. The authors describe students reading and writing independently and also the value of shared or core texts (like a Shakespeare play) in their classrooms: 'We want our students to compare their thoughts and theories and feelings to those of others. . . . We believe there is a synergy – a level of insight – that occurs when an entire class huddles around a core text that does not always happen in independent reading or in small book clubs.'[2] Gallagher and Kittle provide an example for teaching *Romeo and Juliet* as a core text, with that complex work surrounded by other texts. In this workshop model, students might study the play with their teacher while also reading and carrying out small group discussions of different Young Adult literature titles. They might complete reflective writing on themes and ideas ('true love', 'parental power', 'potions and poisons') that connect the play to other texts, and perhaps their lives.

I assign PSTs to choose a companion text from Young Adult or other literature as a reading choice for students that would be one part of a hypothetical unit centred on *Romeo and Juliet*. Rosie Kerin claims that all choices that a literacy teacher makes in planning should be in answer to the question 'What's the value of this text, for these students, at this time?'[3] In secondary ELA classrooms, Young Adult literature titles accommodate a range of student reading levels and interests. Diane Lapp and colleagues argue that these companion texts 'build the background knowledge, vocabulary, and literacy skills needed to critically analyze a more difficult text on the same topic'.[4] Alfred W. Tatum explains that texts that adolescents find meaningful in connection to their own lives can help mediate access to more difficult texts.[5] Rudine S. Bishop offers the important metaphor of the windows and mirrors of these potentially more relevant texts, describing how they support student identity and the development of empathy.[6] Abbey Bachmann's research suggests that students can also be motivated through having a choice of what to read. As it sounds, a book talk is intended to give students a quick familiarity with a possible independent book choice, and it should be an enthusiastic pitch.[7] In this case, PSTs are required to offer a specific rationale for why reading the selected text will help young readers make connections between *Romeo and Juliet* and their own lives.

In other parts of the course, future teachers discuss the cultural capital of Shakespeare plays and the opportunities for arts integration through drama-based pedagogy. PSTs experiment with activities designed to help students (and teachers) feel more at ease with the complexity of the language and more aware of the connections between a 400-year-old play and their human experiences. Reviewing these book talks highlights what may still be missing in preparing PSTs to teach Shakespeare. The book talk assignment has evolved: in one semester these were live presentations made to classmates. Those first book talks tended to be unrehearsed, ignoring the time limits, and focused on plot retelling with cursory attention to *Romeo and Juliet*. So it was a strange blessing when Covid-19 ended the face-to-face meetings, and this book talk project necessarily became a digital one, and more rigorous.

This chapter uses a self-study methodology to analyse ways undergraduate PSTs responded to the 'companion-text book talk' assignment in three semesters. This inquiry is not about 'fixing' students. I seek to learn about my students from their work and thus improve my pedagogy for building a better bridge between theory and practice.[8] As a practitioner in a self-study, I work to articulate my ideals, reframe my practices, and look for evidence of impact on my students.[9] The result is a meaningful intersection between self-study insights and pedagogy-improving revisions.[10] Data sources included notes on the book talks as delivered live; the digital projects submitted in subsequent semesters; the evaluative commentaries offered by peers; and informal written self-evaluations, especially in response to the question 'what connections were you hoping to make?'

My broader purpose is always understanding and supporting the effective teaching of Shakespeare plays and other complex works of literature. The book talks revealed undergraduates' attitudes about teaching and learning *Romeo and Juliet*: some did not hide that they thought the 'old English' of Shakespeare a burden, others questioned whether companion texts should have any place in a literature classroom; some loved the text they selected because of the movie that had been made of it, others asserted that the best companion text would be a *No Fear Shakespeare*-type modern translation; some chose a companion text to speak to race, gender, and class conflict, while others wanted only to savour the romance. As an instructor, the insights and even confusions of the future teachers offered many new ways to consider how both they and young adults may experience Shakespeare plays as texts and adaptations.

Themes emerged from reviewing these book talks that gave me pause for much reflection about how new teachers learn Shakespeare pedagogy, including blaming the difficulty of Shakespeare on 'the language'; focusing on the plot and avoiding 'spoilers'; having fuzzy ideas about fate; imagining connections to adolescent experiences around complicated topics including diversity, gender, and sexuality; and envisioning a teacher's role as offering straightforward moral guidance.

Blaming the difficulty of Shakespeare on 'the language'

Many future teachers commented on how difficult the text was (and is) for them, and they assumed for their future students. Reflecting on her book talk, one PST described becoming motivated on this assignment only after finding a meaningful companion text, writing that she knew this meant admitting that she had her own 'Shakespeare troubles'. Some of the future teachers felt they had learned strategies for overcoming the difficulty of Shakespeare's language, but one said his continuing belief was that Shakespeare's language got in the way of adolescents recognizing 'true passion', which was what a companion text could offer. Another PST was enthusiastic about YA literature because of the 'modern language and [how] students can relate'. A self-described 'Shakespeare lover' wrote that she felt more confident that students would 'get' the play if they read YA Lit books about 'today's romance and conflicts' in understandable words. These comments suggest that future teachers should think about what Shakespeare is, if not 'the language'.

Several PSTs reflected on their high school days where they were largely passive listeners to information about Shakespeare plays and what they meant, and they wrote that imagining students becoming engaged and empowered in reading the plays was 'a stretch' and 'going to take a lot of work'. It seems necessary to put more time into building up future teacher confidence in their own abilities to read Shakespeare plays.

Focusing on the plot and avoiding spoilers

In preparing to write *Shakespeare with Purpose: A Student-Centred Approach*, Ayanna Thompson and I persuaded a generous local high school teacher to allow us to record her entire *Romeo and Juliet* unit with ninth graders. There are many things to learn in fifty-seven hours of video. One eye-popping moment occurred some three weeks in. The teacher began Act 4 with an off-handed comment about 'knowing they were going to die anyway', and the students reacted with shock and unhappiness, accusing her of 'spoiling the story'. The teacher was understandably surprised, as the class had spent a reasonable amount of time on the prologue, which does more than mention 'star-crossed lovers' to make the impending tragedy quite clear.

While I promote Shakespeare pedagogy that prioritizes helping students experience the pleasures of drama and not worry about 'spoilers', a book talk *is* supposed to motivate independent readers. That said, the PSTs went to such lengths to avoid what they called 'giving away' the plot of the companion text that their descriptions were sometimes baffling, or heavy on detail that seemed not particularly relevant.

Many PSTs could not resist using plot machinations and twists as proverbial cliffhangers in their book talks, intending to motivate young readers to keep reading: 'Will their fates be etched into stone? To find out more, READ!' These exhortations highlight the need for PSTs to think further about what motivates readers. Instead of sharing with (imagined) students why they might relate to the characters, the plot-focused book talk implied that students were only reading to find out what happened.

Having fuzzy ideas about fate

The phrase 'star-crossed' was endemic in the book talks, serving as a shorthand phrase sometimes for fate but often to explain a couple's determination to overcome 'outside' forces that get in the way of love. The PSTs used *outside forces* to mean almost anything that kept a couple separated, from terminal illness (see later in this chapter) to societal disapproval. The future teachers tended to use 'star-crossed' and 'ill-fated' interchangeably, and they avoided raising questions with students about their conceptions of fate or destiny. Instead, the PSTs focused on *choices*. Many asked their imagined students: is one or more death preventable? Whose fault is it? The major exception to this was the choice of suicide, as discussed later in the text. The desire of the PSTs to communicate about the importance of good choices was complicated by some of their selections of companion texts.

By far the most popular texts chosen for the book talks were in the 'sick chick lit' genre – medical tragedies, where the lovers are separated by fatal disease. In three semesters I have seen eleven book talks on John Green's *The Fault in Our Stars* (terminal cancers), six more focusing on *Five Feet Apart* (Rachel Lippincott; cystic fibrosis), and four each about *Me Before You* (Jojo Moyes; quadriplegia) and *It's Kind of a Funny Story* (Ned Vizzini; mental health). One PST claimed that the central problem of a medical *Romeo and Juliet* was that 'your fate is written in the stars, you will cross paths one day, but your relationship is destined for tragedy'. The book talks made variations on the point that medical issues were standing in the way of romance and, as one PST said, 'two people were so alike and yet so not meant to be'. The positive advice about making good choices was recast as declarations that what was important was 'having good attitudes' and 'believing in love'.

When the medical destinies are overcome by one of the characters in the end, PSTs celebrated these works as improving on *Romeo and Juliet*. Such was the case with one book talk on Nicola Yoon's *Everything, Everything*, where a young woman is confined to her home because of severe combined immunodeficiency. She surreptitiously meets and falls for the boy literally next door, and when all seems lost, it turns out her mother (an MD) had faked her diagnosis to make up for an earlier tragedy. All's well that ends well.

PSTs might spend more time thinking about their own conceptions of fate before they discuss these with adolescents. 'Can the stars be re-written?' asked one book talk, answering: 'According to both works of literature, the resounding answer is *no* . . . However, *your* choices can alter your life. Make good ones.'

Imagining connections to adolescent experiences around complicated topics

Most of the book talks included an assumption, if not an outright statement, that *Romeo and Juliet* could not be as relevant to students as the companion text. Yet the PSTs sometimes struggled with explaining why a given work should be relevant. It is one thing to make the text easier to understand; it's another to convince students that it matters specifically to them. Often PSTs used diversity, gender, and sexuality as lenses for explaining the relevance of a companion text, framing their book talk around the idea that the selected text offered an update of Shakespeare.

Diversity

The class had discussed what Carla Della Gatta calls the *West Side Story* effect, where the two families 'alike in dignity'[11] are portrayed as of different races, religions, or social status.[12] The implication is that such differences are automatically a site for strife.[13] In describing their chosen books, the PSTs referenced 'feuding families' as obstacles to a central romance and dysfunctional family dynamics (betrayal, divorce, illegitimate births, murders) as a modern feud. The future teachers described these wide-ranging conflicts but rarely raised a critical perspective on the situations that thwarted the lovers, and especially whether these were inevitable. One PST stated that 'the richer family always gets its way', another that 'race divides'. One said she chose Nicola Yoon's *Frankly in Love* because it is about 'two Korean kids [who] fake loving each other to cover up the fact that they're dating white kids', and the book talk assumed everyone would recognize an obvious problem. In Gloria Chao's *American Panda*, its Taiwanese and Chinese families were presumed to be obviously in conflict without suggesting anything about the nature of that dispute. PSTs offered murky distinctions between groups in terms of barriers like 'societal expectations', 'meaningless hatreds', and 'historical enemies'. One PST described 'enemies to love' in Jacqueline Woodson's *If You Come Softly* as 'racism, police brutality and people's general stupidity'. These book talks are evidence that PSTs are attuned to racial and cultural diversity. Unfortunately, the discussions elsewhere in the class on antiracist teaching (reading Jason Reynolds and Ibram X. Kendi's *Stamped*[14] and Deborah Appleman's *Critical Encounters in Secondary English*[15]) did not obviously influence the PSTs' thinking about their companion texts, at least for the book talks. Did the future teachers think raising these interpretive lenses would not be appropriate? While there is a significant difference between preparing a book talk and preparing to teach a book, the PSTs may still need more convincing that recognizing the racialized bodies of their students can be a powerful way of connection.

Gender

Identifying gender issues seemed to be much more comfortable for the future teachers. Some PSTs focused on young women's agency and the barriers encountered. One contrasted Juliet to the young woman in the selected text, claiming that in the 'historical time' of Juliet's life, 'men decide the fate of women, women have to be skilled at hiding their ideas and being part of a patriarchal society'. Another described Juliet and the protagonist as both 'very determined and confident, only falling into the damsel-in-distress trope when society pressured them to behave as such'. Writing on Sara Gruen's *Water for Elephants*, one PST wrote about what she labelled *confinement*: 'Marlena is trapped in the confines of her rickety marriage. Juliet is trapped in the confinement of her family values and morals and is pressured to uphold these ideals when she wants to be free with the one she loves and not the one she's obligated to be with.' This PST hoped her students would respond to Juliet as someone who makes decisions (to escape confinement) and accepts the consequences. Another future teacher offered an interpretation of the balcony scene as Romeo taking instruction from Juliet, who 'pretty much tells him how stupid the family feud is. She tells him that his family name should never have this much power over him'. Each of the feminist readings evidenced how the future teachers were thinking about Juliet's situation in the Shakespeare play, and these revealed something of the text that might be explained to their students. The PSTs who took this approach were all women, and they sought to make common cause with their imagined female students in calling out male domination and unfair discrimination by gender, 'then' and now.

Sexuality

Each semester multiple future teachers chose Benjamin Alire Sáenz's *Aristotle and Dante Discover the Secrets of the Universe*. They wrote and spoke with different degrees of explicitness about the relationship between the two male Latinx teenagers, friends who struggle with racial and ethnic identities, family relationships, and their sexuality. The PSTs who chose this book consistently had difficulty articulating the parallels they saw to *Romeo and Juliet*: they identified societal pressures against gay relationships as similar to having feuding families, and they wanted to make it clear they did not share the same prejudices. One PST wrote, 'I wanted to communicate . . . the intense passion and love the characters in both these novels have for each other. I also wanted to connect the violence that is amplified due to these characters' passion for each other.' In their reflections on this text, PSTs were clear about connecting with students by demonstrating their acceptance of different sexual preferences. In their book talks, they were more circumspect, inclined to talk generally about passion and violence and not draw an explicit parallel between Romeo and Juliet and Dante and Aristotle. Going forward, future teachers may need to understand coming-of-age narratives, with characters and situations developing over time, in contrast to the fever pitch of *Romeo and Juliet*. This could help them situate struggles with sexual orientation outside the violence and death of the play.

Overall, the class should see me model more strategies that connect texts to students and put texts in dialogue with each other. The PSTs understand the basic moves required for 'selling' a text to their students. Their work to introduce the books and promote thematic ties could be aided by considering their purpose in choosing and emphasizing a particular connection, thinking about how they would then frame their teaching of *Romeo and Juliet*.

Envisioning their teacher role in offering straightforward moral guidance

In making one explicit connection to *Romeo and Juliet*, one future teacher said of both works that 'uncontrollable forces keep them apart, but they do have people who want the best for them'. The PST clearly wanted to be seen as one of those people. In their self-evaluations, many PSTs described themselves as being in search of what one called a 'good message' for young adults. Whether they wanted their students to read about Romeo and Juliet and the companion texts to understand 'how your decisions impact your future' or that 'love is worth terrible risks', they often finished their book talks with a strong statement of advice or even purpose. One said: 'Romeo and Juliet risked their whole lives for their love. Maddie and Ollie risked seeing the world for a chance to explore their love. So please don't be afraid to take a chance.'

Sometimes the message to students tried to account for how teenagers feel about love. One book talk tried to echo Friar Lawrence's advice to Romeo and yet concluded, '"love in moderation, softly and safely" . . . But what most of us know is, that isn't what happens'. Often the book talks presented decisions, choices, and consequences, making the suicidal end to Romeo and Juliet (and in some of the companion texts) challenging for the future teachers to rationalize. They were understandably concerned about offering suicide as 'an answer' to anything. One told his audience, 'In both of these scenes, Juliet and Will are making a decision to take their own lives. However, they are not thinking of how these choices will affect the people around them.' Other PSTs noted that in both the play and the text they selected 'deaths lead to deaths or other desperate actions', and they wondered about preparing to talk to students about the dangerous attractions of violence.

Preparation for teaching Shakespeare

Future teachers probably need more explicit discussion in class about the responsibility that comes with connecting to their students' lives. They might also consider the messages they give students about the value of reading, as each semester multiple PSTs recommended choosing a text because it was available as a movie. And the book talks also demonstrate the need for learning about adaptations and appropriations of Shakespeare. Some PSTs selected explicit retellings or modern adaptations of *Romeo and Juliet*, including Meg Haston's *The End of Our Story*, Suzanne Selfors's *Saving Juliet*, and Melinda Taub's *Still Star-Crossed*. PSTs emphasized how helpful the companion texts would be, because background characters from *Romeo and Juliet* came to life in them, and these characters were able to reframe or alter the fate of the central lovers.

PSTs wrote how much easier it was to read a novel, instead of a play, because 'you can know what characters are thinking'. The PSTs liked how the different characters in the adaptations offered new points of view on the Shakespeare play. They may need to think about drama as a genre and how viewing performances could give students more access to the interior lives of characters. In evaluating the book talks, it's not clear whether it is right to assess future teachers for their interpretations of Shakespeare's characters.

Rewatching the digital book talks can lead to angst for what English language arts PSTs still need to become effective Shakespeare teachers. This isn't a pedagogical problem to be solved easily. But the book talks as a collection suggest that focusing teacher preparation on what the future teachers most want to be – above all, open-hearted to the lives of adolescents – does not preclude teaching classic, complex plays like *Romeo and Juliet*. It's a formidable task to address all the approaches in a single English language arts methods class, but future teachers can become their kind of teacher through, and not in spite of, what they teach.

Notes

1 Arnetha F. Ball, 'Toward a Theory of Generative Change in Culturally and Linguistically Complex Classrooms', *American Educational Research Journal* 46, no. 1 (2009): 45–72. doi: 10.3102/000281208323277, 48.

2 Kelly Gallagher and Penny Kittle, *180 Days: Two Teachers and the Quest to Engage and Empower Adolescents* (Portsmouth: Heinemann, 2018), 63.

3 Rosie Kerin, 'Knowing and Planning: A Framework for Planning in English', *Literacy Learning: The Middle Years* 25, no. 2 (2017): 10–15.

4 Diane Lapp, Barbara Moss, Kelly Johnson, and Maria Grant, 'Teaching Students to Closely Read Texts: How and When?' in

Rigorous Real-World Teaching and Learning (Newark: International Reading Association, 2012): n.p. doi: 10.1598/e-ssentials.8022 NP.

5 Alfred W. Tatum, 'Adolescents and Texts: Overserved or Underserved?' *English Journal* 98, no. 2 (2008): 82–5.

6 Rudine Sims Bishop, 'Mirrors, Windows, and Sliding Glass Doors', *Perspectives: Choosing and Using Books for the Classroom* 6, no. 3 (1990): n.p. https://scenicregional.org/wp-content/uploads/2017/08/ Mirrors-Windows-and-Sliding-Glass-Doors.pdf.

7 See for instance Nancy Atwell, *In the Middle* (Portsmouth: Heinemann, 1988) and Penny Kittle, *Book Love: Developing Depth, Stamina, and Passion in Adolescent Readers* (Portsmouth: Heinemann, 2013).

8 Kenneth M. Zeichner and Susan E. Noffke 'Practitioner Research', in *Handbook of Research on Teaching*, ed. Virginia Richardson (Washington DC: American Educational Research Association, 2001), 298–332.

9 Vicki LaBoskey, 'The Methodology of Self-Study and Its Theoretical Underpinnings', in *International Handbook of Self-Study of Teaching and Teacher Education Practices*, ed. Jeffrey J. Loughran, Mary Lynn Hamilton, Vicki LaBoskey, and Tom Russell (Dordrecht: Kluwer, 2004), 817–69.

10 Megan Madigan Peercy, 'Challenges in Enacting Core Practices in Language Teacher Education: A Self-Study', *Studying Teacher Education* 10, no. 2 (2014): 146–62.

11 William Shakespeare, *Romeo and Juliet*, ed. René Weis, in *The Arden Shakespeare, Third Series, Complete Works* (London, New York, Oxford, New Delhi, and Sydney: Bloomsbury, 2020). All references to the play are to this edition (1.1.1).

12 Carla Della Gatta, 'From *West Side Story* to *Hamlet, Prince of Cuba*: Shakespeare and Latinidad in the United States', *Shakespeare Studies* 44 (2016): 151–6.

13 Laura B. Turchi and Ann C. Christensen. 'When the "House" (of Montague) Is a Color not a Clan: Teaching *Romeo and Juliet* Productions Where Difference Signals Inevitable Conflict', *The English Journal* 108, no. 2 (2018): 111–14.

14 Jason Reynolds and Ibram X. Kendi, *Stamped: Racism, Antiracism, and You* (New York: Little Brown and Company, 2020).

15 Deborah Appleman, *Critical Encounters in Secondary English: Teaching Literary Theory to Adolescents*, 3rd ed. (New York: Teachers College Press, 2015).

Afterword

Adaptation studies and interactive pedagogies

Alexa Alice Joubin

The pandemic of Covid-19 has fuelled intersectional forms of hatred and fear that have coalesced around the idea of 'outsiders'. Teaching and learning about adaptations of Shakespeare's canonical plays can change this trend by promoting mutual understanding. In a time when the classroom is subject to racism and misogyny, and governed by content warnings, it is all the more important to use inclusive, and interactive, pedagogies to encourage students to build intellectual communities. This volume reveals the many ways in which Shakespeare offers audiences, teachers, and students new tools for addressing trauma and social justice. If Shakespeare's plays seem to contain unredeemable, sexist, and racist views of the world, what is the role of 'Shakespeare', or early modern history, in the modern classroom? As the foregoing chapters have shown, many adaptations (particularly works aiming at young adults) speak to the prejudices both early modern and modern. We believe criticism of the Shakespearean canon through adaptation as a genre has the capacity for liberation and social reparation, which is why we, in this volume, treat Shakespeare's plays as fundamentally performative narratives that sustain both past and contemporary conventions in adaptation, especially for young adults. As a cluster of complex texts that sustains both past practices and contemporary interpretive conventions, Shakespeare provides fertile ground for training students to listen intently and compassionately to other individuals' voices. The inequities exposed by the pandemic – even as they are cause for grief and anxiety – can spur change for the better in education. We can achieve this through adaptation, one of the most powerful forms of cultural criticism.

Taking stock of the important questions raised by the chapters in the present volume, this chapter theorizes contextualized and interactive pedagogies that link historical texts to our contemporary contexts. Contextualization enables students to find their own voices. Interactivity nurtures student-initiated engagement. Education can be reparative when we practise 'radical listening': a set of proactive communication strategies to listen for the roots rather than only the 'plots' of stories. Students learn to listen for motives behind characters' actions in Shakespeare and in adaptations. Meanwhile, applying radical listening to curricular design, educators can rethink current practices, such as teaching with trigger warnings. Commonly practised in secondary and higher education in the United States, the United Kingdom, and Canada, a trigger or content warning is a statement about potentially traumatizing themes in the reading, typically on the syllabus, to offer accommodation for disability, PTSD, neurodiversity, and different learning styles. It is important to teach with content warnings, but it is equally important to be cognizant of our assumptions about what could be 'triggering' and what we overlook in the first place. The following will begin with the theory of radical listening and proceed to pragmatic concerns in a tripartite approach to teaching, namely communal, contextualized, and interactive pedagogies that foster inquiry-driven learning and evidence-based argumentation.

Radical listening

Adaptations, by virtue of their intertextuality, can help students develop radical listening skills. Adaptations invite multiple, sometimes conflicting, perspectives on what may appear to be the same stories. Radical listening is a set of proactive communication strategies to listen for the roots of stories. This strategy creates 'an egality between teller and listener that gives voice to the tale', as the founder of narrative medicine Rita Charon theorizes.[1] Instead of looking for the what in the plot of Shakespeare, students, using this strategy, can examine the why in characters' motivation and behaviours. This communication strategy emphasizes the listener's understanding of the root cause of the speaker's trauma.

Radical listening also draws on the methodology of 'strategic presentism', a term coined by Lynn Fendler.[2] This method acknowledges the students' position in the present time in terms of their world views. It empowers readers to take ownership of the text by bringing history to bear on our contemporary issues and by comparing our contemporary concerns with those in the historical period. By thinking critically about the past in the present – such as the #BlackLivesMatter movement – students analyse Shakespeare with an eye towards changing the present.[3] In this way Shakespeare ceases to be a white canon with culturally predetermined meanings. This method foregrounds the connection between historical and contemporary ideologies and 'the ways the past is at work in the exigencies of the present'.[4] In particular, adaptations turn the past from what some students mistakenly regard as irrelevant knowledge into one of many complex texts in our exploration of present issues. The past is no longer sealed off in a vacuum.

Another benefit of encouraging radical listening, enhanced by strategic presentism, in the classroom is that this strategy decentres the traditional power structures that have excluded minoritized students, such as differently abled students and students of colour. Previously underprivileged students are now empowered to claim ownership of Shakespeare through presentist adaptations.

In pragmatic terms, radical listening fosters connections between seemingly isolated instances of artistic expression. The ability to recognize ambiguity in literature helps students to more productively analyse multiple, potentially conflicting, versions of what seems to be the same story. As students take into account the ambiguities and evolving circumstances that affect interpretations of the texts through adaptations, the singular, modern edition of Shakespeare's plays is no longer the only object of study. Instead, it is one of multiple nodes that are available for search and reassembly.

For example, through adaptations students can learn that directors filming *King Lear* must carve a path between theatrical elements ('language of drama') and discrete 'cinematic codes of communication'.[5] While readers' interpretations often hinge on their ability to sympathize with Lear,[6] applying the radical listening strategy to the study of adaptations reveals that the question of redemption need not and should not be the sole focus of interpretive strategies. In studying the play, students often find Lear's decision to divide his kingdom in three enigmatic and haphazard. The scene of regal abdication is folkloric in origin, which is why most students would detect the atmosphere of a fairy tale. Lear's trajectory becomes more relatable if we interpret it in relation to Lear's mental illness. Performances of the division-of-the-kingdom scene reflect each director's interpretation of the causes of Lear's madness. Structurally, when the scene begins, there are other divisions paralleling Lear's announcement: Cordelia versus her elder sisters, and Edgar in opposition to Edmund. Lear asks his daughters to publicly confess their love for him and, by extension, their loyalty to the throne. This is a highly performative act, which makes the scene dramatic and memorable.

Is the division-of-the-kingdom scene ceremonial (a premeditated act of policy) or symbolic (a public test of loyalty)? Peter Brook's 1971 film does not treat the scene ceremonially, while other adaptations portray the scene as a solemn ritual without political weight, such as the *Kathakali King Lear*, which premiered in 1989 and toured internationally through 1999.[7] In Brook's film version, Cordelia's asides are cut, which diminishes the weight of a potentially revelatory moment as well as Cordelia's self-discovery. The scene sets a sinister and nihilistic tone for the entire narrative. The film dramatizes Lear's recognition that kingship is a metonymy and that he is but a human subject. To survive, he, like others, depends on sustenance. In contrast, Kalamandalam Padmanabhan Nair performed Lear in the ritualistic, Kathakali style, a genre that originated in temple ceremonies to portray 'non-worldly' characters drawn from the Indian epics. Co-produced by the French director-choreographer Annette Leday and Australian playwright David McRuvie, this adaptation treats the division of the kingdom and downfall of Lear as a cleansing ritual.

Some adaptations try to make Lear more sympathetic through comedic elements. Laurence Olivier's Lear in Michael Elliott's televised film (1983) laughs off Cordelia's initial response ('nothing, my lord')[8] and cajoles her, in a playful manner, to be more forthcoming. As a jolly 'fond old man' (4.7.60), this Lear returns to a childlike state due to his egotistical incredulity that Cordelia could be serious. Lear's line 'Mend your speech a little, / Lest you may mar your fortunes' (1.1.94–5) is spoken with doting tenderness. Lear winks at Cordelia, making his favouritism clear. In most performances the line takes on a sinister undertone, as a stern warning.

Akira Kurosawa's Samurai film *Ran*[9] (1985) also features some elements of merriment in this scene. Warlord Hidetora decides to retire but retain his title of 'Great Lord'. Against the counsel he receives, Hidetora divides his kingdom among his three sons, Taro, Jiro, and Saburo, but asks them to remain united to defend the clan from invaders. Kurosawa frames the scene of division in the historical feudal lord Mōri Motonari's parable, with a twist. Known as 'the legend of the three arrows', the story depicts an ageing father who demonstrates the power of a united front to his three sons. To teach his sons a lesson in unity, Hidetora in the film gives each son an arrow and tells them to break it, an action which they accomplish with ease, similar to the events in the Mōri legend. Hidetora then gives each a bundle of arrows, which the two elder sons are unable to break. However, Saburo (the equivalent to Cordelia), ever the odd one out, breaks the bundle of arrows with his knee to burst the bubble of his ageing father's delusional plan. His act of defiance exposes that his father's childish fable is not suited for adults in a feudal world. It also highlights the irony in Hidetora's delusional and self-contradictory lecture that calls for both a division and unification of his 'kingdom'.

There are also numerous pop cultural references to Lear and ageing as an undignified process. In Christopher Nolan's film *The Dark Knight* (2008), Gotham City's district attorney Harvey Dent says, in a foreshadowing scene, that one either 'dies a hero' young or lives 'long enough to see yourself become a villain',[10] implying that longevity simply brings more opportunities to make mistakes that tarnish one's image. The association of a modern patriarch with a family business has been a popular trope in adaptations of *Lear*. In Francis Ford Coppola's *Godfather* trilogy (1972, 1974, 1990), mafia boss Vito Andolini Corleone holds court to grant favours and, like Lear, to divide up the family business. His two elder sons Sonny and Fredo end up betraying him by working with a rival gang. Similar to Jesse Armstrong's HBO series *Succession* (2018–present), the crisis of succession and the presence of three sons in *Godfather* parallel the story of *Lear*.

More recently, *King Lear* has been connected to the catchphrase 'OK boomer', which went viral after being used as a pejorative retort in 2019 by Chlöe Swarbrick, a member of the New Zealand Parliament, in response to heckling from another member. Radical listening as a mode of thinking will enable students to connect Lear's most eccentric moments (the division-of-the-kingdom scene and the first scene at Goneril's castle) to the generational gap crystallized by the catchphrase. Similarly, analysing contemporary events, such as Brexit, alongside *King Lear* helps students take ownership of Shakespeare's narrative. After the UK's 23 June 2016 referendum to leave the European Union, directors have turned to *King Lear* as a 'Brexit play' – a play about division and dispossession, with the map as its central prop in the opening scene. In Richard Eyre's 2018 film, for example, Anthony Hopkins's exiled Lear finds himself an unaccommodated man in a refugee camp under pouring rain. The film alludes to the issue of migration and the refugee crisis in Europe. In the post-Brexit context, there is dramatic irony in Lear's decision to cut familial and political ties with Cordelia, only to see her return from France to save him from oblivion. Lear's exile and search for refuge, as Stephen O'Neill points out, highlights 'supranational connections' in contemporary UK and in the play.[11]

We will now apply this theory of radical listening to adaptation studies in the classroom in three particular areas of emphasis: communal, contextualized, and interactive pedagogies. Each type of assignment or class activity will benefit from analyses of various adaptations of Shakespeare.

Communal writing assignments

In contrast to goal-oriented pedagogies, the presentist, collaborative learning strategies – enabled by radical listening – are student centred. In the classroom, students can work together to annotate play texts and adaptations. Based on these principles, I have designed assignments that give students substantive opportunities to own their narratives and write with a purpose. These assignments are meant for community building. This is an act that is particularly urgent and meaningful in the era of Covid-19, when students, more than ever, long to be connected to others, even under quarantine and in a remote learning environment. As Ariane M. Balizet points out in her chapter on teaching *Romeo and Juliet* during Covid-19, 'recognizing the force of trauma in students' lives' can 'support a more meaningful engagement with early modern affect'.[12] We can develop students' visual and cultural literacy through innovative digital annotation tools that promote collaborative learning structured around analyses of both texts and films, *contextualized* discussions that connect premodern texts and modern theories, and *interactive* critical writing exercises that sustain student engagement. The digital annotation empowers students to collaborate with one another and contextualize course materials in the time we live in, which leads to a buy-in from more students from diverse backgrounds.

There are many analogue and digital tools to achieve this goal. I use the open-access tool Perusall.com, which incentivizes and supports the collaborative annotation of texts and video clips. Annotations are gathered under thematic clusters as distinct conversations, as Perusall calls them, for analysis. For each assigned text, the class would read, annotate, and comment on a shared document, engaging in close reading and a critical framework of literary interpretation. The interactive nature makes reading a more engaging, communal experience, because readers become members of a community.

The annotation tool, paired with a dynamic digital play text, provides pedagogical advantages over reading a print text as an isolated activity. A typical, codex-book modern print edition would fixate ambiguous textual variants by making editorial choices and by glossing particular words in the text. For example, we worked with the modernized version of the *Internet Shakespeare Editions* (ISE) *King Lear*. The ISE's dynamic digital text shows textual variants when readers mouse over a word.

Research shows that Perusall and similar computer-mediated scholarly communication platforms enhance the quality of collaboration and promote effective learning interactions between students.[13] Writing and circulating rationale for editorial and interpretive choices led to increased awareness of one's own decision-making process, known as 'meta-cognition' in educational psychology.[14]

The Tempest works equally well with this method. Using Perusall, I established a social space where students learned from each other through the creation and circulation of free-form responses to cultural texts. In self-selected groups, some students explored historical meanings of 'cannibal', while others launched a comparative analysis of racialized representations of Caliban in Julie Taymor's film and Greg Doran's stage versions of Shakespeare's *The Tempest*. The course material was thereby transformed into a museum with many rooms. When completing assignments, students wandered into and explored different rooms depending on their interests. There were multiple activation points for knowledge economies. Learning was nonlinear in nature. As a result, students' experiences in class were enriched by their differentiated, individualized, and yet connected explorations.

Another example is an assignment that reveals the context-dependent meanings of a pivotal line. Students analysed the political meanings and affective labour behind Hamlet's line 'A little more than kin, a little less than kind' (F.1.2.63) during Claudius's announcement of his marriage to Gertrude. The meaning of this line depends upon performative contexts. The communal annotation tool enables the class to see it from multiple perspectives. If played as an aside, as Kenneth Branagh's Hamlet mutters under his breath next to a wall of mirrors, without Claudius hearing him, in his 1996 film, in response to Claudius's greeting him as a son, Hamlet's comments could deepen a division within the court. If addressed to Claudius, these lines could publicly challenge Claudius's authority by disrupting the king's orchestrated familial harmony, as is the case in Michelle Terry's gender-bending production at the London Globe in 2018. The king has to decide whether to respond in kind or ignore the insult, as his courtiers are watching. If addressed to his mother, Gertrude, Hamlet could be opposing her remarriage after his father dies, gesturing towards a moral high road. If addressed to the spectators, the prince could be insinuating that his uncle's marriage with his mother has overstepped the boundary of brotherly kinship. Students' writing thus connects them to other racialized communities, times, and places. With collaborative close reading, students claim the language, in recognition of the speech act, rather than just the character in the sense of whether a character is relatable.

Contextualized pedagogy

Contextualization is important in community building. We recently engaged with questions related to the 2021 U.S. Presidential

Inauguration, such as: Why does National Youth Poet Laureate Amanda Gorman read Shakespeare's sonnets for inspiration? What do the sonnets represent? In this framework, the past enables us to rethink the present. As we discover deep connections among seemingly distinct interpretations, early modern texts are no longer what some students assume to be an object of obscure knowledge that is sealed off from our present moment of globalization.

Teaching Shakespeare through adaptations draws attention to dramatic ambiguities and choices that directors must make. In dramaturgical terms, it helps students discover 'how the same speech can be used to perform . . . radically divergent speech acts'.[15] Instead of taking a secondary role by responding to assignment prompts, students examine the evidence as a group, annotate the text and video clips, and ask and share questions that will, at a later stage, converge into thesis statements. Students no longer encounter Shakespeare as a curated, editorialized, pre-processed narrative but as a network of interpretive possibilities. To demonstrate how close-reading adaptations shed new light on dramatic ambiguities, let us return briefly to *King Lear* as a case study. Lear's test of love becomes a trick question in the modern corporate context. The question tests audiences as much as the characters involved. For example, in his 1998 film, Richard Eyre set the scene around a table in a boardroom. Ian Holm's Lear announces the division of his kingdom as a corporate decision in sombre tone without emotional attachment. Another adaptation that sets this scene in a corporate setting is Eric de Vroedt's Dutch production *Koningin Lear*[16] (2015). Betty, the female CEO of Lear Inc., suffers from dementia. She proceeds to divide her shares among her three sons in a family and business meeting in the boardroom atop a skyscraper. While the modern boardroom is a popular choice for staging this scene, some adaptations have opted for a political allegory. Hundreds of balloons in *Lér Konungur* (directed by Benedict Andrews, National Theatre of Iceland in Reykjavik, 2010) call to mind American political conventions, with characters milling around in conservative contemporary business attire on a bare stage. Set in our contemporary period, the production critiques neoliberal, free-market capitalism driven by corporate interests. Analysing these adaptations in a comparative context enables students to see beyond the superficial, fairy-tale-like plotline and explore the motives behind each character's action.

Beyond comparing, side by side, video clips of performances of the same scene from various adaptations, I also asked students to combine textual annotations with a cluster of relevant images they selected from the Folger Library's LUNA, an open-access digital image collection.

In Othello's final speech before his suicide, he alludes, in the 1623 First Folio, to the 'base Iudean', a person of Jewish faith or Judas Iscariot in the Bible, and, in the 1622 First Quarto, to a 'base Indian', Indians of the New World, who 'threw a pearle away / Richer then all his Tribe'.[17] With dynamic toggle view in the *Internet Shakespeare Editions*, a reader of the digital edition could see simultaneously all the variants in a crux that are now open for comparative analysis. The biblical allusion would signal Othello's failed conversion to Christianity, Iago's betrayal as well as Othello's lost soul. The reference to the New World would support interpretations of Othello's internalized status as a 'savage'. Historical engravings and paintings of Othello in the final scene in Folger's LUNA reflected varying assumptions about the choice of word and the weight of the freighted words.

Students can bring their own contexts to bear on the adaptation in an inquiry-driven learning environment. One way to excavate the different layers of meanings within the play and in performances is to compare different stage and film versions from different parts of the world. I encourage my students to translate a key passage in a canonical English text into other languages (and to report back in English) to diversify the class's interpretive approaches (2015). Students may be studying a foreign language, or they may speak a language other than English at home. Students are thus able to bring into the classroom new voices and new ways of seeing the world.

Another type of adaptive assignment involves students' own adaptations of a play. My students have also 'translated' Shakespeare's plays into other media in their own adaptations. Students would examine popular culture examples of a particular theme before moving on to analysing a scene in Shakespeare. Showing popular culture examples first can help students enter into the discussion more freely and openly, without the stress of responding appropriately to the Shakespeare text. When they then view the Shakespeare examples, they can see that many of the same decisions, options, and demands exist for these productions as for the others. After the viewings, students could then engage in an active discussion about both, making connections between them and their readings of Shakespeare. Following this discussion, they could engage in an activity through which they apply what they have learned by creating their own version of a scene they viewed. In this activity, students would have to decide what actors, set, staging, or filming choices they would use and why. They would also need to consider how their choices would affect their entire imagined production and how it would be received by audiences.

By examining a large number of adaptations as common objects of study, students make links among what was previously regarded as distinct and siloed instances of Shakespearean criticism. Our current, active, communal user-centric culture, which prioritizes user participation,[18] is supplanting the more passive and siloed reader-centric experience that dominated the previous centuries, which in turn replaced the oral culture of Shakespeare's age. Performance-oriented understanding of Shakespeare can enhance the collaborative reading of textual variants in multilingual contexts. By creating knowledge collaboratively, students and educators lay claim to the ethics and ownership of that knowledge.

Interactive pedagogies

The core of communal and contextualized pedagogy is interactivity. The malleability of digital video puts play texts and performances to work in an interactive environment. Online performance video archives can encourage user curation and interaction with other forms of cultural records. In practice, this redistributes the power of collecting, rearranging and archiving cultural records away from a centralized authority to the hands of users. Despite the challenge of maintaining net neutrality and equal access, generally speaking, in a decentralized model of networked culture, the users have more direct engagement with narratives and multi-modal representations of events.

My interactive pedagogy reflects the need for racialized globalization to be understood within hybrid cultural and digital spaces. My students and I build a community with shared purposes. Team projects encourage students' ethical responsibility to each other as they grow from recipients of knowledge transfer to co-creators of knowledge. While it is only feasible to teach in-depth by assigning one or two films of *Lear* in a given class, students can expand their horizon by close reading competing performative interpretations of a few pivotal scenes.

Interactivity prompts students to take on the role of an active participant and independent researcher. For example, teaching *Lear* entails teaching each culture's and generation's reaction to the challenging ethical burden within and beyond the play's actions. An inclusive and interactive exercise is collective translation. Teaching Shakespeare through translated versions draws attention to aspects of the plays that have been dormant. Having students translate a key passage into a language of their choice, and report back in English, empowers multilingual students. It turns international students into an asset rather than liability, and it diversifies the class's interpretive approaches. When Cordelia replies 'nothing, my lord' to Lear's impossible question 'what can you say to draw / A third more opulent than your sisters?' (1.1.85–7), what does she mean? That she has nothing (new) to say to her father? That she cannot win a game that is rigged and therefore nothing she says would matter? In collaboratively translating, in small groups, the simple word 'nothing' which is often glossed over, and in analysing the same scene in multiple adaptations, my students were able to bring into the classroom new voices and new ways of seeing the world, including those of their own and those of others. All too often heritage speakers or international students are seen as a liability, but their linguistic and cultural repertoire should be tapped as collective resources. We asked such questions as: Does Cordelia's hanging enhance the tragic pathos surrounding her journey, or does it help to highlight the senseless male suffering? The biggest payoff of teaching *Lear* through video analysis is a rhizomatic, productive engagement with performative variants. Viewing a clip of Cordelia's silent protest from Peter Brook's existentialist 1971 film of *King Lear* and a clip of Lear's reaction from Grigori Kozintsev's *Korol Lir* (1971) enables an inherently comparative approach to scene analysis. Viewing performances in this productively distracted fashion helps to resist the tyranny of the few canonized adaptations and their privileged interpretations. Consuming performances through arbitrary as well as curated pathways sheds new light on performances that do not tend to be discussed side by side.

Conclusion: Intersectional pedagogies

The new normal in education exposes inequities that were previously veiled by on-campus life and resources. Since the true diversity of our lives resides in individualized, embodied experiences, we can make education intersectional by interrogating any paradigm that flattens out the diversity inherent in unfamiliar communities against stereotypes or national profiles. Adaptations can counter the misconception that Shakespeare is only meaningful when performed in white accents. Students write intelligently about films from the Global South to diversify the English curriculum.

In conclusion, interactive pedagogies – enhanced by adaptation studies – recognize the gap between diversity as a statistical notion used to exonerate an institution of discrimination and diversity as a reservoir of meaningful, embodied experiences. Cooperative learning fosters students' ethical responsibilities while drawing attention to the uneven terrain of collaboration in the creation of arts and literature. In this way we hope to liberate Shakespeare from centuries of bardolatrous expectations and show that his works belong to all of us.

Notes

1 Rita Charon, *Narrative Medicine: Honoring the Stories of Illness* (Oxford: Oxford University Press, 2006), 66, 77.

2 Lynn Fendler, 'The Upside of Presentism', *Paedagogica Historica: International Journal of the History of Education* 44.6 (2008): 677–90; 677.

3 David Sweeney Coombs and Danielle Coriale, 'V21 Forum on Strategic Presentism: Introduction', *Victorian Studies* 59.1 (2016): 87–9; 88.

4 David Sweeney Coombs and Danielle Coriale, 'V21 Forum on Strategic Presentism: Introduction', *Victorian Studies* 59, no. 1 (2016): 87–9.

5 Macdonald P. Jackson, 'Screening the Tragedies: *King Lear*', *The Oxford Handbook of Shakespearean Tragedy*, ed. Michael Neill and David Schalkwyk (Oxford: Oxford University Press, 2016), 607–23; 608.

6 Macdonald, 611, 622.

7 'Kathakali King Lear (Leday, 1999)', *MIT Global Shakespeares: Video and Performance Archive*, https://globalshakespeares.mit.edu/kathakali-king-lear-leday-annette-1999/#video=scene-1-kathakali-king-lear-1999.

8 William Shakespeare, *King Lear*, ed. R. A. Foakes, in *The Arden Shakespeare, Third Series, Complete Works*, (London, New York, Oxford, New Delhi, and Sydney: Bloomsbury, 2020). All references to Shakespeare's works are to this edition (1.1.87).

9 *Ran* translates as *Chaos*.

10 Christopher Nolan, *The Dark Knight* (Burbank, CA: Warner Home Video, 2008).

11 Stephen O'Neill, 'Finding Refuge in *King Lear*: From Brexit to Shakespeare's European Value', *Multicultural Shakespeare: Translation, Appropriation and Performance*, 19.34 (June 2019): 119–38.

12 See Ariane Balizet, 'Teaching *Romeo and Juliet* in Plague Time: A Trauma-Informed Approach' in this volume.

13 Miller, Kelly, Brian Lukoff, Gary King, and Eric Mazur, 'Use of a Social Annotation Platform for Pre-Class Reading Assignments in a Flipped Introductory Physics Class', *Frontiers in Education* (March, 2018); J. J. Cadiz, A. Gupta, and J. Grudin, 'Using web annotations for asynchronous collaboration around documents', *Proceedings of CSCW'00: The 2000 ACM Conference on Computer Supported Cooperative Work* (Philadelphia: ACM, 2000): 309–18.

14 Mary Varghese, 'Meta-cognition: A Theoretical overview', *International Journal of Advance Research in Education & Literature* 5.8 (2019): 1–4.

15 Edward L. Rocklin, *Performance Approaches to Teaching Shakespeare* (Urbana, IL: National Council of Teachers of English, 2005).

16 *Koningin Lear* translates as *Queen Lear*.

17 LUNA, Folger Shakespeare Library, https://luna.folger.edu/luna/.

18 Valerie M. Fazel and Louise Geddes, 'Introduction', in Valerie M. Fazel and Louise Geddes (eds), *The Shakespeare User: Critical and Creative Appropriations in a Networked Culture* (New York: Palgrave Macmillan, 2017), 3.

SELECTED BIBLIOGRAPHY

Primary texts

Anderson, Lily. *The Only Thing Worse Than Me Is You*. New York: St. Martin's Griffin, 2016.

Beck, Kiersten Beck. *Much Ado about Magic*. Amazon Digital Services, 2012.

Blackman, Malorie. *Noughts and Crosses*. London: Penguin Books, 2001.

Booth, Molly. *Nothing Happened*. New York: Hyperion Books, 2018.

Burke, J. C. *Faking Sweet*. Sydney: Random House Australia, 2006.

Candle Wasters (Elsie Bollinger, Sally Bollinger, Minnie Grace and Claris Jacobs), *Nothing Much to Do*, 2014, web series, https://www.youtube.com/user/nothingmuchtodovlog/videos.

Capin, Hannah. *Foul is Fair*. New York: Wednesday Books, 2020.

Carey, Jaqueline. *Miranda and Caliban*. New York: Tor Books, 2017.

Draper, Sharon M. *Romiette and Julio*, 1999. New York: Simon Pulse, 2001.

Fiedler, Lisa. *Dating Hamlet*. London: Harper Collins, 2002.

Garcia, Kami and Margaret Stohl, *Beautiful Creatures*. New York: Little, Brown and Company, 2009.

Gehrman, Jody. *Triple Shot Betty*. New York: Dial Books for Young Readers, 2008.

Greene, Robert. 'Pandosto'. In *An Anthology of Elizabethan Prose Fiction*, ed. Paul Salzman. Oxford: Oxford University Press, 1987.

Johnston, E. K. *Exit, Pursued by a Bear*. New York: Penguin, 2016.

Klein, Lisa. *Lady Macbeth's Daughter*. New York: Bloomsbury, 2010.

Klein, Lisa. *Ophelia*. New York: Bloomsbury, 2006.

May, Alison. *Much Ado about Sweet Something*. Camberley: ChocLit, 2013, reissued in 2021.

McCall, Guadalupe García. *Shame the Stars*. New York: Tu Books, 2016.

Oldfield, Jenny. *Much Ado about Nothing*. London: A&C Black, 2008.

Ophelia, directed by Claire McCarthy. Covert Media, 2018.

Peet, Mal. *Exposure*. Somerville: Candlewick Press, 2009.

Quip Modest Productions. *Like, As It Is*, 2015, web series, https://www.youtube.com/playlist?list=PL7Aos6cZ-mUw3t3B9LyKlfXK7-dY6wMwM

Quip Modest Productions. *Twelfth Grade (or Whatever)*, 2016, web series, https://www.youtube.com/watch?v=csp35NipXEU&list=PL7Aos6cZ-mUxgWreHGvC1S5dY5IHq3Am6

Ray, Michelle. *Falling for Hamlet*. New York: Hachette Book Group, 2011.

Ray, Michelle. *Much Ado about Something*. Amazon Digital Services, 2016.

Reisert, Rebecca. *The Third Witch*. New York: Washington Square Press, 2001.

Su, Bernie and Hank Green. *The Lizzie Bennet Diaries*, 2012, web series, https://www.youtube.com/user/LizzieBennet.

Sweeney, Aoibheann. *Among Other Things, I've Taken Up Smoking*. New York: Penguin, 2007.

Tolan, Stephanie S. *The Face in the Mirror*. New York: Harper Trophy, 1998.

West, Jacqueline. *Dreamers Often Lie*. New York: Dial, 2016.

Winters, Cat. *The Steep and Thorny Way*. New York: Amulet Paperbacks, 2016.

Zindel, Lizabeth. *A Girl, a Ghost, and the Hollywood Hills*. New York: Viking, 2010.

Secondary texts

Adelman, Janet. *Suffocating Mothers: Fantasies of Maternal Origin in Shakespeare's Plays,* Hamlet *to* The Tempest. New York: Routledge, 1992.

Alexander, Jeffery. *Trauma: A Social Theory*. Cambridge: Polity Press, 2012.

Appleman, Deborah. *Critical Encounters in Secondary English: Teaching Literary Theory to Adolescents*, 3rd edn. New York: Teachers College Press, 2015.

Balizet, Ariane M. *Shakespeare and Girls' Studies*. New York: Routledge, 2020.

Ball, Arnetha F. 'Toward a Theory of Generative Change in Culturally and Linguistically Complex Classrooms'. *American Educational Research Journal* 46, no. 1 (2009): 45–72.

Bicks, Caroline. *Cognition and Girlhood in Shakespeare's World: Rethinking Female Adolescence*. Cambridge: Cambridge University Press, 2021.

Brenner, Robin. 'Teen Literature and Fan Culture'. *Young Adult Library Services* 11, iss. 4 (2013): 33–6.

Britzman, D. 'Queer Pedagogy and Its Strange Techniques'. *Counterpoints: Vol. 367, Sexualities in Education: A Reader* 367 (2012): 292–308.

Buchwald, Emilie, Pamela R. Fletcher and Marth Roth, eds. *Transforming A Rape Culture*. Minneapolis: Milkweed Editions, 1993.

Butler, Judith. *Precarious Life: The Powers of Mourning and Violence*. London: Verso, 2004.

Callaghan, Dympna. 'Wicked Women in Macbeth: A Study of Power, Ideology, and the Production of Motherhood'. In *Reconsidering the Renaissance: Papers from the Twenty-First Annual Conference*, edited by Mario A. Di Cesare, 355–69. Binghamton: Medieval & Renaissance Texts & Studies, 1992. Quoted in *Shakespearean Criticism*, edited by Michelle Lee. Vol. 100. Detroit: Gale, 2006. *Gale Literature Resource Center*. https://link.gale.com/apps/doc/H1420073544/LitRC?u=ogde72764&sid=bookmark-LitRC&xid=d37e2723 (accessed 27 July 2022).

Carello, Janice and Lisa D. Butler. 'Potentially Perilous Pedagogies: Teaching Trauma Is Not the Same as Trauma-Informed Teaching'. *Journal of Trauma & Dissociation* 15 (2014): 153–68.

Carter, Angela M. 'Teaching with Trauma: Trigger Warnings, Feminism, and Disability Pedagogy'. *Disability Studies Quarterly* 35, no. 2 (2015): https://doi-org.ezproxy.tcu.edu/10.18061/dsq.v35i2.4652.

Charon, Rita. *Narrative Medicine: Honoring the Stories of Illness*. Oxford: Oxford University Press, 2006.

Cho, Alexander, Indira N. Hoch, Allison McCracken and Louisa Stein. *A Tumblr Book: Platform and Cultures*. Ann Arbor: University of Michigan Press, 2020.

Corredera, Vanessa '*Get Out* and the Remediation of Othello's Sunken Place: Beholding White Supremacy's Coagula'. *Borrowers and Lenders* 13, no. 1 (2020): 1–19.

Della Gatta, Carla. 'From *West Side Story* to *Hamlet, Prince of Cuba*: Shakespeare and Latinidad in the United States'. *Shakespeare Studies* 44 (2016): 151–6.

Desmet, Christy. 'New Directions: *Much Ado about Nothing* and Social Media'. In *Much Ado About Nothing: A Critical Reader*, edited by Deborah Cartmell and Peter J. Smith, 155–76. London: Bloomsbury Publishing, 2018.

Enterline, Lynn. *The Rhetoric of the Body from Ovid to Shakespeare*. Cambridge: Cambridge University Press, 2000.

Fazel, Valerie M. and Louise Geddes, eds. *The Shakespeare User: Critical and Creative Appropriations in a Networked Culture*. New York: Palgrave Macmillan, 2017.

Flaherty, Jennifer. 'How Many Daughters Had Lady Macbeth?' In *Shakespeare and Millennial Fiction*, edited by Andrew James Hartley, 101–14 Cambridge: Cambridge University Press, 2018.

Flaherty, Jennifer. 'Reviving Ophelia: Reaching Adolescent Girls through Shakespeare's Doomed Heroine'. *Borrowers and Lenders: A Journal of Shakespeare and Appropriation* 9, no. 1 (2014): 1–21.

Gallagher, Kelly and Penny Kittle. *180 Days: Two Teachers and the Quest to Engage and Empower Adolescents*. Portsmouth: Heinemann, 2018.

Garber, Marjorie. 'Relatable'. *Raritan* 38 no. 4 (2019): 113–29.

Gaskill, Malcolm. *Witchfinders*. Cambridge, MA: Harvard University Press, 2007.

Gillen, Katherine and Adrianna M. Santos. 'Borderlands Shakespeare: The Decolonial Visions of James Lujan's Kino and Teresa and Seres Jaime Magaña's *The Tragic Corrido of Romeo and Lupe*'. *Shakespeare Bulletin* 38, no. 4 (2020): 549–71.

Hateley, Erica. 'Sink or Swim?: Revising Ophelia in Contemporary Young Adult Fiction'. *Children's Literature Association Quarterly* 38, no. 4 (2013): 435–48.

Hateley, Erica. *Shakespeare in Children's Literature: Gender and Cultural Capital*. New York: Routledge, 2009.

Herman, Judith. *Trauma and Recovery*. New York: Basic Books, 1992.

Hulbert, Jenifer, Kevin J. Wetmore Jr. and Robert L. York, eds. *Shakespeare and Youth Culture*. New York: Palgrave Macmillan, 2006.

Hutcheon, Linda. *A Theory of Adaptation*. New York: Routledge, 2006.

Jenkins, Henry. *Convergence Culture: Where Old and New Media Collide*. New York: New York University Press, 2008.

Kafer, Alison. 'Un/Safe Disclosures: Scenes of Disability and Trauma'. *Journal of Literary & Cultural Disability Studies* 10, no. 1 (2016): 1–20.

Kittle, Penny. *Book Love: Developing Depth, Stamina, and Passion in Adolescent Readers*. Portsmouth: Heinemann, 2013.

Lanier, Douglas M. 'Afterword'. In *Shakespeare/Not Shakespeare*, edited by Christy Desmet, Natalie Loper and Jim Casey, 293–306. New York: Palgrave Macmillan, 2017.

Lanier, Douglas M. 'Shakespearean Rhizomatics: Adaptation, Ethics, Value'. In *Shakespeare and the Ethics of Appropriation*, edited by Alexa Huang and Elizabeth Rivlin, 21–40. New York: Palgrave, 2014.

Lanier, Douglas M. 'Text, Performance, Screen: Shakespeare and Critical Media Literacy'. *Cahiers Élisabéthains* 105, no. 1 (2021): 117–27.

Lanier, Douglas M. 'Vlogging the Bard: Serialization, Social Media, Shakespeare'. In *Broadcast Your Shakespeare: Continuity and Change Across Media*, edited by Stephen O'Neill, 185–206. London: Bloomsbury Publishing.

Lehmann, Courtney and Lisa S. Starks, eds. *Spectacular Shakespeare: Critical Theory and Popular Culture*. Teaneck: Fairleigh Dickinson University Press.

Levins Morales, Aurora. *Medicine Stories: Essays for Radicals*. Durham: Duke University Press, 2019.

Malo-Juvera, Victor, Paula Greathouse and Brooke Eisenbach. *Shakespeare and Young Adult Literature*. London: Rowman & Littlefield, 2021.

McCarthy, Carol J. and Joycee Kennedy, 'Transforming Trauma Responses to Sexual Abuse in Adolescents'. In *Trauma Transformed: An Empowerment Response*, edited by Marian Bussey and Judith Bula Wise, 35–50. New York: Columbia University Press, 2007.

Mead, Rebecca. 'The Scourge of "Relatability"', *The New Yorker*, 1 August 2014.

Mendoza, Kristen B. 'Sexual Violence, Trigger Warnings, and the Early Modern Classroom'. In *Teaching Social Justice through Shakespeare: Why Renaissance Literature Matters Now*, edited by Hillary Eklund and Wendy Beth Hyman, 97–105. Edinburgh: Edinburgh University Press, 2019.

Misheff, Sue. 'Beneath the Web and Over the Stream: The Search for Safe Places in *Charlotte's Web* and *Bridge to Terabithia*'. *Children's Literature in Education* 29, no. 3 (1998): 131–41.

Molyneaux, Heather, Susan O'Donnell, Kerri Gibson and Janice Singer, 'Exploring the Gender Divide on YouTube: An Analysis of the Creation and Reception of Vlogs'. *American Communication Journal* 10, no. 1 (2008): 1–13.

Moore, Amber. '"I Knew You Were Trouble": Considering Childism(s), Shame Resilience, and Adult Caretaker Characters Surrounding YA Rape Survivor Protagonists'. *New Review of Children's Literature and Librarianship* 24, no. 2 (2018): 144–66.

Moore, Amber. 'Traumatic Geographies: Mapping the Violent Landscapes Driving YA Rape Survivors Indoors in Laurie Halse Anderson's *Speak*, Elizabeth Scott's *Living Dead Girl*, and E. K. Johnston's *Exit, Pursued by a Bear*'. *Jeunesse: Young People, Texts, Cultures* 10, no. 1 (2018): 58–84.

O'Neill, Stephen. *Shakespeare and YouTube: New Media Forms of the Bard*. London: Bloomsbury Publishing, 2014.

Orem, Sarah and Neil Simpkins. 'Weepy Rhetoric, Trigger Warnings, and the Work of Making Mental Illness Visible in the Writing

Classroom'. *Enculturation: A Journal of Rhetoric, Writing, and Culture* 16 December (2015). http://enculturation.net/weepy-rhetoric.

Osbourne, Laurie. 'Reviving Cowden Clarke: Rewriting Shakespeare's Heroines in Young Adult Fiction'. In *Shakespearean Echoes*, edited by Adam Hansen and Kevin J. Wetmore, 21–35. New York: Palgrave Macmillan, 2015.

Peercy, Megan Madigan. 'Challenges in Enacting Core Practices in Language Teacher Education: A Self-Study'. *Studying Teacher Education* 10, no. 2 (2014): 146–62.

Perni, Remedios. 'Ana and Mia: Ophelia on the Web'. *Shakespeare Quarterly* 67, no. 4 (2017): 503–14.

Peterson, Kaara L. and Deanne Williams, eds. *The Afterlife of Ophelia*. New York: Palgrave Macmillan, 2012.

Pihlaja, Stephen. '"Hey YouTube": Positioning the Viewer in Vlogs'. In *Rethinking Language, Text and Context: Interdisciplinary Research in Stylistics in Honour of Michael Toolan*, edited by Ruth Page, Beatrix Busse and Nina Nørgaard, 254–66. New York: Routledge, 2018.

Pipher, Mary and Sara Pipher Gilliam. 'The Lonely Burden of Today's Teenage Girls'. *Wall Street Journal*, 17 August 2019, C3.

Pipher, Mary and Sara Pipher Gilliam. *Reviving Ophelia: Saving the Selves of Adolescent Girls*. New York: Riverhead Books, 2019.

Quiros, Laura and Beverly Araujo Dawson. 'The Color Paradigm: The Impact of Colorism on the Racial Identity and Identification of Latinas'. *Journal of Human Behavior in the Social Environment* 23, no. 3 (2013): 287–97.

Refskou, Anne Sophie, Vinicius Mariano de Carvalho and Marcel Alvaro de Amorim. Introduction to *Eating Shakespeare: Cultural Anthropophagy as Global Methodology*. Edited by Anne Sophie Refskou, Vinicius Mariano de Carvalho and Marcel Alvaro de Amorim, 1–24. London: Bloomsbury Publishing, 2019.

Rocklin, Edward L. *Performance Approaches to Teaching Shakespeare*. Urbana: National Council of Teachers of English, 2005.

Rokison, Abigail. '"Our Scene Is Alter'd": Adaptations and Re-Workings of Hamlet for Young People'. *Literature Compass* 7, iss. 9 (2010): 786–97.

Royster, Francesca T. 'Introduction to "Shakespeare's Female Icons": Sorcerers, Celebrities, Aliens, and Upstarts'. *Upstart Crow: A Shakespeare Journal* 31 (2012): 5–13.

Schwebel, Sara L. *Child-Sized History: Fictions of the Past in the U.S. Classroom*. Nashville: Vanderbilt University Press, 2011.

Showalter, Elaine. 'Representing Ophelia: Women, Madness, and the Responsibilities of Feminist Criticism'. In *Shakespeare and the Question of Theory*, edited by Patricia Parker and Geoffrey H. Hartman. 84–101. New York: Methuen, 1985.

Simon, Bennett. 'Hamlet and the Trauma Doctors: An Essay at Interpretation'. American Imago 58, no. 3 (2001): 707–22.

Stebbins, Anne. 'Fun Home: Questions of Sexuality and Identity'. Journal of LGBT Youth 8 (2011): 285–8.

Stein, Louisa. 'The Digital Literary Fangirl Network: Representing Fannishness in the Transmedia Web Series'. In Seeing Fans: Representations of Fandom in Media and Popular Culture, edited by Lucy Bennett and Paul Booth. 707–22. New York: Bloomsbury Publishing, 2016.

Tal, Kalí. Worlds of Hurt: Reading the Literatures of Trauma. Cambridge: Cambridge University Press, 1996.

Tassi, Marguerite. Women and Revenge in Shakespeare: Gender, Genre, and Ethics. Cranbury: Associated University Press, 2011.

Tatum, Alfred W. 'Adolescents and Texts: Overserved or Underserved?' English Journal 98, no. 2 (2008): 82–5.

Thompson, Ayanna and Laura Turchi. Teaching Shakespeare with Purpose: A Student-Centred Approach. London: The Arden Shakespeare, 2016.

Tribunella, Eric L. Melancholia and Maturation: The Use of Trauma in Children's Literature. Knoxville: Tennessee University Press, 2010.

Turchi, Laura B. and Ann C. Christensen. 'When the "House" (of Montague) Is a Color not a Clan: Teaching Romeo and Juliet Productions Where Difference Signals Inevitable Conflict'. The English Journal 108, no. 2 (2018): 111–14.

Varghese, Mary. 'Meta-Cognition: A Theoretical Overview'. International Journal of Advance Research in Education & Literature 5, no. 8 (2019): 1–4.

Wetmore, Kevin J. 'Shakespeare and Teenagers'. In The Edinburgh Companion to Shakespeare and the Arts, edited by Mark Thornton Burnett and Adrian Steele, 377–87. Edinburgh: Edinburgh University Press, 2011.

Young, Alan. Hamlet and the Visual Arts, 1709–1900. London: Associated University Presses, 1984.

INDEX